Women and
Culture Series

*The Women and Culture Series is dedicated to books that illuminate the lives,
roles, achievements, and status of women, past or present.*

LESLIE W. RABINE is winner in the Hamilton Prize competition for
1983. The Alice and Edith Hamilton Prize is named for two
outstanding women scholars: Alice Hamilton (educated at the
University of Michigan Medical School), a pioneer in environmental
medicine; and her sister Edith Hamilton, the renowned classicist. The
Hamilton Prize competition is supported by the University of Michigan
and by private donors.

Reading the Romantic Heroine

Reading the Romantic Heroine)

Text, History, Ideology

Leslie W. Rabine

Ann Arbor
The University of Michigan Press

1988   1987   1986   1985   4   3   2   1

Library of Congress Cataloging-in-Publication Data

Rabine, Leslie W., 1944–
  Reading the romantic heroine.

  (Women and culture series)
  Bibliography: p.
  Includes index.
  1. Love stories—History and criticism.   I. Title.
II. Series.
PN3448.L67R3   1985   809.3'85   85-13955
ISBN 0-472-10068-8 (alk. paper)

For Beatrice and Henry Wahl

Preface

While intellectuals refer to our cultural era as postromantic, contemporary women are devouring mass-market romances by the millions. Thus romantic love narrative remains on the agenda for literary and cultural criticism. The study undertaken here concerns neither romanticism in general nor romance in general, but narratives, be they romances or romantic novels, that have, since the twelfth century, made romantic love a cultural model which continues to dominate women's imaginations even today. Gottfried von Strassburg's *Tristan and Isolde* (twelfth century), Prévost's *Manon Lescaut* (eighteenth century), Stendhal's *The Red and the Black* (nineteenth century), Charlotte Brontë's *Shirley* (nineteenth century), Alain-Fournier's *Big Meaulnes* (early twentieth century), and Harlequin Romances (contemporary) have all contributed to this tradition. Their study can help build a theory that finds connections between an unconscious feminine personality structure, the culture that shapes women's consciousness, and women's social situation.

Romantic love, although a myth that does not exist in daily experience, remains the ideal model for interpersonal relations. As a heterosexual, private, total, exalted love, it is supposed to give meaning to an otherwise drab existence, and allow us to transcend daily life to a higher plane. Whether fatal passion or happily-ever-after fantasy, it has always been a total love, combining sexuality, emotional intimacy, and self-reflecting intellect. In twelfth-century courtly love poetry and chivalric romance, romantic love combines sexual passion with the spiritual love previously reserved for religion, and serves to make the lovers more self-conscious. In the nineteenth-century novel it becomes the central human relation around which all other relations revolve. While today feminist theorists, historians, novelists, and poets are challenging the myth of romantic love's pivotal position in the solar system of human relations by foregrounding mother-child and same-sex relations, romantic love continues to reign supreme in the most widely read literature—mass-market fiction. Romance outsells all other mass-market genres and sells to an exclusively feminine audience. As a form of feminine sexuality, romantic love is not about to disappear. Vast numbers of women remain passionately attached to it, and the fantasies it evokes merit serious study.

From the Tristan romance to Harlequin Romances, romantic love has held at its heart an intense contradiction, which can perhaps explain its seduction. On the one hand, it provides one of the few accepted outlets through which women can express their anger and revolt against their situation in a patriarchal order. On the other hand, it idealizes and eroticizes women's powerlessness and lack of freedom. One of the purposes of this study is to read that contradiction in a series of romantic love narratives, where the two aspects battle against each other in a more or less intense way, but where neither wins out over the other. It is this double and contradictory attraction of romantic love narrative that has made it so resilient as a literary form and so potent as a cultural myth.

Because at certain periods of history romantic love has exerted a dominant force in shaping the consciousness, desires, and choices of a large section of a population, and has also acted as one of the most fundamental and fertile literary forms in Western literature, I have been led to seek a critical method that can analyze the relation between literary texts and history. Such a method needs to study the underlying logic governing sexuality and textuality in a given narrative, as well as the connections between text and historic context. It needs to bring history into the closed circle of literary criticism in spite of the attendant risks, given the problematic nature of both disciplines. Thus the following attempts to challenge the romantic quest have themselves taken the form of a quest, not for identity and fulfillment, but for a critical method that can integrate the study of text, history, and ideology.

Acknowledgments

I would like to thank the friends and colleagues who helped me write this book. To Ray Giraud, Diana Rebolledo, and Judy Taylor, who read this manuscript and provided many insightful and valuable criticisms, I am deeply thankful. I am also grateful for the many helpful editorial comments and for the encouragement of Domna Stanton, Martha Vicinus, Louise Tilly, Judith Newton, Margaret Homans, Judy Walkowitz, and Carol Jacklyn. Many thanks are extended to Ross Chambers for his support and encouragement.

Joan Ariel, the University of California Irvine women's studies librarian, was tireless in giving bibliographic and library assistance, and my thanks go to her for this.

I would also like to acknowledge the Committee on Research and Travel of the Academic Senate of the University of California Irvine for funds to do research on this project, and Dean Kendall Bailes of the UCI School of Humanities for a Faculty Fellowship, which allowed me to complete the manuscript.

Finally, my thanks to my husband Merle and to my parents Beatrice and Henry Wahl for their support.

Contents

Chapter 1

Problems of Textuality, History, and Ideology

The dichotomy between the bad reputation romanticism enjoys among intellectuals and its popularity with a feminine public is not new, and in fact reflects a split at the heart of romanticism itself. It has at various times in the past found itself simultaneously the object of intellectual disdain and popular acclaim, but considerable variation has marked both the reasons for its bad reputation and also the social composition of its enthusiastic audience.

At the beginning of the twentieth century, literature that carried on the legacy of nineteenth-century romanticism was still read by middle-class readers of both sexes. A reactionary critic like Pierre Lasserre could identify it with "emotional disorder" and "theories . . . that cast malediction and vengeance upon society";[1] and Irving Babbitt could associate it with "excess."[2] But today, when the audience for romance consists of working women, it is avant-garde criticism, much of it with a feminist thrust, that warns of its dangers. Julia Kristeva speaks of the need to avoid "naive romanticism,"[3] and Candace Lang reviews the way that modern criticism has identified romanticism with phallocentric illusions of a "unified, unique, ineffable self" existing as a private and stable entity.[4]

This difference between conservative criticisms of the past and avant-garde criticisms of today indicate more than a simple evolution in which yesterday's revolutionary movement hardens into the reactionary target of today's new radical trends. While this cyclical rhythm is itself a product of nineteenth-century romanticism, the contradiction between reaction and revolt has always been fundamental to romantic love narrative. Since the birth of courtly love poetry in eleventh-century Europe, romantic love literature has been simultaneously both a chaotic revolt against established order and an imposition of rational order on chaotic passions. This internal contradiction can even help explain its popularity.

Discussing the role of Heloïse and Abelard in the early love literature, Peggy Kamuf quotes Paul Zumthor's preface to an edition of their letters, in which he remarks that "the passions of love remained at the margin of the conceptual universe, and therefore all the more tenacious—unconquered, deprived of both language and of that relative security which results from insertion in an order." The Provençal poets changed this, creating "the rational frame that love needed in order finally to assert itself as a cultural value."[5]

The double action of courtly love poetry, both recuperating and expressing the passions that threaten order, have remained inherent to romantic love narrative, from the chivalric romances of the twelfth century through the romantic novels of the nineteenth to the mass-produced paperbacks of our own time. What has changed are the social structure of that order and the social composition of groups whose desire to disrupt it needs to be both repressed and expressed. For medieval aristocratic *mal-mariées,* nineteenth-century isolated bourgeoise housewives, or contemporary working women, the romantic forms of sexual desire have given voice to fantasies of revolt and have contained their disruptive force within strong bonds.

As the cultural space of a privileged encounter between individual sexual passion and rationalized social order, romantic love narrative encodes two of our most cherished myths. The first is the changing yet stable myth of romantic love, which underpins and shapes our culture's bonds of interdependence/antagonism between the sexes. The second is the myth of history itself, which grows out of the quest form of romance. Critics as varied as Harold Bloom, Northrop Frye, Georg Lukács, and Lucienne Frappier-Mazur have defined romance narrative in terms of a quest for transcendence.[6] Lost in the realm of alienation, the romance hero seeks a return to authentic identity. In Greek, Roman, and Christian romance the hero is alienated from nature or God and seeks reunion with nature or God. But as romance is transformed into the romantic novel in the eighteenth and nineteenth centuries, the hero, alienated from himself, seeks to return to self-identity; and his quest takes the form of an exalted passion for an unattainable heroine. This quest form provides one of our most powerful cultural codes, determining how we conceive both sexual relations and historic process. The traditional romantic quest narrative, which puts at its center the development of a single, individual hero, and which rests on strongly end-oriented, rationally ordered, monolinear chains of cause and effect, provides the conceptual form in which history is thought to happen.

In studying narratives that join these two powerful myths, sexual and historic, I have asked why they are so inseparably intertwined and why the romantic form of history works so well to contain and bind disruptive passion. I have also examined disruptive sexual and historical forces within the text which the mythic forms can contain but not suppress. In order to do so I have worked toward a method that reads literary texts in relation to history.

Structures and Codes

In an effort to avoid reducing literature to an apparently unproblematic reflection of an apparently unproblematic historical period or unified "world vision," most contemporary literary critics have avoided historical criticism. Articles in contemporary journals of critical theory discuss the need to relate history and literature in new ways, but one finds relatively few critics who relate them in doing practical criticism.[7]

One of the first modern critics to open the way for new methods of historical criticism, Lucien Goldmann, also left unsolved problems for his successors. His theory of "genetic structuralism" goes beyond examining the content of a literary work as a reflection of historical reality. It holds instead that "the *structures* of a work's universe are homologous to the mental *structures* of a social group, or are in an intelligible relation with them."[8] Instead of seeing literature as "the reflection of collective consciousness," genetic structuralism, claims Goldmann, posits literature as "one of its most important constitutive elements" (p. 353).

One problem of genetic structuralism has been discussed by Fredric Jameson. According to him, Goldmann's method assumes identity between the various levels of a text and between a text and what he calls its social text.[9] It ignores the multiple and conflictual nature of literary texts, which do not emit a single message and do not have a single structure, although, as in the case of romantic love novels, one structure may dominate and hide the others. Moreover, it inserts this homogeneous text into a historical period which it also assumes to be homogeneous. Yet recent historical research, much of it feminist, has shown that a given historic moment is really a point at which a multitude of heterogeneous periods intersect. Relevant to this book is the fact that, as historians like Louise Tilly, Suzanne Wemple, Joanne McNamara, Darline Gay Levy, and Bonnie Smith have shown, the periodization of women's history takes a different course and assumes a very different form from that of men.[10]

In order to ask why and how texts mask their own multiplicity and have themselves influenced us to view literature and history as homogeneous and self-identical, more recent critics like Roland Barthes and John Berger went beyond a focus on structure in texts to study textual and artistic codes.[11] As sets of rules that generate linguistic, narrative, and/or visual structures, codes determine models of representation and interpretation and also govern our responses to literature and art. Textual codes are thus active in shaping ideologies and even social realities.

Producing unconscious models for interpreting and representing our social world, they determine not only *what* we see in reality, but also *how* we see. The world is visible, comprehensible, and knowable to us only if we read coherence into it, and popular, traditional, deeply rooted literary forms like that of romantic love narrative give us the models for such coherent reading. The codes through which we interpret reality exist not only in literature, but also in us. Therefore, as Jameson points out, we need in reading literature to become conscious of codes as historic constructs (pp. 53–54).

The problem of consciously historicizing codes is complicated by the fact that they exist not only in literary texts, in social texts, and in us, but also in historic texts. The "history" which acts as the unavoidable context for literary works in a study like this one is not historic practice, but a representation already coded by the very forms of romantic monolinearity that this book seeks to challenge. The problems multiply when literary texts from different historical moments are studied in diachronic succession, because, as Jameson says, "individual period formulations always secretly imply or project narratives or 'stories'—narrative representations—of the historical sequence in which such individual periods take their place and from which they derive their significance" (p. 28).

This problem is especially acute when the sequence of texts from different periods includes works that have already instilled and affirmed a notion of history as inevitable evolution, as *Tristan and Isolde*, *Manon Lescaut*, *The Red and the Black*, and *Big Meaulnes* have done. Their succession cannot help but be implicated in the myth of history as a linear, end-oriented evolution. Each of these narratives centers itself firmly on the hero with his strong teleological development. Moreover, each inevitably presents itself as a stage in the rise and decline of the masculine romantic self, and thus in the rise and decline of the masculine bourgeois self.

In seeking to modify such a perspective on history, I have situated the hero's development and the narrative form which supports it as background for a study of the heroines as textual figures. These feminine textual figures do not conform to an evolution in two ways. First, in the succession of narratives, from Isolde, to Manon, to Mathilde, to Shirley, to Yvonne, to the Harlequin heroines, there is no evolutionary line. Second, within each novel, the heroines do not proceed through a teleological development. With the exception of the Harlequin heroines, they are fragmentary figures, suggesting only potential, as yet unknown, forms of development.

The lack of cultural codes for feminine personal and historical development in romantic love narrative can be illustrated by contrasting briefly what I have called the feminine historicity of Mathilde de La Mole in Stendhal's *The Red and the Black* and of the two heroines in Charlotte Brontë's *Shirley*. By feminine historicity I mean the desire on the part of a feminine character to enter the historic process and to become an active agent of history. In order for her to achieve this, history would have to take a very different form from the one encoded in the narrative in question.

Since *The Red and the Black* (1830) and *Shirley* (1848) were written within a twenty-year span, one by a male author and one by a female author, and since both are historical novels, they form an appropriate pair for a contrastive study of feminine historicity. In *The Red and the Black*, Mathilde's fragmentary historical development is differently coded than that of the hero Julien, with the result that she appears repulsive and monstrous, defying reader identification (see chap. 4). The potential development of feminine historicity in *Shirley* remains on the other hand uncoded, unspoken, implicit, dispersed in the symbolism of the text (see chap. 5).

Reasons for this difference about which more will be said later could be traced to the gender difference between Stendhal and Brontë, to important differences in the French and English novel traditions, to the difference between Stendhal's membership in an urban bourgeoisie with aristocratic pretensions and Brontë's membership in a rural middle class. But the differences also remain to a certain extent arbitrary, and indicate the lack of models for women's development.

The heroes' development in each text and through the succession of texts has been decentered by a focus on feminine historicity, and is also challenged in another way. I have studied the hero's development and the narrative form which bears it along at one remove, as ideological illusion which masks textual and historical multiplicity. When these illusions are isolated as illusions, the other conflicting elements within the text become more apparent.

Locating the Feminine Other within the Text

If these conflicting elements are seen as historical contradictions working within the text, then history is not only external to the text, but also internal to it. A study of historic forces within the text deepens a study of texts in relation to their specific sociohistoric contexts but cannot replace it. Yet using the two methods together does tend to render more ambiguous the dichotomy between an inside and an outside of the text, since historic forces as well as textual codes work both in the text and in society.

Several writers have developed theories that show historic forces at work within literary form. Fredric Jameson's theory of literature as a "socially symbolic act," symptomatic of a "political unconscious" (p. 20), analyzes in the relation between a literary text and a cultural text the "*interference* between levels" or the "subversion of one level by another" (p. 56, italics in text). Mikhail Bakhtin's theory of "dialogism" shows how the heterogeneous dialects of different social groups in a national language, "upon entering the novel, combine to form a structured artistic system."[12]

Julia Kristeva has adapted this theory by studying how conflicting social discourses are transformed into the unified language of a particular text through the mediation of logical paradigms called "ideologemes."[13] According to her, ideologemes are "principles of textual organization" (p. 52) that define genres or types of narrative by the way they integrate heterogeneous discourses into a unified, ideologically significant textual and linguistic structure. The "ideologeme of the sign," which according to Kristeva originates in courtly love poetry and governs the structure and language of the classical novel, can help to analyze conflictual feminine discourses in the androcentric romantic narratives studied in this book. But before Kristeva's concept is brought to bear on sexual conflicts in these romantic texts, a description of how they work is necessary.

In each narrative studied here, masculine and feminine discourses in a given historical moment speak at different levels of the text. Where better than in romantic texts can one find feminine voices inscribed in masculine narratives? And where more than in romantic narratives can one find the forces that mask conflict and the conflict between different voices more intensely joined in contradiction? Romantic textual structure combines masculine and feminine voices in a struggle which on the one hand veils and idealizes, on the other hand clarifies and reveals the sexual power relations of their society.

The dominant masculine voice of traditional romantic narrative imposes a totalizing structure on romantic narrative and represses an independent feminine other. Reducing the heroine to a reflection of himself, the hero makes of her an "intermediary," as Simone de Beauvoir says,[14] through whom he can realize his desire to return to a mythical union with himself. While by no means all nineteenth-century French novels are based on this structure, it is noteworthy that most of the prominent novelists wrote one such novel and that none of them wrote more than one. A list of these novels includes Chateaubriand's *René*, Constant's *Adolphe*, Sainte-Beuve's *Volupté*, Balzac's *The Lily in the Valley*, Stendhal's *The Red and the Black*, Dumas's *The Lady of the Camellias*, Nerval's *Sylvie*, and Flaubert's *Sentimental Education*. Discussing how the romantic quest in these novels entails "the sanctification of woman as mother and mediatrix," Lucienne Frappier-Mazur says: "Ultimately immobilized in timeless perfection, she shows the way and represents a necessary stage in the hero's quest for identity but never appears as the subject of that quest."[15]

The hero and/or narrator in each of these works posits the heroine at first as an autonomous other and then in the end absorbs her back into his own identity. In so doing they conform to the ideologeme of the sign that governs each narrative. As a logical paradigm, the ideologeme of the sign works in two steps, first positing two different terms, and then claiming, in Kristeva's words, "a resemblance and an identification between the elements that it connects, in spite of the radical difference between them that it postulates at first" (p. 56). The logic of the novel "absorbs the duplicity (the dialogism) of the carnival scene, but submits it to the univocity (monologism)" of its own logical form and thus "guarantees a transcendent moment" (p. 62). In such a way is the independent feminine voice submitted to the totalizing masculine voice of romantic narrative.

Yet an autonomous feminine voice remains in the romantic text, in the form of a fragmented excluded other. She is just as much a part of romanticism as the unified masculine romantic subject although in a form that differs greatly from his explicitly realistic presence. She can be found in aspects of the heroine that have been excluded from explicit representation of the text, in aspects of other female characters, or in other elements of the text. Her silenced voice gives evidence of itself not in overt utterances, but in the conflicts between levels and elements of the text that disrupt the dominant narrative voice. This sexual conflict between different levels of romantic texts is also consistent with the ideologeme of the sign.

Working not only on the levels of narrative structure and voice, the ideologeme of the sign also works on the levels of representation and textual productivity. Its double movement of positing difference and absorbing it into identity also takes place in the relation between signified and signifier. The signifier is absorbed into the signified as its simple reflection, so that its only role is to represent, as Kristeva says, "a 'real' already there, preexisting this signifier" (p. 73). The romantic narrative puts itself forward as simply recounting a chain of events that have already ended in the "real world" before the narrative began, and thus hides the productivity of the text. Whatever does not fit its representational codes is hidden from the reader. As Kristeva says: "the very act of writing passes to a second level and presents itself in its totality as secondary: as a transcription-copy, as a sign" (p. 76). The logic of the novel masks the difference between the levels of finished representative narration and productive writing, just as it masks the voice of an autonomous feminine other. In the narratives studied here, that fragmentary feminine voice reveals this textual productivity and denies the totalizing effect of representation.

Why and how the masculine voice comes to impose this apparent univocity on the romantic text has to do with the historical transformation of romance into the romantic novel. According to Harold Bloom, romanticism "is an internalization of romance, particularly of the quest," in which "the poet takes the patterns of quest-romance and transposes them into his own imaginative life."[16] In the case of the novel, the author also transposes them into the imaginative life of his fantasy alter ego hero. With this inward turning of romance, the heroine as active agent of the quest disappears. Northrop Frye, in his study of Greek and Latin romances with their themes of mysterious birth, magic, enchantment, and shipwreck, finds many heroines who guide the plot and are active subjects of the quest.[17] But when romance turns inward and becomes the romantic novel, the magic disappears, and along with it the "sprawling octopus of a plot" (p. 40) and the questing feminine subject.

The plot of the classical romantic novel, as it traces the quest for self-identity, follows a closed and closely knit circle. In its movement, this plot is akin to the circle of Hegel's Self-Consciousness as it emerges from an immediate form of self-unity, suffers alienation, and seeks to return to self-identity in the higher form of "the fundamental oneness of the Absolute."[18] Like Hegel's Self-Consciousness, each of the heroes in the nineteenth-century romantic novels listed earlier and in the novels studied in this book finds that his feminine object of desire is "[his] own object in which [he] finds [him]self reflected" (Hegel, p. 86). He arrives at true self-knowledge when he "knows [his] object [his object of desire, his heroine] to be [him]self" (Hegel, p. 97).

That this "circle of the self" (Hegel, p. 654) in both the Hegelian and the romantic plot is male-centered, everyone seems to agree. For Hegel the feminine principle is "eternal love that merely feels" (p. 784), while only the masculine principle is the "self-driving force of self-conscious existence" (p. 726). And Harold Bloom refers to the imagination, that higher self of the romantic hero-poet, as the "Real Man" (p. 10). That the underlying logic of the romantic circle is phallocentric has been suggested by such French theorists as Luce Irigaray, Hélène Cixous, and Julia Kristeva.[19] While in the chapters of this book specific passages from their works will be studied in relation to specific novel texts, a few of their basic concepts will be briefly discussed here.

The Heroine as Phallus and the Feminine as Other

Both the monolinear plot of the romantic hero-poet's quest and his rejection of difference are inherent to the structures of subjectivity and selfhood he seeks to fulfill. Seeing this subjective structure as historically a product of Western Greco-Roman and Judeo-Christian tradition, Cixous, Irigaray, and Kristeva have shown it to be exclusively masculine and repressive of feminine difference. They base their analyses on notions from Lacanian psychoanalysis.

Developing through the male-centered model of the Oedipal complex and the castration crisis, the masculine subject comes into being as a necessarily split, alienated subject, driven to heal its unhealable split. It in fact comes into existence as multiply split. It first recognizes, or rather misrecognizes, its "self" as an object reflected in a mirror, and so can know itself only as an other. It then becomes a speaking subject—or in Lacanian terms enters the phallic symbolic order—through a radical separation from its unconscious drives and from the maternal body.[20] Formed in the gap between its unconscious drives and its image in the mirror, the subject seeks a unified "I" that can bridge the gap. This multiple split, fantasized as castration, brings the subject into existence with the irremediable feeling that he has "lost" an essential part of himself, which is fantasized as the phallus. His desire, therefore, whatever shape it may take, remains a desire to return to what he imagines as lost, to retotalize himself, or to reunite himself with a lost Oneness.[21]

As Luce Irigaray and Juliet Mitchell have maintained, there is nothing parallel to the Oedipal model for the development of women. In psychoanalytic theory the girl passes through the masculine model, becoming a "normal woman"[22] by accepting that she is always/already castrated. Within the terms of the phallocentric model of development, women are lacking men and/or pure lack which reflects masculine being. "Femininity," as Mitchell says, "is, therefore, in part a repressed condition that can only be secondarily acquired in a distorted form."[23]

In the nineteenth-century romantic novels listed earlier, the hero is the quintessentially phallocentric subject, and the heroine figures as the lack which promises his plenitude. He desires to heal his split and thus yearns for a return to the pre-Oedipal mother, which the romantic heroine, in her multifold role as a metaphor for everything that the hero desires, also represents. She moreover represents to the hero the unconscious from which he is barred, and of course the imaginary phallus. He projects onto her both his own lack and also the guarantee of its transcendence.

As metaphor for the hero's lack and for everything that fills it and heals his split, the romantic heroine is, in Lacanian terms, more than an object of desire; she is an object of love. For Lacan, and for Kristeva who develops his notion of love in *Histoires d'amour*, to figure as an object of love is to occupy the mythical place of the "Other." While Woman, according to Lacan, "represents, in the phallocentric dialectic the absolute Other,"[24] the place of the Other as law of the symbolic order is both "an indeterminate place" which preexists the subject and also the place "of the unconsciousness."[25]

As the source of the "chain of language" that constitutes the subject, the Other is the source of the subject. But this chain produces language through "the double play of combination and substitution in the signifier,"[26] processes that require lacks and gaps in the chain in order to operate. Therefore, the Other, as the place of that play, is really the place of the lack without which the subject could not exist as a speaking subject. And the phallus, as the master signifier of the language chain, is not a "lost object or the truth of the subject's being." It is not an object at all, but an ever-fleeing absence that governs the chain, since as absence it creates the necessary gaps wherein and whereby combination and substitution can play.

Describing how the subject projects onto the Other the illusory source of his original "lost" "identity" and "wholeness," Jacqueline Rose says: "The Other appears to hold the 'truth' of the subject and the power to make good its loss. But this is the ultimate fantasy."[27] Rose also says that as guarantor of masculine identity, "the status of the phallus is a fraud" (p. 40). Romantic love narrative, by putting the heroine in the place of the Other, and having her affirm the hero's identity, gives the illusion of reality, at least on one of its contradictory levels, to this phallic fantasy, and this has been one of romanticism's most basic ideological roles.

To occupy the place of the Other and there to figure as an object of love means, in Lacanian terms, to be for the subject an object of identification. For the romantic hero, the heroine is more than an object of desire; she is the means of his identification with his own ego ideal. This means that he desires her to identify with him, or in other words to affirm his identity, to recognize him as both object of desire *and* subject of desire. By joining in this way the hero as subject and the hero as object, she would allow him to see reflected in her his "reunified," "whole" self. As metaphor or substitute for the Other, the image of the romantic heroine condenses in herself all the other mythical figures that the masculine subject puts in the place of the Other: the pre-Oedipal mother, the Divine, the phallus. She is everything but the subject of her own autonomous language, of her own desire, and of her own history.

But while romantic narrative gives on some levels the illusion of reality to phallocentric fantasy, it also, on other levels, unmasks that fantasy and reveals the Other as the place of the text's unconscious process. The autonomous feminine other, which I have tried to locate in the cracks and crannies of romantic texts, belongs to that textual process which contradicts the illusions conveyed by phallic representation. Yet it is also, and more crucially, the development of a nonexistent feminine subject, for whom there exists no developmental model within the logic of phallocentric and/or romantic narrative. As a form of development which is not monolinear, which does not seek a return to oneness and identity, and which tolerates gaps, lacks, and difference, it reveals itself in symptomatic fragments in the texts under question.

A study of this fragmented voice and the textual process that represses it can reveal the romantic text as a battle between historically specific masculine and feminine forms of discourse, logic, and sexual desire, even, as in the case of *Tristan and Isolde,* between two historically differentiated civilizations. The dominant form of discourse, logic, and desire in each text presents itself as unique, universal, and total. These universalist forms come into being through a process of exclusion, and the excluded remains by definition unrepresentable within them. In romantic culture, the feminine has been the excluded other, on whose exclusion the coherent representation of masculine desire and history depend.

In romantic love narrative the feminine other, which has to be repressed in order to ensure the unified, ordered forms of the hero's history, is also a different form of historicity, one that would challenge the privileged myth of monolinear, end-oriented development. She suggests other potential historical practices that are also other ways of loving and other unwritten novels within a closed, seemingly unified text. Taking a series of discontinuous historic moments, each chapter of this book studies in a particular text a feminine historical process that differs in temporality and form from masculine history. While this feminine historical process has been buried by official His-

tory, it is incorporated into the textual unconscious of narrative literature. Each chapter also studies in a particular text the process of
ideological production which masks this other history.

Romanticism and Its Others

While in each narrative studied, the heroine is supposed to act as the
negative term of the hero's circular dialectic, the feminine figures in
these texts cannot be wholly contained by this function in the narrative structure. What I have called the repressed feminine other in
the text consists precisely in those elements which refuse to confirm
masculine romantic self-identity. Such refusal threatens to disrupt the
line of the narrative quest and the form of historical development it
implies.

Romantic narrative, as Georg Lukács has discovered, is structured
by the hero's "search to discover the secret totality of life," which has
been irremediably lost from this world and exists only in a transcendent "beyond."[28] According to Paul de Man, this very need for totality determines the dominance of monolinear temporality in the romantic novel.[29] Feminine historicity within the text appears similar to
this quest for an imaginary original totality, but is in fact very different. Instead of a desire to return to an original unity of self and other,
feminine historicity in many of the narratives studied reveals itself as
the desire to heal the devision of society into the separate spheres of
the feminine domestic and the masculine sociopolitical, which according to many feminists grounds the social and sexual oppression of
women.[30] Rather than a *synthesis,* these feminine voices seek to re-
discover the already existing but invisible *interconnections* between domestic and sociopolitical, public and private, sexual and historical
spheres.

Rather than a unified totality, the feminine voices seek a network of
difference. The wholeness they seek does not transcend history and is
not a resolution of contradictions, but an entry into history which
women have been denied. Read from the perspective of the repressed
feminine voice, the romantic love passion, which seems to epitomize a
private, self-enclosed relation, leads back into the network of social
contradictions. It was mentioned before that romantic narrative combines on an ideological level the twin cultural myths of phallocentric
sexual relation and androcentric historical development. The level of

the repressed feminine other also establishes unbreakable interconnections between sexuality and history, but in a quite different way.

Texts and Their Contexts

Although I have chosen texts whose narrative structure strikingly
embodies the circular Hegelian dialectic, I have included only one
text from the previously mentioned list of nineteenth-century French
romantic novels—Stendhal's *The Red and the Black.* Rather than examine repeated examples of this structure in nineteenth-century France,
I wanted to go in two other directions. On the one hand, I have
studied narratives from different periods, in order to examine how
the structure and the cultural myths it upholds have undergone
changes at different historic moments. I especially wanted to study
the twelfth-century Tristan romance and the eighteenth-century
novel *Manon Lescaut,* because in these two preromantic texts we wit-
ness the birth process of the internalization of romance.[31] These two
texts, then, also recount the emergence of masculine romantic subjectivity out of historically different forms of subjectivity, which related
in different ways to different kinds of femininity.

On the other hand, Brontë's *Shirley* contrasts with the classical nineteenth-century French romantic novel both in that it is written by a
woman and in that it belongs to the more flexible, less tightly ordered
narrative forms of the English tradition. It is perhaps no coincidence
that in this novel tradition, where the Hegelian dialectic is less in
evidence, women writers had a greater autonomous voice than in
nineteenth-century France. The only major woman novelist in nineteenth-century France is George Sand, and her novels represent, as
Frappier-Mazur says, a "displacement"[32] of the masculine romantic
form rather than a different form that can encompass and go beyond
it.

My intent in including Brontë's *Shirley* was to examine conflicts
between masculine and feminine discourse in a novel authored by a
woman as compared to those authored by men. Most of the narratives
included in this book are authored by men[33] for a double reason. By
studying how phallocentric literary texts repress feminine discourse, I
hoped to gain insight into how this repression works in our social text.
For the same reason, I wanted to study how the repressed feminine
discourses can break into and speak through masculine discourses,
and speak against their objectifying forms.

The male-authored narratives included in this study were chosen because they have most powerfully and seductively produced and perpetuated the twin myths of phallocentric romantic love and androcentric history; they also contain the most powerful forces of disruptive passion. They have therefore been the most widely read and adapted into operas—like *Tristan* and *Manon Lescaut*—and films— like *The Red and the Black* and *Big Meaulnes*. In many cases their titles have become, more than titles of particular texts, emblems of cultural legends. The name Tristan has come to symbolize fatal passion, and Manon Lescaut the fatal charms of Woman. Julien Sorel of *The Red and the Black* has come to symbolize individualist revolt.

While *Big Meaulnes* is not now a widely read novel, it was influential on the generation of French intellectuals that grew up during and after World War I and again in the 1950s and 1960s. For the members of this earlier generation in their adolescent years this novel epitomized the unattainable, the marvelous, the mysteriousness of a lost world, and it even provided the model on which Simone de Beauvoir as an aspiring young writer based her first, unpublished, novel.[34] In the 1950s it was again considered the model of the fantastic novel (see chap. 6).

In addition to the cultural influence these narratives have exerted, certain of their formal qualities make them especially suitable for inclusion in this study. In *Tristan and Isolde, Manon Lescaut, The Red and the Black*, and *Big Meaulnes*, the narrative structure of the circular dialectic takes a particularly strong and controlling form. Yet at the same time the text of each work offers a particularly strong conflict between the dominating masculine voice and the repressed feminine voice. In other words I have selected those works in which the feminine other is at the same time especially forcefully excluded and also especially disruptive of masculine self-completion. In *Manon Lescaut* and *The Red and the Black* the formal workings of the text exert a great deal of energy toward silencing this feminine other which refuses to confirm the identity of the hero and the unity of the narrative.

Harlequin Romances were chosen, or rather they forced their choice upon me, because they present themselves as the obvious progeny of the romantic love genealogy in contemporary times. But Brontë's *Shirley* presents itself as the exception among all these narratives. The question of how Brontë's work differs from the others studied here is also the question of the unavoidable connection between a text and its sociohistoric context. The social situation of writers, their position in historically specific hierarchies of race, sex, and class, cannot help but affect their authorial voice, and also their relation to the generic and narrative forms which culture and tradition have dictated they write within. If masculine discourses repress feminine discourses in a literary text, they must also do so, in different ways, in the social text within which authors speak and write. If, as Harold Bloom says, the romantic author's writerly project is an internalized form of the hero's narrative quest, does not that internalized writerly quest exclude a feminine other just as the romantic narrative quest does?[35] How then does a woman author of a romantic love novel speak within, break through, or subvert its masculine authorial discourse? How do the differences between male- and female-authored romantic novels implicate differently the status of a subversive feminine voice within the text?

While chapter 5 of this book, "Feminine Romantic Desire: Charlotte Brontë's *Shirley*," does not claim to give a complete answer to these questions, it does compare one romantic novel by a female—and feminist—author to novels by male authors. I have avoided giving a single rigid definition to the terms "feminine" and "feminist," because they are used today in so many different ways, and their meaning is in a process of change. In general, however, "feminist" refers to a consciously articulated discourse which criticizes the oppression of women. In this sense Brontë is a feminist author, and *Shirley* is a feminist novel. I have used "feminine" in the French poststructuralist sense of an unnameable other excluded from the phallocentric symbolic order. Designating neither an eternal essence in opposition to the masculine, nor the complementary reflection of the masculine within our phallocentric symbolic order, the feminine is that which the symbolic order has had to exclude in order to establish itself as a unified structure. Yet it is not the formless, inchoate "outside" of that structure. It is rather the unrealized potential for other forms of discourse, desire, and development that cannot be spoken within our order. *Shirley* gives evidence of the feminine in this sense.

As a historical novel, *Shirley* explicitly thematizes those problems of feminine historicity, sexuality, and subjectivity that act as implicit interference within the other narratives studied. Although a feminist novel, its narrative is necessarily couched in masculine discursive forms and structured around events of masculine history—the War of 1812 in its effects on male factory owners, the Luddite revolts of

1812, and the class war between male property owners and male workers from which women are excluded. Beyond its explicit feminism, limited in the confines of these discursive and historical forms, the text harbors a deeper, more implicit, uncoded feminism which can be read in the symbolic networks dispersed throughout the text. The conflict between narrative and symbolism works at several levels of the novel. It suggests potential, as yet unformulated, feminine alternatives to the models of personal and historical development encoded in *Shirley*, and it also suggests alternatives to traditional representation. The dominant discourse objectifies the world and represents a supposedly exterior and preexisting reality. The repressed discourse, nonrepresentational, does not give us any preexisting image but challenges the illusions of objective representation (see chap. 5).

In *Shirley* and the four male-authored novels, a masculine discourse dominates the narrative and a feminine discourse subverts it. Yet the two kinds of novels differ in qualitative ways. In "The Internalization of Quest Romance," Harold Bloom maintains that in romanticism, the poet becomes the hero of the romantic quest. Through his own poetry he becomes "not a seeker after nature but after his own mature powers" (p. 26). The same is true of the male novelists studied here. Although Prévost, Stendhal, and Alain-Fournier may not identify with des Grieux, Julien Sorel, and Augustin Meaulnes in an autobiographical sense, the authors do identify with their heroes as allegories of their own internalized quest. Speaking in the codes of masculine self-identity they can, in recounting this quest, have the illusion of expressing their own "self" in a language that seems natural. But a feminine author who seeks to express feminine desires for historical agency, subjectivity, and sexuality does not have such a luxury. The forms of narrative and language in which she must speak are themselves obstacles to the realization of those desires. She must speak in a borrowed tongue and use forms that are constructed to exclude the very forms of history, subjectivity, and sexuality she wants to express.

In the texts of these male authors the repressed feminine other threatens to undermine the hero's identity, but in the end identity and unity prevail in the novels. While the threat is not entirely silenced, it can be ignored by readers well schooled in the codes of romantic narrative. A reader hears what is excluded only if she or he is conscious of the need to listen for it. In Brontë's novel, on the other hand, where the repressed feminine is a weapon in the hands of the author, it disrupts the narrative itself. Almost all the commentators of *Shirley* have seen that the narrative does not succeed as a narrative, that it is not ordered and unified as a traditional narrative should be. While some critics have analyzed these disruptions as flaws in the novel, other critics, like Susan Gubar,[36] have focused on showing the ways that the novel does work very powerfully. It might also be worthwhile to show why the novel does not work and to uncover some deeper powers within the text that prevent its traditional narrative form from cohering.

In asking this "why," chapter 5 studies how Brontë breaks chinks in the walls of masculine discourse and also how these walls imprison her. *Shirley* shows us the relation between the masculine and feminine forms of discourse, the way in which they entwine and double each other inseparably. Phallocentric discourse, which is structured, syntactical, grammatical, is coded to represent what we see as "reality." The different feminine discourse is unformulated and uncoded, but the two are interdependent. The structures of phallocentric discourse could not exist without the productivity of feminine discourse, which is always working in and through it. Women authors, who have had to speak in the tongues of men, can show us how to make masculine tongues more permeable and vulnerable to their other.

Textual Seduction

As long as the masculine language structure remains impermeable and undisputed, the dominant voice of masculine romantic narrative exerts a double seduction on the reader. Seducing readers into the myth of romantic love, they also seduce them into accepting the interpretation or limited range of interpretations offered by the voice of the narrator. We automatically agree to see what the dominant masculine voice of narration shows us and to ignore what it masks because the narrator tells his story through codes of interpretation which readers have already internalized, and which seem as natural as the ideologies of linear narrative and romantic heterosexual relations. These interpretive codes are simply more invisible. They encode the shared values that underlie the "interpretive community" that Stanley Fish talks about,[37] and the "agreement" between implied reader and implied author that Wayne Booth postulates: "The author creates, in short, an image of himself and another of his reader; he makes his reader as he makes his second self, and the most successful reading is one in which the created selves, author and reader, can find agreement."[38] Yet many feminist critics, recognizing their exclusion from this "community of readers" (Fish, p. 109) have developed strategies which critically analyze the author/reader agreement itself.

Recognizing in classic works and in their interpretive codes a community of values in which they do not share, feminist critics have engaged in readings which consciously resist and violate the complicity between author and reader upon which rests much of the seduction of classic texts.[39] In my readings of romantic heroines, I have sought to separate the stories narrated from the charm of the narrator's voice that frames them in what seems a necessary, natural, and factual interpretation, and to discover to what extent the stories exceed this frame and its implicit value system. The contradictions inherent in romanticism also mark my attitude toward its literary classics. I am seduced by their beauties and repelled by their active complicity in forming a cultural value system which has systematically excluded women from humanity. The study of a contradictory relation between women and romantic love has also been the study of a contradictory relation between a feminine reader and the most seductive texts of a masculine culture.

Chapter 2

Love and the New Patriarchy

Tristan and Isolde

The fascination of romantic love narrative for contemporary feminine readers sinks it roots into a long history. The first women in Western culture to enjoy it belonged to the aristocratic and royal courts of late-twelfth-century Europe. One of their favorite romances, judging by the number of different manuscript versions which have come down to us, was *Tristan and Isolde*,[1] the original and archetypal tale of fatal passion.

Written by clerics in the personal service of aristocrats, these romances synthesized the Provençal courtly love lyrics with northern Celtic and Arthurian legends, transforming both genres to create the romantic love narrative.[2] As the lyric moment of sexual passion develops into narrative, it becomes the shaping force of the hero's and heroine's entire life span, and thus becomes a temporal form which structures their destiny. The authors of the Tristan romances, Béroul, Thomas, and Gottfried von Strassburg, helped to create the new cultural force of romantic love, which for the first time turned sexual love between a man and a woman into an exalted ideal and a central theme of literature. According to René Nelli, it combines sexual desire with a total spiritual union previously reserved for religious experience.[3]

Modern critics like R. Howard Bloch have interpreted this legend as reflecting the "birth of subjective conscience" and "the designation of the individual as an autonomous legal entity,"[4] but this interpretation accounts only for Tristan's story, and excludes Isolde's story, which tells of the destruction of a different kind of individuality. While the Tristan story recounts the development of masculine individualism, the Isolde story, which has remained invisible to readers, recounts the birth of modern "femininity," without which masculine individualism could not exist.

Yet *Tristan and Isolde* does not explicity recount this historical development, since it does not "realistically" represent social reality, nor does it consciously reflect history. In the vernacular literature that preceded medieval romances and remained popular after their advent, women were either barely present, as in the epics which treat the love of men for each other, or presented as evil, as in the clerical writings which treat the love of man for God.[5] But courtly love lyrics and romances replace the love of men for God and each other with the love of men for women, at least in the world of literature.

While this new prominence of women in literature might suggest a parallel rise in their social status, most historians agree that their status did not improve. While Joan Kelly-Gadol, looking backward from the perspective of women's lower status in Renaissance culture, says that by comparison courtly love "represents an ideological liberation of their sexual and affective powers that must have some social reference," other historians, like Joanne McNamara and Suzanne Wemple, looking forward from the perspective of women's role in early feudalism, find that women's freedom suffered.[6] The Ideal Woman and the reality of women's lives start to split into two dichotomous directions.

Their status did not exactly fall in a quantitative sense; instead their relation to society was changed by the restructuring of the feudal order that occurred in the late twelfth century in what is now northern France. *Tristan and Isolde* produces an ideological structure which assigns femininity its place within this changed social order, not by the way the romance represents historical change, since it does not directly do so, but by the way it combines the courtly love lyric and Celtic legend to produce romantic narrative. While critics have noticed that the first part of the romance is marked by Celtic myth elements and the second part by courtliness and have debated about the predominance of one genre over the other,[7] little analysis has been done of the relation between them, and of how the conflict between Celtic logic and courtly logic in the same text works to produce a new ideological structure, a new literary form, a new concept of sexuality, and a value system for a new European culture.

This culture developed in the course of a profound revolution in every aspect of life, from the shape and form of the sociopolitical world to the most intimate forms of consciousness and sexuality. What emerged were the first shadowy outlines of our world, with its individualistic, self-conscious form of masculine subjectivity, its repressed and obsessive sexuality, the beginnings of a bureaucratic state, and a market economy. What also emerges is a form of patriarchy that has remained strong in capitalism.

The nobility, whose membership had been fluid, became at the end of the twelfth century a closed class with hereditary membership passed from father to son. And while feudalism was tightening into a hierarchical system, it was also being contested by the rise of cities, which had all but disappeared in the early medieval period. The cities reintroduced world commerce and the use of money, and created an urban class, the bourgeoisie.[8] The establishment of a new hereditary aristocracy meant that the many-branched mixed matrilineal-patrilineal family networks of the early feudal period were being replaced by an exclusively patrilineal family system, marked by strict linear descent. In this system, an aristocratic man could begin to define himself as an isolated entity in relation to his property and to his name rather than in relation to the concrete, immediate reciprocal connections to mixed-lineage, complex kinship groups.[9] Women, by contrast, retained and maintained these connections, even as they were losing their old importance and power.

In general the old feudal social structure as a concrete network of direct dependence relations and mutual service, having for its foundation a many-branched, mixed-lineage kinship network, was transformed by the beginnings of an abstract state, of a cash nexus, of a unilineal patriarchal family system, and of an abstract legal code which began to separate codified law from practical living laws. The Capetian state also began to stand as an abstract, unilateral institution separate from the social world; and although it lacked the elaborate mechanisms and power of the state in later periods, it bore a sharp contrast to the personal, direct relations of early feudalism. The emergence of an abstract realm felt to be autonomous and separate from lived experience, yet which mediated the lived reality of masculine individuals, became a crucial structuring element of a new mentality which is expressed through the text of *Tristan and Isolde*.

In these historical transformations, the rupture of concrete relations between people in favor of relations that link isolated individuals to abstractions is connected to the changed situation of women. During the early feudal period, when there had been no distinction between public and private law, the lord—and the lady—of the manor held the entire manor as their household and administered all the affairs upon it. The new legal system, distinguishing the public realm from the private family, also regulated more strictly who could administer what, so that women were excluded from active roles they had played before. Between 950 and 1150, women fulfilled functions in greater numbers as property holders and managers, judges, participants in assemblies, and even on occasion military leaders in the absence of the lord of the manor. Abbesses controlled monasteries, schools, and entire fiefs.[10]

Joanne McNamara and Suzanne Wemple show how aristocratic women lost power as the family lost its public role and its functions as a central institution of society. They also lost property rights and inheritance, as property ownership became more important and more tightly controlled.[11] David Herlihy finds that by the end of the twelfth century, even the children of peasant and artisan families ceased to inherit through their mother or to take their mother's name with the same frequency as earlier.[12] And in order to ensure that the newly won privileges and hereditary wealth of aristocratic men would be passed to legitimate heirs, women found their sexual chastity much more stringently enforced.

Although the early feudal system was far from the preclass societies Eleanor Leacock analyzes in *Myths of Male Dominance*, its replacement by a stricter system of authority involved, as she says, "not so much a replacement of a formal system by another, as the substitution of formal stabler units for informal, unstable ones."[13] The development of formal hierarchies in all feudal institutions tended to exclude women from active decision-making roles. Ineligible for posts in the new state bureaucracies and for education in the new universities, they were also denied their independent feminine monasteries, as these were placed under the authority of bishops.

Into this lessening of feminine public activity in the aristocracy comes the courtly love culture, where the adoring knight pledges "fealty" to his distant lady. In courtly love a metaphorical power replaces real social status, while the high position of the single great lady compensates for the lowered position of women as a social group. In a society where abstract systems of power and authority begin to replace more informal social networks, courtly literature, through its treatment of women, helps to produce forms of logic that create and isolate an ideal markedly separate from reality.

The Story of Tristan and Isolde

In *Tristan and Isolde* the textual production of form includes the radical separation of a transcendent ideal from concrete experience, and the transformation of an open, fluid network of myth and legend into a closed, unilinear narrative system. Its thematic elements include exiling Isolde from a land where women have independence and power; duping her into believing she is marrying the man of her choice so as to force her into a despotic marriage with a man she has never seen; and suppressing matrilineal kinship relations. Yet the text retains strong traces of a dissident feminine voice which conflicts with the final narrative and ideological structures.

An analysis of formal production in *Tristan and Isolde* presents certain difficulties, because the manuscripts have come down to us in a fragmentary state. I have used the Gottfried von Strassburg text, because, being the most complete, it offers the best version for an analysis of the text as a whole. Since Gottfried claims that he bases his version on Thomas, and since the Thomas fragment takes up where Gottfried's ends, I have used Thomas in analyzing the romance's conclusion. For further evidence for the continuity between the Gottfried and Thomas versions, I have used Friar Robert's Old Norse *The Saga of Tristan and Isond* since it is the only complete version that remains from the Middle Ages. For points of comparison, I have on occasion brought in other versions. Since this romance may be unfamiliar to today's readers, an analysis of it will be deferred in order to scan briefly its main events here.

The romance begins, as do most legends, before the hero's birth. His father, Rivalin, Prince of Loonois, comes to the court of King Mark in Cornwall, where the king's sister Blanchefleur falls in love with him and conceives Tristan out of wedlock. The lovers then marry just before Tristan is born, but Rivalin dies in battle, and Blanchefleur dies of grief just after giving birth. Ignorant of his parents' identity, Tristan is raised by his father's trusted liegeman Rual Lefoitenant.

As a young adolescent, Tristan is kidnapped by merchants and ends up in Cornwall at Mark's court. Unaware of their kinship, they are nevertheless drawn to each other by "blood instinct," and Tristan swears to protect Mark's domain with complete loyalty. When they do finally learn of their kinship, Tristan is adopted as Mark's heir. At this time, the fearsome knight Morold is harassing Cornwall, demanding yearly tribute on behalf of King Gurmun of Ireland, his sister's husband. No one has been willing to fight against Morold until the arrival of Tristan, who does kill him but receives from him a poisoned wound. Just before Morold dies, he tells the hero the wound can be cured only by his sister Queen Isolde of Ireland, and so the mortally wounded Tristan is put in a boat set for Ireland. As the queen's "mortal enemy," he must hide his identity under the name of Tantris in order to be cured by her and her beautiful, wise, and talented daughter the Princess Isolde.

Upon Tristan's return to Cornwall, Mark's barons, jealous of Tristan and envying him his position as Mark's heir, force the king to marry in order to produce another heir. Mark insists that he will marry only Princess Isolde. Offering to obtain Isolde for Mark, Tristan again goes to Ireland where a dragon is now ravaging the land. The king of Ireland has promised to grant the hand of his daughter to the one who will slay the dragon. Again only Tristan will slay it, but no one knows of his deed. He cuts off the dragon's tongue and puts it in his pocket, where it begins to poison him. As he lies hidden in agony, the cowardly steward of the Irish court, seeing the dead dragon, cuts off its head and goes to court where he claims Isolde's hand.

Isolde, refusing this match, and disobeying her father's authority, takes her mother to find the real dragon-slayer. For a second time the two women save Tristan's life. Princess Isolde bathes Tristan to cure the poison, but while he is in his bath, she notices that a notch in his sword matches a fragment of sword she had taken from the skull of her dead uncle Morold. Preparing to avenge her uncle's death, she raises the sword to kill Tristan, but he dissuades her.

Isolde leads Tristan to her father, and it is only here for the first time that Tristan, talking to the king, reveals his intention to take Isolde for King Mark. On the boat for Cornwall, Isolde laments her hatred for Tristan. By accident, during the boat voyage, Isolde's maid gives the two young people a magic potion, specially prepared by Queen Isolde for her daughter to drink with King Mark. The powerful philter makes the two people who drink it together love each other exclusively and eternally unto death.

Having drunk the fatal potion, the lovers are forced by their love to live a life of treason and adultery. From perfect loyal knight, Tristan becomes the traitor to his kinsman and liege lord Mark. Mark's barons discover the illicit passion and denounce Tristan, who goes off into exile. He and Isolde live for four years in the isolation of the Morois Forest, after which Isolde returns to Mark's court while Tristan continues his knightly adventures in the service of Kaherdin, whose sister he marries, because her name, also Isolde, reminds him of his beloved. After a series of adventures, more numerous and discontinuous in some versions, more unified toward a single conclusion in Gottfried, Tristan is again mortally wounded in battle. Isolde leaves her position and reputation in Mark's court and comes to cure him, but a plot by Tristan's wife prevents her from arriving before her lover dies. She arrives in time to die beside Tristan as the two are finally united in death.

Denis de Rougemont's Love in the Western World

The most famous and influential interpretation of this romance is Denis de Rougemont's *Love in the Western World*.[14] Since his theory repeats in a curious way the production of the same ideological structure that the Tristan romance produces, a discussion of the theory can show how the same patriarchal logical process operates in the romance and in twentieth-century critical discourse. Therefore, an analysis of the romance will again be deferred for a short discussion of de Rougemont's theory.

Briefly, his theory holds that the twelfth-century legend constitutes a cultural myth which both "expresses and veils" (p. 16) the foundations of Western consciousness. By falling in love, Tristan and Isolde willfully but unconsciously choose to desire what they cannot have, because the object of their passion is not each other but their own suffering, through which Western man gains his self-consciousness. Their ultimate object of desire is death, in which they find the absolute they seek. Thus the love philter symbolizes, like a Freudian symbol in a dream, this unconscious will, the internalization of formerly exterior repressive forces, and a secret death wish. The philter hides from us and from the lovers the fact that they choose to repress their sexuality by turning away from their guilty passion, because they really do not love each other. They love instead the ideal represented by their love, or their own ideal self, their "deified Ego" (p. 239), which is reflected in their love.

Like other critics, de Rougemont neglects to examine how the role of Isolde modifies his theory, and in two self-contradictory ways. On the one hand he assumes her to be the *same* as Tristan and simply merges them together in his analysis. On the other hand, he sees her as Tristan's objectified *other*. Merging her with Tristan, he says: "They are in love, but each loves the other only *for the sake of the self, not for the sake of the other*. Their misery arises from a false reciprocity, the mask of a double narcissism" (p. 43, italics in text). Here he sees Isolde as a subject of narcissistic desire, but in other passages he denies the possibility that she could be the subject of any kind of desire or engage in any kind of reciprocity with a man: "For Tristan, Isolde was nothing but the symbol of luminous Desire: . . . Therefore, Isolde had to be the impossible" (p. 239). Forgetting about reciprocity in love, he says: "Isolde is always the stranger, the very strangeness of woman" (p. 238).

As in the romance itself, in de Rougemont's theory the exclusion of women from membership in humanity flows out of a logic that separates spiritual ideals from social reality. To support his main contention, that romantic love is a completely and exclusively destructive force, "the *anarchic invasion* into our lives of a spiritual heresy to which we have lost the key" (p. 158, italics in text), de Rougemont states a connection between the Tristan legend and the twelfth-century Catharist heresy with its Manichaean theology. Other critics have made this connection, which in itself is quite compelling, but de Rougemont does so by creating his own new and fantastic version of the pre-Christian Celtic religion in which *Tristan and Isolde* ultimately extends it roots. He claims that Celtic paganism is fundamentally identical to this Christian Manichaeism, which posits a rigid and absolute separation between earthly life and the life of the spirit: "Every dualist, Manichean conception sees in daily life misery itself; and in death the ultimate good, . . . reintegration into the One. . . . The fulfillment of Love denies all earthly love. . . . Such is the great background against which our myth stands out" (p. 53).

While Celtic Druidism is in fact very far from this Manichaean

doctrine, de Rougemont holds that in Druidism, as in Christian Manichaean heresies, the Christian idea of incarnation would be the "supreme scandal . . . for our reason which in no way can accept this
unthinkable confusion between the finite and the infinite" (p. 53).

De Rougemont claims to take his information on Druidism from
Henri Hubert's work, but Hubert, as well as the Rees brothers and
Jean Markale, point out that although the Druids were concerned
with death and the afterlife, the boundaries between this world and
the other world in that religion were remarkable for their fluidity and
permeability to each other. The confusion of the finite and the infinite, far from "unthinkable," was accepted as the normal state of
affairs.[15]

This distortion of Druidism permits de Rougemont to transform
women from the active participants in the college of Druids that history shows them to have been into an ahistorical emanation of male
Druids' minds.

> In the eyes of the Druids, woman constitutes a divine and pro-
> phetic being. She is the Velleda of the *Martyres,* the luminous
> phantom who appears to the vision of the Roman general lost in
> his nocturnal revery. . . . Eros has taken on the appearance of
> Woman, symbol of the beyond and of that nostalgia which
> makes us despise earthly joys. . . . The Essylt of sacred legends,
> "object of contemplation, mysterious spectacle," was an invita-
> tion to desire what is beyond bodily forms. She is beautiful and
> desirable in herself . . . and yet her nature is fleeting. "The Eter-
> nal feminine pulls us forward," Goethe will say. And Novalis:
> "Woman is the goal of man." (P. 51)

Besides noting that de Rougemont cannot see women outside the
"eyes," the "visions," or the quotations of men, one can also note that
there exists no "sacred legend" of Essylt (the Old Welsh version of
Isolde) that has come down to us. This is a complete fabrication of de
Rougemont. The only extant references to Essylt are in two very brief
Welsh Triads and a catalog of the "leading ladies of the Island" in the
Welsh Mabinogion *Culhwch and Olwen.*[16]

De Rougemont's "dualism," whose irreconcilable separation between matter and spirit makes spirit (masculine spirit) the primary or
even the only reality, is really a rigid monism. Finding "scandalous"

the "confusion" of matter and spirit, it necessitates this desire to return to "the One"—to the *mono*tony of pure spirit and the vision of *one* sex. It is a monologic ideology that preserves its dominance by negating that which differs from or does not conform to it.

This same ideological form takes shape in the course of *Tristan and Isolde,* but in the opposite direction from that which de Rougemont proposes. For de Rougemont, the romantic love of the Tristan legend "surfaced with the same movement that raised into the half-light of consciousness . . . that Feminine Principle" (p. 105) always/already buried within it. But the romance traces precisely the opposite process. It first transforms concrete women into an abstract "Feminine Principle," then interiorizes that principle into the hero's spirit, and finally suppresses an independent feminine presence. This gradual suppression of feminine difference in the course of the narrative is precisely what differentiates *Tristan and Isolde* from Celtic mythology. The Tristan legend does not "revivify . . . ancient religions," as de Rougemont says (p. 119), but on the contrary marks a rupture with them, as is illustrated by the way Celtic myth elements in the romance serve to represent that which is disappearing and are themselves gradually excluded from the text in which they leave their very telling traces.

Women and Celtic Culture

Those Celtic myth elements in *Tristan and Isolde* retain the feminine activity that marks so strongly the original myths. In Celtic literature—Irish legends and Welsh mabinogi—feminine characters have greater prominence and power, a wider range of action, and a different function in the structure than in romantic narrative. The inclusion and ensuing repression of those myth elements in the romance entail the inclusion and repression of a powerful, active femininity. Since they are so decisively at play in the text of *Tristan,* the analysis of the romance will once again be put off, to allow for a short analysis of these myth elements.

Preserved in oral form by Druids and by an official class of bards called Fili, Celtic legends were compiled and written down by Christian clerics in Ireland from the seventh to the ninth centuries, in Wales in the twelfth century, and are still transmitted orally today. The compilers divided Irish legend into four cycles, each of which relates, in a combination of myth and history, the stories of four successive peoples who invaded and inhabited Ireland.

The first cycle, the "mythological cycle," recounts the adventures of the Tuatha de Danaam (Tribe of Danu). The earliest known inhabitants of Ireland, the tribe is said to trace its descent back to its primal ancestress Danu, who is also the mother of the gods, and whom Robert Graves associates with the Great Goddess, worshipped in the Eastern Mediterranean during the second millenium B.C.[17] When defeated by the second group of invaders, the Gaels, the Tuatha de Danaam become the ever-living supernatural beings of the Other World, where women continue to have the power of enchantment and the sexual freedom they now lack in This World. An illustration of this double feminine sexual code—freedom to bear children out of wedlock for women of the Other World and severe punishment for adultery for women of this world—appears in the fairy tale "The King of Erin and the Queen of the Lonesome Island."[18] In the Tristan romance, Isolde confronts a similar split, freedom in Ireland, severe punishment for adultery in Cornwall.

In the mythological cycle of Irish legend, women are not passive incarnations of the "Feminine Principle," but warriors, founders of capital cities, physicians, and Druids. Even in the third or "heroic" cycle and the fourth or "Fenian" cycle, the greatest heroes like CuChúlainn and Finn MacCumhail are trained by women warriors who live away from men and who teach the heroes secrets of invulnerability. Only women, like "the mother of Fear Dubh who is more violent, more venomous, more to be dreaded, a greater warrior than her sons," outsmart Finn and CuChúlainn and defeat them in battle.[19]

In the extensive critical debates over how much *Tristan and Isolde* retains elements from Irish and Welsh legend, Gertrude Schoepperle Loomis's work, often considered the most authoritative and extensive work on sources, claims that what has been incorporated into the Tristan legend are *motifs* from Celtic and especially Irish folklore. Important among these motifs is the *Imrama* or "Voyage," in which a young hero sails, guided by magic forces, to the supernatural Other World, often called the Land of Women, as Tristan sails to Ireland to find Isolde.[20] Another motif is the "Elopement," in which a young married woman runs away from her old husband with a younger man, of which the most famous example is the story of *Diarmuid and Grainne.*

But Schoepperle points out that while the first part of *Tristan and Isolde* is folkloric, the later part, with its celebration of adulterous, distant love between Tristan and Isolde, falls entirely into the courtly ethos (pp. 120 and 177). This seeming dichotomy is really a process which first integrates and then excludes elements of Celtic culture and by so doing gives form to an ideology that is patriarchal not only in the narrow sense of male kinship descent, but in the broader sense that it justifies, naturalizes, and totalizes the institutions and thought structures that make masculine hegemony seem natural.

Elements of an ideology more open and more inclusive of feminine difference appear in the first part of *Tristan and Isolde*, and also characterize early medieval Irish culture. The social structure of early medieval Ireland is in some ways similar and in other ways very different from that of early medieval Western Europe. Based on a patriarchal kinship structure, the clans of Ireland still retained up to the end of the twelfth century traces of matrilineal descent; and Henri Hubert notes in Irish writings the feminine elements we have already seen: "the epics, history and laws of the Celts . . . contain memories of important remnants of the uterine family."[21] The Irish legal code, although repressive to women in the sixth century, had by the ninth century given equal property rights and "equal lordship" to the majority of women.[22]

Technically less "matrilineal" than early medieval Western Europe, medieval Irish society, until the Norman invasions of the late twelfth century, maintained its ancient clan structure in a stable form, and so incorporated to a relatively high degree that informal decision-making structure which Leacock sees as so favorable to women. The only part of Europe never conquered by Rome, Ireland continued to develop a flourishing, energetic culture, which, unlike that of the rest of Europe, was not interrupted by the fall of the Roman Empire, did not succumb to the anarchy of early feudalism, and did not experience a Dark Age. This culture grew in a context free from the Roman property system, legal system, and government bureaucracies.

The Irish property system, combining individual ownership and collective clan ownership, did not give women inheritance of property, but gave both men and women the right to keep the products of their own labor. In the frequent case of divorce, the woman took back with her the products of her labor along with the instruments that produced them, while the property she had brought into the marriage went back into her clan. This floating of property between rival

clans coincided with the absence of a separate state bureaucracy or
police force above the clan. In ninth-century Ireland there were no
towns and no central government. The kingship and other positions
of leadership tended to be elective, temporary, and limited in scope,
without the vast privilege, wealth, and unilateral power associated
with inherited positions.[23]

While Celtic law gave the husband authority over the family, that
authority was undercut by many other laws. If the wife had equal or
greater property, she had equal or greater authority in the marriage.
Moreover, since the clan remained primary over the family, the woman remained a member of her own clan even in marriage. The clan
protected her from the power of her husband because it protected in
her its own property, and it also raised her children through the
institution of fosterage.

Although female adultery was as severely punished as anywhere
else in Europe, the divorce laws manifest, according to Donncha
O'Corráin, a "care for the individual personality of the woman" that
was unheard of anywhere else in Europe.[24] A woman could divorce
for a sexually unsatisfactory husband, for maltreatment by him, or for
his revealing sexual secrets of the marriage or violating her privacy.
In addition to keeping her property after divorce, the woman also
received compensation and a fine.

In certain ways the Irish system of property tenure has the features
that, according to anthropologists like Eleanor Leacock, Rayna Reiter,
Kathleen Gough, and Karen Sacks, differentiate egalitarian societies
from patriarchy.[25] In societies where the clan is more important than
the individual family and maintains its right over the woman's property even when she marries a man from another clan, the status of
women is doubly strengthened. Private property ownership and the
power it confers do not consolidate in the hands of one man, but float
among different clans. In addition, the woman's clan protects her
from her husband, allowing her more independence and respect.

In such a society the ties between husband and wife are loose, and
the social role of the biological father relatively unimportant. Instead,
the clan forges sacred bonds between brother and sister, and between
maternal uncle and sister's children. Much has been written about the
remnants of this kinship structure that are found in medieval epics
and romances as exemplified by the relation between Roland and
Charlemagne. Lancelot and Arthur, Tristan and Mark, but little has

been written about the relation between Isolde and her maternal uncle Morold that will be discussed here.

When private, inherited property replaces the collective and/or floating property of the clan, private, male-headed families become dominant over the clan. They seclude women to ensure their sexual purity, isolate them from the clan relations that give them independence from their husbands, and place them under the control of one man, and a stranger at that. The clan gradually disappears, fragmenting into a collection of separate families on the one hand, and an abstract state ruling from above on the other.

Celtic society, combining as it does contradictory elements of both matriliny and patriarchy, produces a literature, exemplified by the four mythical cycles and the CuChúlainn saga, whose structure is based on multiple logic and opposes the unilogic or monologic we have seen in de Rougemont's analysis of Celtic society. Celtic legends with their women warriors like CuChúlainn's enemy Macha, and their passive men like Pwyll, husband of the warrior goddess Rhiannon in the Welsh Mabinogion "Pwyll, Prince of Dyfed,"[26] do not have a rigid categorization of "male" qualities and "female" qualities. Furthermore, characters can adopt the form and attributes of the other sex. For instance, in the CuChúlainn cycle, Macha puts a curse on the Ulster soldiers that make them periodically experience labor pains and menstrual weakness. The most extreme example of the fluid exchange of sexes appears in "Math son of Mathonwy" where King Math punishes his sister's sons Gwydion and Gilfaethwy by changing them first into a hind and a stag who mate and bear a fawn. Then he changes the hind into a wild boar and the stag into a sow. After the two mate and produce a piglet, the boar is transformed into a wolf bitch and the sow into a wolf. The final result is that each of the two men ends up "bearing the other's child."[27]

A telling example of this sexual fluidity is found in the varying versions of what we now know as the Cinderella tale. While children today believe that there is only *one* version of the tale in which the handsome, active prince puts the shoe on the passive, obedient Cinderella because only she has a dainty enough foot to fit it, the Irish versions, of which there are many,[28] show a different logic and set of sexual values. In a tale like "Fair, Brown, and Trembling," it is the heroine who must fit her foot into the shoe, but in a tale like "The Thirteenth Son of the King of Erin," it is the hero who must fit his foot into a boot in order to marry the princess. Moreover, the shoe does not fit the maid because her foot is small enough and dainty enough to meet a set and rigid visual model of femininity. Instead the size of the shoe *changes* to fit the maid or the lad who has done the actions showing the most desirable moral qualities.

In this literature is found the logic based on multiplicity and contradiction that will appear in the first part of *Tristan and Isolde.* Irish and Welsh legends contrast to the type of romanticism that denies contradiction and sees the relation between man and woman as one in which the man cancels out the autonomous difference of the woman and absorbs her into identity with him. In Celtic legends the relation between man and woman is irreducible to oneness. Instead of intolerance of difference as in de Rougemont's "dualism," there is a true dialogic that promotes ambiguity and contradiction, defies linear logic, and rejects hierarchies.

Contrary to de Rougemont's characterization of women in Celtic myth, they appear as both desirable maidens and as ugly but powerful old hags. The same woman in a given myth often takes both forms, and she can with her magic powers make the same man both young and desirable or old, weak, and ugly. The legendary women are not only desirable, as de Rougemont says, but also desiring, and their relations with men, especially in the Fenian cycle, are marked by complex patterns of desire and rejection on both sides, of hostility and alliance.

In sexual relations, and in human relations generally, hierarchies in the legends tend to cancel each other out. Class hierarchies begin and end in the Other World, whose inhabitants, as Rees says, are at the same time the lowest—scapegoats, serfs, and outcasts from this world—and also the highest, since they are gods and goddesses (p. 145). In the Irish myths in the Curtin edition, supernatural gods visit this world in the form of servants, cowherds, and henwives.

Most of the Celtic legends concern the fluid exchanges and interpenetration of boundaries between this world and the Other World: figures who are both mortal and gods; relations between people and gods who exchange form; gods visiting this world and mortals voyaging to the Other World, as Tristan voyages to Ireland. This fluidity between the earthly realm and the supernatural realm, between masculine and feminine, between matter and spirit, is completely opposed to de Rougemont's notion of a separate, isolated spiritual realm and the desire to return to its oneness. Here the spiritual realm is not transcendent, but multiple and always present in matter.

The mutual existence of contradictory and equally true visions of a same reality is illustrated by the voyage to the Other World, the Land of Women, in the legend of Bran.

> It is what Bran thinks, he is going in his curraugh over the wonderful, beautiful clear sea; but to me from far off in my chariot, it is a flowery plain he is riding on.
>
> What is a clear sea to the good boat Bran is in, is a happy plain with many flowers to me in my two wheeled chariot.
>
> It is what Bran sees, many waves beating across the clear sea; it is what I myself see, red flowers without any fault. . . .
>
> Let Bran row on steadily, it is not far to the Land of Women; before the setting of the sun you will reach Emhain, of many-coloured hospitality. (Gregory, p. 105)

Women in this kind of culture do not have "equality" in the abstract sense that "equal" people are the "same" as each other, or that they all have some identical attribute. The respect, freedom, and independence women have are based on a multiplicity and ambiguity of relationships which work against the establishment of hierarchy and prevent unilateral dominance of one group over another.

The Establishment of Patriarchy in Tristan and Isolde

The multiple and ambiguous logic found in Celtic legend marks the first part of the romance, before Tristan and Isolde drink the love potion, not only by the inclusion of Irish myth elements in a romance structure, but in that two different forms of logic, the multilogic of Celtic culture and the more unilinear logic of patriarchal culture, cohabit. Ireland itself appears as a double place, at once mythic Other World and historically situated land in this earthly world.

While Tristan's first voyage resembles the mythic *Imrama* to the Other World, his second voyage is a voyage of conquest of a real historical land. Not only does he conquer Isolde; he also subjugates the feminine freedom of both the historical and the mythic Ireland. This contrast between the two voyages is underscored by Queen Isolde. The first time Tristan comes to Ireland, she tells him: "I will restore your life and body to you in perfect health and looks. I can give or refuse: both are in my power [both are in my hands]."[29] But during his second voyage, by the time Queen Isolde discovers he is the Tristan who murdered her brother Morold, she has lost the power over him because she has by now pledged to protect him as the dragon-slayer: "Alas, alas, lord Tristan, that I should ever have you in my power as well as I have now, yet not so as to be able to use it or so that it could serve me" (Gottfried, p. 177).

The dragon episode is a crucial turning point in the development of monologic in *Tristan and Isolde*. It places both the mother and the daughter in a double bind where they are forced to choose one or another undesirable alternative and so must deny doubleness, contradiction, and at the same time freedom. The queen must either let her enemy live or betray her pledge to save the dragon-slayer, while Princess Isolde is at an even more tightly determined crossroad. In deciding whether or not to kill Tristan, she must either forsake the vengeance of her uncle or marry the evil steward who has falsely claimed to kill the dragon. Like her mother, she faces an impossible but necessary choice between two disastrous situations and thus loses her freedom of will and of action. With either choice Isolde also loses her power.

Although the romance tells us that Tristan, by killing the dragon, becomes Isolde's defender, the real effect of his act is to subjugate her. To understand why this is so we must look not only at the episode's function in the narrative, by which it robs her of her power to choose and delivers her to the will of Tristan, but also at its connection to ancient myth. Here we are looking not at a single early medieval myth but at a long series of sedimented "archaeological layers" of the dragon myth as it is transmitted into different contexts.

In Mediterranean areas, sculptures of the ancient Great Goddess, dating from ca. 2000 B.C., often portray her holding serpents, the most common symbols of goddess power. Serpent worship was a widespread practice in areas like Minoan Crete where matrilineal culture was highly developed.[30] Myths that reflect the subjugation of these cultures after 1500 B.C. often portray the serpent as an evil force, still associated with women (as in the myth of Adam and Eve), whose power must be destroyed. Many Celtic peoples, including the Gaels who later settled in Ireland, participated in conquering those

Mediterranean lands at that period, and there is some evidence that the Tuatha de Danaam came from this area in the second millenium B.C.[31] In the Irish legends concerning Finn and the Fenians, the matrilineal Tuatha de Danaam become an ominous enemy force, and Finn must defeat a constant stream of feminine enemies: witches, hags, and "urfeists" (serpents), who threaten to take over and/or disrupt this world.[32] Like Finn, Tristan in killing the dragon, called a "serpent" in the romance, overthrows matriliny and establishes patriarchy.

Gottfried's sentence—"the King swore by his royal oath that he would give his daughter to whoever would make an end of it [the serpent]" (p. 159)—is rich in latent significance. Whoever kills the dragon not only wins the daughter, but also reduces her to the position of "being given away" by her father, and moreover gives the father the power to dispose of his daughter. Indeed, after Tristan kills the dragon, Isolde loses the power granted her as niece of her *maternal uncle* and must submit as daughter of her *father*. Once he gives her away and she leaves her native land, both Ireland, as representative of an accessible Other World, and Queen Isolde disappear forever, while Princess Isolde loses her wisdom and her healing power.

In clanic societies, especially if they have any form of matriliny, men play a significant role not as husbands and fathers but as brothers of the women and uncles to their sister's children. Blood ties are all-important. Bell and Farnsworth see in the emphasis on maternal uncle-nephew relations in the medieval epic the survivals of ancient matriliny, and George Duby's study of ninth-century Macon shows the historical existence of matriliny.[33] But if *The Song of Roland* represents, as Bell and Farnsworth say, the uncle-nephew relation in its perfect form, *Tristan and Isolde* traces the breaking of this bond.

Critics have noted that Tristan, by loving his uncle Mark's wife, betrays that most sacred of bonds with his closest kin, after which he becomes an isolated individual. Just as important, however, Isolde, by failing to kill Tristan in his bath, also betrays her sacred tie to her uncle Morold, but with the different result that she loses her magic power and her prestige. Both characters break the bond, before which they have equal and very different forms of power. Afterward the hero develops his individualism, and the heroine falls into a subservient and relative existence.

When, during Tristan's second voyage, Isolde raises the sword to kill him as the murderer of her uncle, she is exercising not only a duty but also a right. The right over Tristan's life and death, as the right to avenge her uncle, is the source of her power and independence in Ireland. When she allows herself to be persuaded by Tristan not to kill him, she falls under his power, becomes an object for him to dispose of at will, and is taken away from her clan to a land of strangers. Tristan says to her father King Gurmun: "Your majesty, remember your word—I am to dispose of your daughter" (Gottfried, p. 189). When the exchange is concluded, Gottfried tells us: "Gurmun solemnly surrendered Isolde into the hands of Tristan her enemy" (Gottfried, p. 191). When she fails to kill her uncle's murderer in his bath, she loses her matrilineal rights.

She also, by this act, loses her place in the mythic world of feminine supernatural power. In one of the major Celtic myths, the story of the god Llew Llaw Gyffes, Llew is killed in a bath with the complicity of his wife Blodeuwedd. According to Robert Graves, this is also a common motif in god myths of Eastern Mediterranean, pre-Achaean goddess religions.[34] By failing to murder Tristan in his bath, Isolde loses her connection to the Celtic goddesses.

Isolde's active, independent life while she is in Ireland, as well as her magic healing powers, come to her not through a mystic source but because she is surrounded by kinspeople and retainers who protect and defend her actions. The early section of *Tristan and Isolde*, which emphasizes the all-important relations between Tristan and his maternal uncle, as well as Isolde and her maternal uncle, also accents in Gottfried, Thomas, and the Old Norse versions the close ties between mother and daughter, which aid Isolde to be free and independent. It is her mother who helps Isolde refuse her father's order to marry the steward and go out on her own to find the real dragon-slayer.

Repeatedly, when Isolde, after she has left Ireland for Mark's court, complains of her weakness, she attributes it not to her weak womanly nature but to the fact that she has been put among strangers. When she is spied upon, entrapped, and denounced for her adultery by Mark's barons, she says to Mark:

"And so I am not surprised to be the victim of such talk. There was no chance that I should be passed over and not be accused of improper conduct, for I am far from home and can never [find helpers here, nor] ask here for my friends and relations. Unfortunately there is scarcely a soul in this place who will feel disgraced with me." (Gottfried, p. 245; German version, ll. 15494–98)

In Bédier's Thomas version, Isolde's fall from a former high status protected by close kin is expressed even more clearly. She tells Mark: "For the sake of your love I have left all my support: father, mother, kin and friends, honor, joy and power!" (p. 186).

After Isolde's marriage to Mark, the courtliness which then comes to dominate the romance works as a sign that sexual relations between people not related by blood overtake in importance blood relations. Courtly mores accompany the new hegemony of sexual ties between people who choose each other as individuals without regard for the needs of the clan. But in the Middle Ages such sexual love always takes place outside of marriage, which remains an economic arrangement between powerful families in which the bride has no say. Therefore the courtly adultery in *Tristan and Isolde* also has as its corollary Isolde's revolt against subjugation to her husband, her lack of legal and also physical freedom, the constant portrayal of her as hemmed in, trapped, spied upon, pushed into a corner, able to escape only by the most desperate of measures.

One such desperate move appears in the scene where Isolde must swear, on pain of carrying red hot iron, that she has been faithful to Mark. She makes Tristan disguise himself as a poor pilgrim and carry her across a stream on his back in front of Mark's court. She then swears that "never did a man born of woman approach my body, except you, sire King, and the pitiful pilgrim who carried me from the boat and who in front of you fell on top of me" (Thomas, p. 201).

Critics like de Rougemont, who have criticized Isolde (in itself a dubious practice of literary criticism) for her "feminine ruse" and her "blasphemy,"[35] neglect to see her reacting in the total context of the legend, as a formerly "happy and carefree" (Gottfried, p. 186) woman who has been reduced to the state of a hunted animal, or as she says in Bédier's Thomas version, "a prisoner of war" (Thomas, p. 207), by foreign marriage laws of which she had no knowledge, and by a despotic marriage which she did not choose.

Another significant contrast between multiple logic in the first part of the romance and unitary logic in the second part is found in the notion of love itself. While in the second part the only model for love is the fatal romantic passion between Tristan and Isolde, the first part has two different models of love. One is the love of Tristan's mother Blanchefleur for his father Rivalin, which resembles the fatal passion of the second part, but which does not structurally dominate the narrative as Tristan's and Isolde's love will after they drink the potion. The second model is Isolde's love for Tristan when he is in Ireland and before she discovers he has killed her uncle. This love of Isolde is so much outside our cultural framework that some critics deny she loves him. Hatto, for instance, says:

> Sentimental critics, wise in the wisdom of latter-day psychology, attribute Isolde's inability to kill Tristan to her being more or less consciously in love with him, even before drinking the love potion, a conception which was foreign to Gottfried. Gottfried's own explanation, which one may be excused for preferring, despite its not being entirely free from prevarication, is that Isolde's womanly instincts forbade her to kill.[36]

Hatto's logic, based as it is on an "eternal feminine," is reminiscent of de Rougemont's. While Hatto does note that Tristan appeals to Isolde's femininity in order to dupe her, he does not mention that Gottfried *invents* these "womanly instincts," nor that the more primitive Eilhart version, as well as the Old Norse version, are more explicit in telling us that Isolde loves Tristan. In these two other versions, she is prevented from killing Tristan by the thought that if she kills him, she will have to marry the steward instead of him.

This "conception" is "foreign" to Gottfried not because he is too premodern, but because he is too modern. Yet the very structure of the dragon episode makes it impossible to suppress entirely from the Gottfried text Isolde's preromantic, prepatriarchal form of love. When Isolde says: "Never will I consent to what my father wants, to marry this man [the steward]" (Thomas, p. 119), and when she goes out to find the real dragon-slayer, she is not only rejecting her father's authority, but also going out to *choose her own husband* according to her ancient Celtic right. Only later does she find out that Tristan has come to seek her as Mark's wife, and Tristan is very careful to hide this fact from her when, handsomely naked in his bath, he is persuading her not to kill him.

In the Irish myths of the Curtin collection, the heroine almost always chooses her own husband, and significantly enough, this choice is never directly expressed. But when she helps a warrior to accomplish exploits that would be impossible without her aid, or when she saves his life, or when she asks him to save her, this means, according to the code of that literature, that she has chosen him to marry her. The legends do not say that she loves the hero, do not analyze her motives, and never show her reflecting on her love. But the man who rejects such a marriage is considered unfaithful enough to receive harsh punishment, and when women are sold into marriage without their consent, as in "The Weaver's Son and the Giant of the White Hill," it is treated as a disastrous situation. Each of these stories states that the father or brother gives the heroine to the hero who can accomplish a dangerous exploit, but no hero can gain victory unless the daughter or sister chooses to help him, to save him from danger, or to heal him when he is wounded. Contrary to what Hatto says, he himself, in denying that Isolde loves Tristan, projects modern psychology onto the romance.

Isolde's psychology is that of the mythical Celtic maidens. Like them, she chooses, while she is still unaware of Tristan's identity, to bring him back to life and to prove he really killed the dragon, because she knows she is destined to be the wife of the dragon-slayer. According to the multiple logic she operates under, the fact that her future is determined would not prevent her from exercising her power to choose and to realize her own desires. Although her resistance to her father and her intention to seek and choose Tristan as her husband are much more explicit in other versions of the romance, Gottfried, even by having Tristan as part of his disguise claim to have a wife already, cannot prevent traces of this older version from breaking through, especially since polygamy still existed in Celtic culture.

In the crucial scene where Isolde, having discovered that the dragon-slayer is also the man who killed her uncle, tries and fails to kill Tristan, Gottfried expresses her conflict as a purely psychological one between abstract, eternal forces. But it is also a mythical and historical conflict between the past status and the future status of women.

Those two conflicting qualities, those warring contradictions, womanhood and anger, which accord so ill together, fought a hard battle in her breast. . . . Thus uncertainty raged within her, till at last sweet womanhood triumphed over anger, with the

result that her enemy lived, and Morold was not avenged. (Gottfried, p. 176)

While this "sweet womanhood" seems to signify an eternal force, the
language in the passage also makes it a historical quality that comes
into being in this moment. By bringing into opposition "womanhood"
and "anger," this passage gives both terms a new meaning in relation
to each other. Womanhood now excludes anger, and no longer con-
notes the women of Irish legend, but a more subdued type of femininity, while anger, formerly associated with the ancient bisexual
clanic duty of vengeance, is now reserved for "manhood." The "tri-
umph" of womanhood signifies that by this nonvengeance of Morold
the maternal uncle, femininity becomes defined as submission.

In the Old Norse version, Isolde goes so far as to ask Tristan to be
her husband (p. 61), but we can see why this un-self-reflecting, unspoken, but very active love of Isolde, which resembles that of the
maidens in Irish folklore, is not considered "love" when we compare
it to Blanchefleur's love for Rivalin, characterized by a self-reflective
anguish and torment which conforms to our modern conception of
love. Because Blanchefleur experiences love as a mysterious "suffering" (Gottfried, p. 44), it leads her to self-questioning and self-consciousness, and thus resembles the romantic love de Rougemont defines. Likewise, Isolde's passion for Tristan after drinking the potion,
in opposition to her love for Tristan while they are still in Ireland, also
brings her to self-reflection, since in her anguish she tells herself
explicitly for the first time that she loves Tristan.

But beyond attributing this self-consciousness and suffering to
guilt, de Rougemont does not say what causes it. Blanchefleur suffers
because her love is forbidden for reasons of her brother's political
power in a set hierarchy, his lineage which must be protected, and the
difference of rank between herself and her lover Rivalin. In other
words, all those accoutrements of patriarchal society force her to repress her love.

For Isolde the role of patriarchy in making her reflect upon her
love and try to repress it is even more striking. She is no longer free to
love the man of her choice because the purpose of her marriage is to
provide Mark "a wife from whom he could get an heir" (Gottfried, p.
151) other than his nephew Tristan. Mark's barons, by forcing their
king to reject his sister's son as heir and to take only his own child, are
committing much more than a mere act of envy. They are suppress-

ing the principle of matrilineal succession and enforcing the exclusive principle of patrilineal succession. Both Tristan and Isolde experience forbidden love as tormented self-consciousness because Isolde must ensure the purity of patriarchal inheritance.

Isolde's loss of freedom is most clearly expressed in the famous "Isolde's Lament," chanted while the two are on the boat for Cornwall, after Isolde has submitted to Tristan and right before they drink the love potion.

> She wept and she lamented amid her tears that she was leaving her homeland, whose people she knew and all her friends in this fashion, and was sailing away with strangers, she neither knew whither nor how. . . . The loyal man hoped to comfort the girl in her distress. But whenever he put his arm around her, fair Isolde recalled her uncle's death. . . .
>
> "But lovely woman, am I offending you?"
>
> "You are—because I hate you!"
>
> "But why? dear lady?" he asked.
>
> "You killed my uncle!"
>
> "But that has been put by."
>
> "Nevertheless, I detest you, since but for you I should not have a care in the world [I would be free from cares and woes]. You and you alone have saddled me with all this trouble, with your trickery and deceit. What spite has sent you here [to Ireland] from Cornwall to my harm? You have won me by guile from those who brought me up, and are taking me I do not know where! I have no idea what fate I have been sold into [how I have been sold], nor what is going to become of me!" (Gottfried, p. 193; German version, ll. 11552–95)

When Tristan reminds Isolde that without him she would have had to marry the steward, she answers:

> "You will have to wait a long time before I thank you, for even if you saved me from him, you have since so bewildered me with trouble that I would rather have married the Steward than set out on this voyage with you." (Gottfried, p. 194)

The themes of losing power and freedom by losing family and defenders, and of succumbing to her uncle's murderer and therefore renouncing the matrilineal kinship rights, are repeated here, but with the added emphasis on personal humiliation through submitting to Tristan's clever manipulations; Tristan's rational calculation has conquered Isolde's magic power. In interpreting Isolde's hatred, Jackson says:

> The reasons she gives are perfectly logical—he murdered her uncle and has taken her from her parents. Yet they are unconvincing. The first was, so far as Isolde was concerned, a technical offense. . . . Tristan haunts Isolde's cabin, and she shows an anger toward him which seems so excessive as to be akin to love. . . . It is against this emotional background that Gottfried introduces the *Minnetrank,* the draught of love.[37]

Like Hatto, Jackson projects onto Isolde a modern psychology. Her reasons are unconvincing only from a point of view that adopts an exclusively patriarchal logic. It has been shown that from a prepatriarchal point of view, Tristan's offense is far from technical and Isolde's anger far from excessive, given the momentous upheaval Tristan has just accomplished. It is entirely probable that Isolde's formerly forthright love really has turned to hatred, and that there is quite another reason why her lament is juxtaposed to the love potion scene.

If we study the love potion scene, we find that the potion affects the two characters differently. De Rougemont assumes that since the love between Tristan and Isolde is "reciprocal" (p. 43), it is also symmetrical, but such is not the case. After drinking the potion, each of the lovers experiences a conflict of a far different order from that of the other. Tristan's conflict sets feudal codes against individualist codes: "When Tristan felt the stirrings of love he at once remembered loyalty and honor, and strove to turn away. . . . The loyal man was afflicted by a double pain. . . . Honor and Loyalty harassed him powerfully, but Love harassed him more" (Gottfried, pp. 195–96). Tristan's conflict is one of guilt, which as R. H. Bloch points out, internalizes the external prohibitions of a clan society and replaces them with the self-imposed inhibitions for the autonomous subject of the abstract corporate state. For Tristan, the onslaught of this forbidden passion serves "the emergence of a divided guilt-ridden self" (Bloch, p. 247).

Isolde also experiences conflict: "And so it fared with her. Finding her life unbearable, she, too, made ceaseless efforts" (Gottfried, p. 196). But the text says nothing about her experiencing guilt, and indeed she has no reason to. Although Gottfried does not, as he does for Tristan, explain directly the cause of her conflict, he does juxtapose it to her lament, and he does say: "Isolde's hatred was gone. Love, the reconciler, had purged their hearts of enmity" (Gottfried, p. 195). Isolde's conflict is that she loves the cause of her misery, her subjugation, and her loss of personal autonomy. She loves that which for every reason she should hate.

But the love philter, as the mechanism which internalizes repression, also represses the memory of what came before the establishment of this internalized censor, of her hatred and of the enslavement and humiliation of feminine autonomy which lie at the origin of romantic love. Perhaps this is why critics cannot go behind its origin to another form of psychology and another form of love.

Romantic Love as a Double Force

Yet Isolde is now caught in a contradiction even more intense than Tristan's. For her (as for us) there is no way back to the mythical matrifocal culture. The only route for her to express her refusal to her enslaving marriage, her resistance to it, and her yearning for freedom is through her adulterous love for Tristan, the man who caused that enslavement. Because de Rougemont's notion of "reciprocity" is a false reciprocity which reduces Isolde's role to a function of Tristan, he does not see that romantic love is a double and contradictory force, but denounces it as only destructive (pp. 31 and 42). His view of Isolde as a function of Tristan and his view of love as a single, unambiguous force go together.

It is not only inaccurate but futile to view romantic love as a uniformly destructive force to be condemned. It is the love of its historical epoch, belonging to it just as much as the state, the market economy, the patriarchal family, and the monologic ideology; with the one major difference that romantic love is a double force, since it is a protest against this social order from within it. Just as patriarchal ideology is characterized by the separation between a material and a spiritual realm, so does romantic love open up the mind/body split. But at the same time it is a yearning to heal the split and must be seen in this dual light.

Although when they first drink the potion, Tristan and Isolde love each other "with all their senses," after the Morois Forest episode they separate and increasingly Tristan loves the image of Isolde as preserved in memory and sculpture. The personal sexual relation which replaces the feudal relation is more and more, like the individual's relation to the state, an *imaginary* one. Tristan's love is conclusively transferred from the real woman to the internalized image within him upon his meeting of the second Isolde, Isolde of the White Hands, whom he marries because her name reminds him of his beloved. His meeting with Isolde No. 2 brings his memory of Isolde No. 1 even more prominently to his mind: "she reminded him strongly of the other Isolde, the resplendent one of Ireland" (Gottfried, p. 290). This image of Isolde No. 1 inhibits Tristan from having sexual relations with his wife.

This doubling of Isolde and the introduction of a second purely material Isolde succeeds in completing the idealization of Isolde No. 1 and the separation of the ideal object of love from the material woman for Tristan. Isolde of the White Hands is like the heroines of nineteenth-century novels who in the eyes of their lover must always represent and reincarnate an ideal preexisting in his mind, which she can never quite measure up to. Isolde of the White Hands is the Great Ancestress of heroines like Flaubert's Madame Arnoux in *L'Education sentimentale,* where the hero Frédérique falls in love with her because she "resembled the women in romantic books,"[38] but ceases to love her when she becomes accessible.

Tristan's love is more and more a relation to this image within himself, or in other words a relation to himself in which both Isolde No. 1 and Isolde No. 2 are nullified except as mediators. The apparently reciprocal and mutual love of the beginning becomes a one-sided, linear relation. After Tristan leaves Isolde, he calls her his "other life" (German version, ll. 19157) or as Hatto translates it, his "other self" (Gottfried, p. 293).

While an autonomous feminine other is ejected from the exterior world of the romance, the masculine self projects into it his own alter ego as a fictive other. For Tristan this exteriorized self is Tristan the Dwarf, appearing only at the end of the Thomas version, whom he meets at the end of his adventures, and who takes on more reality for him than either of the two Isoldes. He is mortally wounded when he takes up Tristan the Dwarf's battle and so really dies for the sake of his alter ego rather than for the sake of his mistress.

Throughout *Tristan and Isolde* the transformation of Tristan's personal identity from social and dialectical to individualist and linear can be traced through the series of his loyalties. He is first loyal both to his maternal uncle Mark and to his liege man and foster father, Rual Lefoitenant; then to Isolde the single object of desire; then to the internalized image of Isolde as his "other life"; and then to his alter ego Tristan the Dwarf. Although at the beginning of the romance, Tristan's identity comes from his position in a complex of kinship ties, through the idealization of Isolde, who becomes more and more like his mirror, he gains an identity based on self-reflection. The process of producing this new form of identity merges the autonomous feminine into the masculine spirit.

This new form of identity also serves to suppress social contraction within the romance. In the last part of the romance, Tristan's love seems "more refined" and "noble" (Jackson, p. 41), and no longer makes him disloyal to Mark. But what really happens is that the contradiction between feudal ethics and courtly love ethics which so haunted Tristan after he drank the potion has now been smoothed over, because Tristan has transferred his love to the image in himself and gone away to serve another lord. His form of selfhood serves a society which cannot recognize its own internal contradictions, especially that between patriarchal marriage and sexual love, and so dissolves them in imagination into identities, as the relation to the other turns into a relation to the self. The social oppression of women and the ideological repression of an autonomous feminine presence serve complementary purposes.

In conformity with this new monologic, Tristan also develops in the course of his legend a new art form, based on self-reflection. In the Thomas version, after he has left Mark's court, Tristan builds a statue grotto representing Isolde and the characters from all his past exploits, in figures described as more lifelike to Tristan than they appeared in life. The statue grotto also expresses the rupture between ideals and reality, since it is removed from lived reality and represents realistically that which is absent from reality. Moreover, like the courtly love lyric, the statues, offering Tristan a pretext for isolated meditation, serve to make him more self-conscious. But beyond this, the statue grotto "episode" is not really an episode like the other adventures which continue the legend, expanding it beyond itself in an open-ended, infinite way. Instead it repeats and reflects the past episodes, internalizing them to the text, and idealizing them in a purifying mirror of the romance. This self-reflection makes the text identical to itself and also closes it in upon itself.

While Tristan's unity of self develops through appropriating the other to the same within the structure of a unified totalizing narrative, his meditations in the statue grotto are sporadic; he remains very much in the world of adventure. In addition to neglecting the difference between the development of Tristan and that of Isolde, Bloch, in interpreting the passion of Tristan and Isolde as tending to "isolate the couple from the rest of society and thus to discourage their participation in and responsibility to the community as a whole" (p. 216), has also been inaccurate. Tristan's passion only prevents him from fulfilling his responsibility to his maternal uncle, and isolates him from the matrilineal kinship system. After the Morois Forest and sermon episodes, he again becomes the "hardy warrior" (Eilhart, p. 461) and the honorable, loyal feudal knight, but under the vassalage of Kaherdin's family.

The person who does become isolated and who must completely change her way of life is Isolde. It is she whose life becomes totally identified with love because there is nothing else for her. Her only escape from her enslavement is through romantic love. But love succeeds as an escape only if it cures the mind/body split and allows the ideal to be practiced in reality. For Tristan and Isolde, who must remain physically separated, the ideal can be practiced only in death.

But contrary to de Rougemont's analysis, their inevitable death is not caused by the romantic myth *in and of itself*. The necessity of fulfillment in death is more precisely located in the paradoxical *relation* between the ideal represented by the myth and the society that produces it. In and of itself, the romantic myth represents the ideal of love not as an unattainable absolute, but as the opposite of the mind/body split. Courtly love and the romantic love of Tristan and Isolde before Tristan goes into exile represent a higher form of love than that practiced before, a total love which for the first time in society combines in its ideal form emotional, mental, and sexual faculties in the relation between a man and a woman. The twelfth-century lyric poet Le Châtelain de Coucy expresses most eloquently this ideal as represented by the legend of Tristan.

C'onques Tristanz, qui but le beverage,
Pluz loiaument n'ama sanz repentir:
Quar g'i met tout, cuer et cors et desir,
Force et pooir, ne sai se faiz folage;

[Even Tristan who drank the potion
Never loved so loyally without repenting;
For I commit my all: heart and body, desire,
Strength and will; I know not if this be madness;][39]

But this ideal of a total love becomes unattainable by the very way it is produced. It emerges in a society based on fragmentation, structured, as we have seen, to fragment the old clanic order, to isolate women and separate them from their sexuality, and to separate the spiritual from material and social life.

Romantic love then serves a double purpose in such a society. It represents the quest for freedom from a society that fragments human relations and isolates people, alienates the masculine individual and subjugates women; but at the same time romantic love perpetuates alienated individualism and feminine oppression. This second and destructive facet of romantic love plays the dominant role as long as the rigid sexual roles and gender divisions, initiated in the twelfth century, and finally entrenched in the nineteenth, remain in force, along with a social order which promotes the rupture between mind and body, the dominance of one group over another, and an ideology which cancels out difference and the autonomy of the other.

The transformation of an ideology recognizing contradiction and otherness to a monologic ideology in *Tristan and Isolde* can be summarized if we remember that there are two Isoldes not only at the end but also at the beginning. The first pair of Isoldes, by their close mother-daughter relationship, ensures the strength of an autonomous feminine vision cohabiting with a masculine vision and the mutuality of matter and spirit. The second pair of Isoldes, each making the other only half a woman, symbolizes the separation of matter from spirit and the collapsing of the feminine into an adjunct of the masculine. In this society which tolerates neither contradiction nor autonomous feminine activity, romantic love becomes the place of refuge for both.

Chapter 3

Sex and the Single Girl at the Dawn of Liberalism

Manon Lescaut

In the course of the thirteenth century, romantic love fades out of French literature and is replaced by less tragic, less intimate, and more playful forms of eroticism. It does not really come back to the center stage of French literature until the 1660s with Racine's tragedies and Mme. de Lafayette's *The Princess of Clèves*.[1] These works recall Zumthor's definition of romantic love as destructive sexual passion molded by a rationally ordered frame. In the seventeenth-century texts, built around the consequences of repressed sexual desire, violent passions are restrained both by the characters, through strict self-observation, and by the form, through elaborate formal rules. In this literature a more rationalist, self-conscious mode of thought takes shape.

After the classical age, romantic love as a structuring force in narrative again fades out of French literature until nineteenth-century romanticism. But in the eighteenth century, among the more loosely constructed novels of Rousseau and Marivaux, Prévost's romantic narrative *Manon Lescaut* stands out as a tightly structured anomaly, and is for that very reason a more intriguing and more revealing text than *La Princesse de Clèves* for the purposes of this study. Considered the first preromantic French novel, *Manon Lescaut* follows in the tradition of *Tristan and Isolde*. Structured by what the narrator/hero le chevalier des Grieux calls "my destiny which carried me to my ruin,"[2] the novel gives form to a passion which is literally fatal, if not for des

Grieux, at least for his mistress Manon, who does not have a destiny, but whose death makes des Grieux's destiny possible.

Unlike *Tristan and Isolde,* where the two lovers share the lethal consequences of fatal passion, *Manon Lescaut* parcels out the accoutrements of romantic love, giving a figuratively fatal destiny to des Grieux, and the literally fatal consequences of love to Manon. But like the twelfth-century romance, the eighteenth-century novel harbors in the workings of its text a conflict between sharply diverging masculine and feminine historicities, and again this conflict is not overtly represented—Manon's historicity is in fact rendered unrepresentable—but occurs as a conflict between two masculine discourses and an absent or silenced feminine discourse.

Masculine and Feminine Historicities

With respect to these conflicting historicities, the novel presents a world characterized by an extraordinary social flux. Both narrators, Renoncourt and des Grieux, speak in terms of old aristocratic values that take for granted a stable social order where a person's identity is based on the relatively fixed institutions of family, church, and estate, and where privilege and power are bestowed by birth. Yet the action of the novel takes place in a world beset by the birth pangs of more dynamic social forms based on an urban commodity-producing economy, individualist psychology, and the acquisition of power and privilege through money. This gap in *Manon Lescaut* between the conceptual categories of narrative discourse and the social reality represented recalls Paul Hazard's characterization of the period: "It was one of those moments, striking to come upon, in which the screen becomes blurred, in which different images work upon it, one which delays its disappearance, another which still lacks sharpness and clarity. The nobleman is fading out, the bourgeois, slowly, is taking form and color."[3]

Albert Soboul's dating of the period in which the novel was written suggests further its undecided or blurred quality. According to him, the classical age ends between 1720 and 1730, while the Age of Enlightenment begins sometime between 1748 and 1750.[4] This dating, by which *Manon Lescaut* would almost fall into the gap between two cultural ages, helps to explain the rootlessness of its characters and the seemingly chaotic, disarticulated world they inhabit, as well as the conflicting literary conventions which encode the narrative.

The screen against which *Manon Lescaut* is played appears blurred in yet another way. In the early eighteenth century both an outmoded economic system and an equally outmoded estate system mask the reality of newer class relations. The estate system places all aristocrats—from the most destitute *hobereaux* to the most wealthy and powerful *robin* nobles—in one category, and all commoners—from the wealthiest bourgeois through artisans and day workers, to the poorest peasants—in another. And this at a period when high bourgeois financier-manufacturers who marry into the aristocracy and nobles who invest in commercial ventures may have more in common with each other than with the more obscure members of their estate.[5] This dissonance between the semantic categories that mediate social experience and the realities of that experience will also figure prominently in the narrative process of *Manon Lescaut*.

Cutting across this flux is another historical process, the steady worsening of the feminine work situation in a period of economic expansion. As historian Joan Kelly-Gadol points out: "One of the tasks of women's history is to call into question accepted schemes of periodization. To take the emancipation of women as a vantage point is to discover that events that further the historical development of men, liberating them from natural, social or ideological constraints, have quite different, even opposite effects upon women."[6] This is certainly the case for the early eighteenth century. While bourgeois men were being liberated from the family economy to engage in new commercial and financial activities outside the family, bourgeois women found virtually no jobs or professions available to them. While the newer forms of commercial organization excluded women almost entirely, artisan class women were also being kicked out of the traditional women's trades, as men were taking them over.[7] Single women of the third estate were the poorest of the poor.[8]

In this respect it is noteworthy that Manon is the first bourgeoise heroine of romantic passion in a romantic love narrative to be read by a bourgeois audience. Manon's ostentatiously class-conscious aristocratic lover, le chevalier des Grieux, pointedly stresses the class difference between himself and his mistress at the very beginning of the novel: "Of common birth, she was flattered to have made the conquest of a lover such as myself," he says in the 1753 edition of the novel. His remark seems even more pointed when one considers that this class difference has widened since the 1731 edition of the novel, where the same passage makes Manon "without a title, although of fairly good birth."[9] Critics have contrasted Prévost's Manon to Marivaux's Marianne, pointing out that *La Vie de Marianne* has the heroine narrate her own story and so reveals her inner development as a subject, while Manon appears solely as other through the first-person narration of des Grieux.[10] But if Marivaux has Marianne narrate her story in the 1730s, he is also careful to give her a presumed noble birth.

As a commoner, Manon's unstable life epitomizes this world of flux where free market capitalism hesitantly emerges. But it also shows how much women's historicity takes place outside dominant historical frames. The world outside the family economy was expanding but not for women; and yet the domestic ideology which idealizes the family role of woman as housewife and mother had not yet been elaborated as it will be in the Enlightenment. Whereas an enterprising young middle-class man at this period could make his way to fame and fortune, there was very little for an enterprising young woman to do.

In *Manon Lescaut*, these historical conflicts concerning forms of governance, modes of production, and the changing place of middle-class women are not explicitly expressed. The text of *Manon Lescaut* expresses historic process not by directly representing it but by incorporating conflicting ways of representing reality. The text is rent by what Roland Barthes calls a "rupture" or "collision" between codes,[11] in this case between a "classical" code and a "realist" code. But however much these two codes may enter into conflict with each other, they eventually merge in the text to exclude an unspoken feminine bourgeois code.

The terms "classical code" and "realist code" would be inadequate tools to offer insights into seventeenth-century classical texts or nineteenth-century realist texts, since these texts exceed the descriptive labels and categories that literary history has devised. But they are useful terms if employed in a limited way to show how a text violates and contradicts the literary conventions it consciously sets up as models. And there is no doubt that the framing narrator of *Manon Lescaut*, Renoncourt, holds consciously to literary conventions of classicism which the narrative disturbs. Insights can also be gained from bringing into play literary categories that are thought to be mutually exclusive, in this chapter "classicism" and "realism," in order to explore how conflicts between them in a text can take it beyond literary conventions.

Conflicting Codes

Like any codes, the ones organizing *Manon Lescaut* are meant to be a set of social, linguistic, and literary conventions that can organize what would seem a disparate mass of incoherent detail into what appears a natural, normal, explainable event. They should make the world represented in the novel be perceived as the "true," "real," "normal" world of possible experience, and should allow the details and events in that novelistic world to form a meaningful, understandable, coherent, and orderly whole. But none of the codes working to organize *Manon Lescaut* totally succeeds in doing this. One reason that *Manon Lescaut* has such depth and elusiveness, and gives us a haunting sense that there is always something more to the novel than analytic language can grasp, is that neither of the literary codes informing its text is complete. An aristocratic code, relying on conventions of classical literature, is disintegrating, while a bourgeois code, marked by certain elements of realist literature, is just emerging and not fully formed.

As opposed to *Tristan and Isolde,* which is rent by two different logical forms, a bisexual multilogic and patriarchal monologic, the two masculine codes in *Manon Lescaut* fall within the same logic. While codes order and normalize details and elements of a world, forms of logic determine which details and elements will be perceived as existing in the world at all. The logic that dominates romantic love narrative makes cause and effect appear to happen in linear chains, is strongly end-oriented, and excludes as intolerable the play of contradiction, difference, and reversibility in the world (see chap. 1). But conflicting with this monological form in *Manon Lescaut,* a second logic comes into play which would express the middle-class feminine situation in the eighteenth century. It operates, however, only in the form of fragments which point to its absence.

A literary code which uses classical terminology organizes the introductory paragraphs of *Manon Lescaut* and the words of the framing narrator, the nobleman Renoncourt. Since the principal narrator of the story, le chevalier des Grieux, is an "unreliable narrator,"[12] he is coupled with a more reliable narrator, the older, more stable, established and respected Renoncourt, whom the reader already knows and trusts from the other volumes of his fictional *Mémoires d'un homme de qualité,* of which *Manon Lescaut* is the fourteenth volume. He assures us of des Grieux's perfect sincerity as a storyteller in spite of his naive, distorted vision of events and people, and presents des Grieux as an unworldly noble adolescent lost in a world of heartless greed.

Renoncourt places himself in the tradition of a classical literary code by telling us that the purpose of the story we are about to read is "to instruct while pleasing us," to affirm our moral sense by showing us a stunning example of immorality. Nowadays it goes without saying that such is not the real purpose or moral of the story. But Renoncourt's opening remarks can nevertheless teach a valuable lesson, concerning not Renoncourt's ideas but the unconscious assumptions underlying them.

Renoncourt's introduction is structured according to the concept of *vraisemblance,* which Gérard Genette analyzes as a "world vision" and "value system" based on a perfect correspondence between general maxim and particular behavior, where the maxim explains the behavior, and the behavior implies the maxim.[13] But as Renoncourt exposes his philosophy, it becomes clear that a historic process has driven a wedge in this correspondence, so that it separates from itself and disintegrates. According to his analysis, we can be sure that particular events really do happen, and that general maxims really are true. The only problem is that they have nothing to do with each other. He says:

> No one can reflect upon the precepts of morality, without being surprised to see them both valued and neglected at the same time; and one wonders about the reason for this oddity of the human heart, which makes us delight in the ideas of good and perfection from which we depart in practice.

Continuing with a discussion of how classical and neoclassical authors treat this love of the good, Renoncourt plunges into the heart of his topic.

> How does it happen then that we fall so easily from these elevated speculations, and that we find ourselves so soon at the

common level of men? I am mistaken if the reason that I am going to propose does not explain very well this contradiction between our ideas and our behavior; it is that, since all the precepts of morality are only vague and general principles, it is very difficult to put them to use in a particular application to the details of manners and actions.

Let's take an example. Well-born souls feel that gentility and humanity are agreeable virtues, and are led by inclination to practice them; but when we come to the moment of execution, we often remain in doubt. Is this really the occasion? Do we know the correct measure to exercise? Are we not at all mistaken about the object? A hundred difficulties stop us. We fear becoming dupes in wanting to be beneficial and liberal; being seen as weak in appearing too tender and sensitive; in a word, to exceed or not to fulfill enough our duties, which are enclosed too obscurely in general notions of humanity and gentility. In this uncertainty, there is only experience or example which can reasonably determine the penchant of the heart. However, experience is not at all an advantage that everyone can freely have; it depends on the different situations where fortune places us. There remains then only example to serve as a rule to a number of people in the exercise of virtue. It is precisely for this sort of reader that works like this one can be of extreme utility, at least when they are written by a person of honor and good sense. (Pp. 30–31)

Even though Renoncourt does see the "contradiction" between "ideas" and "behavior," and even though he sees the moral "precepts" and "general notions" as useless in practice, he never calls their validity into question. On the contrary, they are not relativized as "our" precepts or as "old" precepts, but reaffirmed as "the" precepts—the only possible ones. In the same way, the "general notions," however obscurely they enclose our duties, nonetheless do enclose them. Renoncourt's attempt to resolve the original contradiction only deepens it.

On the one hand he adopts a more modern empiricist method of guiding action by using particular examples rather than maxims as models. But instead of replacing the use of general maxims, the apparently new method really serves to rescue and revitalize them.

Through a process of infinite regress and circular reasoning, Renon-court tells us that since principles are too "vague and general," action must be guided by examples. But those examples find their validity in the "honor and good sense" of the person who chooses them. But "good sense" is the *most* vague and general of the classicist notions: it has no articulated definition, because its operative force depends on the mutual understanding of an initiated social group, the court and robe nobility of the ancien régime. Since to know the implicit code is to be initiated into the group, to articulate the code to the general public is to destroy its initiatory function.

The aristocratic ideology, then, when put into contradiction with des Grieux's experience, falls apart just enough to reveal what ide-ologies are meant to conceal: that standards of behavior are deter-mined not by universal principles, nor by neutral models, but by the members of a ruling class. If the classical code has lost its ability to conceal the source of social dictates, a realist code, which begins to emerge in *Manon Lescaut,* will conceal this much more convincingly.

Notable in Renoncourt's discourse is the absence of any awareness that this separation between general maxims and particular behaviors has been brought about by a historical process. His general maxims can explain and dictate behavior only in a society where people will live and die within the confines of the situation they are born to, and can count on following all their lives a limited set of behaviors fixed by their assigned relations to familial, religious, community, and class authorities. This society is disappearing in *Manon Lescaut,* and does not exist for des Grieux. In the city streets, gambling dens, and free market economy that he floats through, standards of behavior and social roles fluctuate according to one's ever-shifting position in the networks of monetary exchange.

Des Grieux's actions often appear, as Renoncourt tells us, inex-plicable, because the new behaviors are uncodified and therefore not enclosed in a form where they seem natural and logical. The aristo-cratic codes are inadequate both because of their form, that is to say the form of the general as a guide to action, and because of their content, which consists of the chivalric concepts of honor, generosity, bravery, and frankness. Whenever des Grieux lets one of those con-cepts inspire his actions in the urban world, it does nothing but get him into trouble. Codes that could guide him must somehow be based on the particular: the self-interest of the individual and the pragmatic necessities of the moment. The outlines of such a code will eventually emerge in *Manon Lescaut.*

In fact the first small traces of it appear in the language Renoncourt himself uses to describe Manon. Renoncourt first meets des Grieux and Manon at Passy where Manon, chained in a group of six prostitutes, is being deported to New Orleans. Des Grieux, in despair, has generously given away all his money to her extortionate guards in order to remain close to her, and he is now reduced to begging from Renoncourt. This introduction, which lays stress on des Grieux's innocence and indifference to money, has the effect of impressing upon us his innate, natural nobility, but it also shows us his complete lack of equipment for surviving in the urban jungle that, he tells Renoncourt and the readers, Manon has led him into.

Renoncourt's introduction of Manon bears out the observation of both Raymond Picard and Jacques Proust that Manon never really is described throughout the novel: "We are ignorant of everything up to the color of her hair," says Picard.[14] But if Renoncourt's description does not let us see Manon, it does tell us a great deal about the way the male narrator/characters see her. The language Renoncourt uses to describe her contrasts to the language he uses to describe des Grieux. Renoncourt's language in describing des Grieux serves to depict him as wholly reflecting his true being in his outer appearance, while he describes Manon as violating this unity of being and appearance. This first impression will never change no matter what each of the two characters does in the novel.

Of des Grieux, Renoncourt says: "He was dressed quite simply; but one distinguishes at the first glance a man of birth and education. I approached him. He stood up; and I discovered in his eyes, his face and all his movements, an appearance so fine and noble that I felt naturally inclined to wish him well" (p. 35). This description of des Grieux falls within the classical code. The hero's true essence shines through because it coincides perfectly with his class and his descent (or birth). No matter what degrading actions he commits, his noble, honorable demeanor continues to translate his noble, honorable inner being. Paradoxically, this is the very reason that he is such a successful cheater at cards: "They claimed that there was much to be hoped for from me, because since there was something in my face which exuded the *honnête homme,* no one would suspect my artifices" (p. 74). At the end of his adventures, after all his violent exploits—

rebellion, murder, cheating, etc.—des Grieux can still say to Renoncourt: "I am of a naturally gentle and tranquil temper" (p. 38).

Completely other is Manon's being and the language used to describe it.

> Among the twelve wenches who were chained in groups of six by the middle of the body, there was one whose manner and face accorded so little with her condition, that in any other state I would have taken her for a person of the first order. Her sadness and the dirtiness of her linen and clothing succeeded so little in making her ugly that the sight of her inspired in me respect and pity. She tried nevertheless to turn away, as much as her chain would permit, so as to conceal her face from the eyes of spectators. The effort she made to hide herself was so natural, that it seemed to come from a feeling of modesty. (P. 34)

Throughout the novel we are given to believe that everything about Manon is the opposite of what it "seems," that she is a double character whose surface hides a contrary depth. The language of this paragraph which introduces her is in like manner a double language whose surface meaning implies an opposite metaphorical meaning. From the beginning, the language of the text surrounds Manon with an ambiguous aura. While it refers explicitly to her apparent gentility in the midst of a group of prostitutes, it also refers metaphorically to her duplicity. In the body of the novel, she will be viewed as a scheming temptress. In this second implicit sense of the passage, her "manner" hardly conforms to her "condition" because she gives herself the airs of a delicate aristocrat when she is really a vulgar bourgeois. She allows herself to be "taken for" a person of the "first order" when she is of a birth low enough that des Grieux's father will not permit their marriage. Since, in the eyes of des Grieux's father and the other male characters, her surface appearance of honor and fidelity carefully conceals a true selfish, greedy nature, to "hide herself" is indeed "natural" and only "seems," as Renoncourt says in the passage, motivated by "modesty." Even though the actions of Manon and des Grieux are similar, his appearance *is* his essence according to the aristocratic code, because his essence equals his social role and social position, while for Manon appearance *hides* a contrary essence because she refuses her position.

Des Grieux tells us that Manon's "penchant for pleasure" leads her to refuse her social and familial role and to seek "liberty" (p. 15). Depending on one's point of view, her desire for liberty is either a dangerous, destructive force or a creative force. The narrator's interpretation constantly leads us to believe that it is a destructive force. But without this feminine revolt against family constraints and conventional morality on the part of Manon, Isolde, and the nineteenth-century romantic heroines, romantic love could not exist; nor could it have its depth and strength as a cultural ideal. Even more dismally than the revolt of these other heroines, Manon's will fail—not only fail to succeed, but fail to be recognized in the way the hero's revolt is, as a quest for individuality. Yet it does signify, much more than des Grieux's confusion, that world in which romantic love will flourish, the world of bourgeois individualism.

The double language used to describe Manon encodes the more ambiguous social structure in which individualism, at least among writers and intellectuals, is a prime value. It also encodes the language of the realist novel. In Balzac's and Stendhal's novels of romantic love, written a hundred years later, when bourgeois individualism and romanticism are recognized cultural ideals, the realist code has a more complete form. In these novels, it leads us to interpret both the characters and the language of a text as making sense if they are divided by a dichotomy between surface and depth. This dichotomy, creating what Robbe-Grillet has called "myths of profundity,"[15] allows us to interpret seemingly inexplicable and illogical behaviors of a character as coherent and logical if they offer clues to a true nature hidden underneath the surface. In a completely realist text des Grieux's behavior would not remain so inexplicable as it does to Renoncourt in *Manon Lescaut*.

The myth of profundity also creates for the reader the realist illusion that we can, as Barthes says, "go behind the paper"[16] to discover the "real life" of the characters, a life which they live more fully outside the fragments of their life shown us in the novel. The narrative techniques of Renoncourt and des Grieux create this illusion for the reader with respect to Manon but not with respect to des Grieux. We have already seen how the transparent character of des Grieux is introduced by the transparent text, immediately yielding its meaning, while Manon's ambiguous character is introduced by the double text where one level of meaning points to another. Des

Grieux, since he not only tells his own story, but also comes guaranteed as entirely truthful by the prestigious Renoncourt, seems wholly present to us in the voice of the text. There is nothing else of des Grieux outside the narration. Moreover, although his desires may lead him to distort reality, his sincerity is never in doubt.

On the other hand, des Grieux tells of Manon and her actions in such a way as to create an ambiguity, which constantly leads us to ask: Who is the *real* Manon? and which makes us want to "go behind the paper" to a Manon we can really see and analyze for ourselves. We are led to see her either as duplicitous or as hiding a mystery behind her enigmatic facade. Alfred de Musset expressed the artistry of this illusion (or is it his own entrapment in it?) in his poem *Namouna*, where he asks:

> Pourquoi Manon Lescaut, dès la première scène
> Est-elle si vivante et si vraiment humaine,
> Qu'il semble qu'on l'a vue et que c'est un portrait?
>
> Why is Manon Lescaut, from the very first scene,
> so alive and so truly human, that you feel you have
> seen her, and that this is a portrait?[17]

Emphasizing the mystery behind her façade, Musset calls her "Amazing Sphinx! true siren," and declares: "How I believe in you! how I love you and hate you! . . . How I would love you tomorrow, if you were living!" The reader is tempted to treat her as if she were a living person rather than the projection of a masculine narrator.

Critics have commented on the fact that Manon is frequently described as at least partially "hiding" or "hidden."[18] Yet in a sense all of her is revealed since she is nothing more that the fragmentary images shown in the novel, and which exist nowhere but in the language of the text and the narrator's voice. There is no more complete physical appearance and certainly no hidden inner essence, no key to the real Manon. While the fragmentary images do not add up to a revelation of the mystery of Manon, they do, when put together, reveal the hidden strategies of representation that make Manon so mysterious.

The eventual putting together of those fragments calls for a reading of *Manon Lescaut* which goes against the grain of the interpretation given us by the narrator and which violates the "agreement" between implied author and implied reader.[19] Des Grieux is the narrator, and his interpretation is embedded in the story he recounts to Renoncourt when they meet a second time. It is two years later, and the younger man is returning to France from Louisiana, mourning Manon's death. The framing narrator Renoncourt now becomes the exemplary sympathetic audience for des Grieux's tragic story. At the age of seventeen, on his way home from school, where he had been in every way a model pupil, he meets Manon, even younger than he, but much more experienced in the ways of the world and of the heart. She is being sent to a convent, "doubtless to arrest her penchant for pleasure, which had already declared itself, and which subsequently was to cause all her miseries, and mine," des Grieux tells his listener. Having thus explained how we should interpret the events of his story, des Grieux goes on to narrate how Manon, exercising her irresistible charms, persuades him to run away with her to Paris, where they "defrauded the rights of the Church," and lived together for twelve days, until Manon manifested her "perfidious" habit of "inconstancy."

"It is certain," says des Grieux, "that, naturally tender and constant as I am, I would have been happy my whole life, if Manon had been faithful to me" (p. 20). Again laying his interpretation rather heavily upon us, des Grieux recounts how his father refused to let him marry this commoner, and also to send them money in Paris. The hero tries to persuade Manon to exercise her charms on his father, but she refuses, saying that she can get money from her own relatives. Des Grieux notices certain expensive improvements in their food and in Manon's attire but does not worry even though he notices the wealthy farmer-general Monsieur B—— hanging around the apartment. He does not worry, that is, until his father's servants arrive to remove him with force from his Paris apartment and lock him in a room in his father's chateau. Only with the help of Manon, des Grieux's father convinces his son, could M. B—— have located the father to inform him of his son's whereabouts. Des Grieux is confused and amazed: "I didn't know my own heart better than hers. 'No, no,' I reproved myself, 'It is not possible for Manon to betray me. She is not unaware that I live only for her.'" He is thus an unreliable narrator in that the reader cannot tell where begins and where ends this tendency to see Manon as conforming to his preexisting idea of her and a more general tendency to confuse reality with his own desires of how it should be.

Having lost Manon, des Grieux becomes an ecclesiastical student at St. Sulpice, where once again his reputation for study and virtue spreads. But two years later that "perfidious creature" shows up, and he is once more enflamed by her spell. He runs away from St. Sulpice with her, and she leaves M. B——. When their money runs out, des Grieux, through the agency of Manon's "brutal and unprincipled" brother, gets a "job" cheating at cards. He carefully keeps Manon ignorant of any financial matters or worries; but when their money is stolen, she finds out and immediately makes herself the mistress of Monsieur de G—— M——. When an outraged des Grieux confronts Manon, she says: "I had hoped you would consent to the project I had created to reestablish our fortune a little, and it was to spare your delicacy that I began to execute it without your participation, but I am giving it up, since you don't approve" (p. 73). The reader is left in doubt as to her sincerity and veracity here.

The lovers run off with the jewels and money the older man has given his mistress-to-be. As a result, des Grieux ends up imprisoned in St. Lazare and Manon in l'Hôpital. Driven by the news of Manon's fate, des Grieux escapes in order to liberate her, and in spite of the best intentions fatally shoots a St. Lazare porter in the process. Having been informed while in hiding with Manon that his little affair has been excused, he rents an apartment, and the couple seem about to settle down to a stable life. But they meet the son of M. de G—— M——, who tells des Grieux that he wants Manon for his own.

Des Grieux agrees to participate in a scheme to make money off of M. de G—— M——, Jr., in which Manon will pretend to go off with M. de G—— M——, Jr., and then return the same night with his gifts. But "the perfidious Manon" does not return. When des Grieux again confronts Manon with her "crime" (p. 142), she again agrees to obey his wishes, but persuades him that they should avenge themselves on M. de G—— M——, Sr. Des Grieux has G—— M——, Jr., kidnapped for a few hours, while the lovers eat his dinner and sleep in his bed, where they are found by the guards of M. de G—— M——, Sr. They are both imprisoned again, but this time, G—— M——, Sr., works with des Grieux's father to free des Grieux and send Manon to New Orleans.

The narrative, having circled back to its beginning, now plunges into the American interlude, where des Grieux and Manon appear to be finally living out the solid middle-class virtues of American pioneers. But the Louisiana governor's nephew demands her hand in marriage. Des Grieux fights a duel, mistakenly believes that he has killed the nephew, flees with Manon to the "desert," sees her die of exposure, buries her, wishes to die himself, and returns to his old life of virtue in the French aristocracy.

In the scene of Manon's death at the end of the novel, as in the scene of her introduction, des Grieux uses double language in describing a surface/depth dichotomy. But this time the dichotomy is in himself, and the double language has undergone a transformation. Instead of symbolizing duplicity, mystery, and revolt, the metaphorical language signals des Grieux's own transformation, from a character encoded by a spontaneous chivalric ethos to a character encoded by an emergent individualist ethos.

Death of the Individualist Heroine;
Birth of the Individualist Hero

The scene of Manon's death is similar to the scene introducing her since here too the language works on two levels in an interchange of metaphors.

> It was not difficult for me to open the earth in the place where I was. This was a plain covered with sand. I broke my sword to use it for digging, but I obtained less help from it than from my hands. I opened a wide grave. I placed within it the idol of my heart, after taking care to envelop her in my clothes, in order to prevent the sand from touching her. I did not do all this until I had kissed her a thousand times with all the ardor of the most perfect love. I gazed upon her for a long time. I could not make up my mind to close the grave. Finally, since my strength was beginning to weaken, and I feared losing it altogether before completing my task, I buried within the earth the most perfect and beautiful creature that had dwelt upon it. Afterwards, I lay down on the grave, my face turned toward the sand, and, closing my eyes with the intent of never opening them again, I invoked the aid of heaven. (Pp. 185–86)

In this passage, words referring to the earth and words referring to des Grieux's body act as metaphors for each other: the hero envelops Manon's corpse in the earth and also in his own clothing; she is buried in the "bosom" of the earth and also in his own bosom. With her burial, des Grieux turns away from the world to her image within him. Whereas before her death his emotions were on the surface, ready for spontaneous expression, now they too are more deeply buried and more difficult to express.

> Pardon me, if I complete in as few words as possible a story which is killing me. I am telling you about a misfortune without previous example. My whole life is destined to mourn it. But although I carry it incessantly in my memory, *my soul seems to draw back in horror every time I attempt to express it.* (P. 184, emphasis added)

Manon's death, transforming the subjective structure of des Grieux into one that seeks its essence within itself, effects three interrelated changes: (1) The hero changes from a spontaneous, impetuous actor into a self-reflecting subject; (2) he changes from an irresponsible, aimless adolescent into a responsible subject of the state; (3) he changes from the doer of adventurous deeds into the teller of his story.

The turning point of this change occurs with the words:

> Do not insist that I describe to you my feelings, nor that I report to you her last expressions. I lost her; I received from her marks of love at the very moment she expired. (P. 185)

The emergence of des Grieux's new form of subjectivity, one which speaks self-consciously and self-reflexively, recalls Julia Kristeva's analysis of how a Western patriarchal-capitalist form of the subject emerges on two levels, in history and in the individual. On the level of history, this subjective form is not eternal and natural but historically produced, subject to change, and molded in the shape of capitalist ideologies. This form determines how an individual child of a given historical moment will become a (masculine) subject, or as Kristeva says, following Lacan, how it will enter language and become a "speaking subject" by going through the castration crisis.[20] Des

Grieux goes through the process of becoming a speaking subject as he passes simultaneously from a childlike state into an adult state and from one historical mode into another. As he goes through this passage, ordered autobiographical narrative emerges out of chaotic, unreflected experience through a symbolic castration crisis.

According to Kristeva, symbolic castration also takes place on both the individual and the socio-historic level. An individual infant, in the earliest period of its life, relates immediately to physical gratifications in the world, mainly represented by its mother, through its instinctual erotic drives or processes. As the child develops, the castration crisis completes the rupture, or what Kristeva calls the "cut," from those drives so that what we call consciousness emerges by being "cut" from instinctual processes. The "cut" does three things: (1) It represses or buries those processes, so that they form the unconscious; (2) it acts as a barrier between consciousness and the unconscious; (3) it thereby forms the psychic structure conscious/unconscious that Kristeva sees as the product of Western patriarchal society, and that is the basis of romantic desire.

Kristeva, following Lacan, sees consciousness as a linguistic construct. To pass through the castration crisis is to enter the world of the symbolic, which relates the subject to the world through the mediation of language, with its linear syntax, its ordered grammar, and the muscular constraints it exerts through pronunciation. To speak in syntactic language requires self-restraint; it requires precisely the repression of immediate erotic impulses. This is what happens to des Grieux when he buries Manon: he passes from living his passion for Manon to telling about it, from the realm of immediate eroticism and unreflective gratification of impulses to the realm of self-restrained language, so that in telling about his love, he raises it from a sordid adventure to a true romantic destiny.

As Freud shows in *The Interpretation of Dreams,* and as Kristeva maintains, symbolic language refers ultimately not to an external referent, but to the impulsive processes buried in the speaker's unconscious. This too is true for the language in the passage where des Grieux relates the burial of Manon. In that scene, the breaking of the sword would symbolize castration for Freudians, but for Kristeva castration is a "phantasmic deviation"[21] of the "cut" which "buries" erotic impulses and permits the acquisition of language. Such castration symbols, relating to the genesis of individual subjects in an individualist society, replace the broader social myths of a collective society. According to Kristeva, in collective societies the "cut" signifies the genesis of the social order itself: "It is through murder . . . that every known archaic society has to represent this cut which installs the symbolic order."[22]

The "symbolic order" for the individual is syntactic language and for the society the rule of law. Des Grieux enters, and also brings forth, both orders. As Prévost achieves the textual murder of Manon, he transforms his hero des Grieux from the subject of an older corporate society into the subject of an individualist order. At the same time, des Grieux acquires the ability to use language, or, in other words, he is transformed from the adventurer into the teller of adventures. The exact point of that double transformation is also the exact point of the textual "murder." It is the phrase "I lost her."

Do not insist that I describe to you my feelings,
nor that I report to you her last expressions.

I lost her;

I received from her marks of love at the very
moment she expired.

The words "I lost her" symbolize the cut in two ways, on the level of the narrative circle as a whole, and on the level of the syntax of this particular sentence. First, this moment of final loss cuts des Grieux from a life of immediate and violent passion. After this moment he *repeats* his life but in the sublimated form of speech. Second, the phrase "I lost her" separates the two parts of the passage, the first of which ("do not insist that I describe . . .") tells us that his last emotions and her last expression cannot be spoken or narrated; and the second part of which actually *repeats* the same scene, telling us in an oblique way ("the marks of love") that which des Grieux had refused to say in the first part.

The narrative language itself shows that des Grieux acquires language at the expense of repressing spontaneous, immediate impulses. As he approaches the moment in his life history where he acquires the possibility of narrating it, des Grieux is for the first time in the narration unable to speak about his life spontaneously and directly. One of the difficulties in analyzing separately the adventures and their narration is the very circularity of the novel. To come to the end of des Grieux's adventures is also to come to the beginning of the narration of those same adventures. Another difficulty is that during most of the narrative, as opposed to the above passage, and as opposed to the narratives of more alienated nineteenth-century heroes, the movement of language coincides closely with the movement of des Grieux's passion.

The immediacy of des Grieux's erotic and angry responses, as well as the close union between movement of action and movement of language, characterize the style throughout most of *Manon Lescaut*. Des Grieux describes his first meeting with Manon: "I found myself all at once enflamed to the point of rapture. At that time I had the fault of being excessively timid and easily flustered; but in this instance, far from being stopped by this weakness, I advanced toward the mistress of my heart" (p. 39). In this early passage the narrator's style gives the impression of a spontaneous flow of speech that translates the character's spontaneity of passage from thought to action.

Whatever self-reflection there is seizes the reflected consciousness, the reflecting consciousness, and their external situation as one totality, as in the following passage: "I have been amazed a thousand times, in reflecting upon it, how so much boldness and facility in expressing myself could come to me; but we wouldn't make a divinity out of love if it didn't often work wonders" (p. 40). Here the times of past reflection, of past action, and of present narration create an intertwined and almost inseparable unit. In this passage three different forms of expression—the hero's expression of love to Manon, his telling of his experience to his listener, and even his expression of his own private thoughts to himself—intertwine as a single spontaneous expression. And in narrating his story, des Grieux repeats that "facility of expression" he found with Manon.

The language of *Manon Lescaut* resembles that of the neoclassical age, which Michel Foucault calls "the spontaneous analysis of representation . . . , the most immediate, the least deliberate, the most profoundly linked to the movement of representation itself."[23] Des Grieux resembles that Cartesian subject which Foucault sees as "the *doubling* of a consciousness that never separates from itself and does not split." How different is the alienated language of Stendhal's Julien Sorel and Balzac's Felix de Vandenesse.

The beauty of this narrative style in the novel is the beauty and seductiveness of des Grieux's character, but also its sordid ugliness. The same spontaneity and passion which would make him truly brave and honorable in a world regulated by aristocratic institutions push him to murder, cheat, and betray his friends in a world that demands calculation and self-restraint. The very nobility of his value system makes him wicked in the world ordered not by frameworks that enclose people in their family, caste, and community, but by networks of money. Prévost wrote at a time when he could portray the effects of this problem but not articulate it as Stendhal would in 1830.

Des Grieux, unable to find a larger explanation for his wickedness, blames it on Manon and her "penchant for pleasure." In the history of Western Europe, as clear and external frameworks guiding behavior disintegrate, structures that control antisocial behavior come to be situated in the (masculine) self. As bourgeois men reject their immediate passions, women even more than before are portrayed in literature as embodiments of those destructive passions that must be repressed, or buried. Manon then is the first of a long series of romantic heroines who die, like Chateaubriand's Amélie in *René,* Constant's Eléonore in *Adolphe,* Dumas's *La Dame aux camélias,* Balzac's Mme. de Mortsauf in *The Lily in the Valley.* Des Grieux can then internalize this symbol of repressed passion, at the same time transforming it from destructive presence into beloved memory.

The end of *Manon Lescaut* retraces this process of interiorization. As an exterior force Manon disrupts the social order; dead and transformed into repressed passion, she permits the hero to enter society as the autonomous self-reflecting subject: "I *voluntarily* renounce ever leading a happy life again" (p. 185, emphasis added), says des Grieux. When Manon is alive, Tiberge, des Grieux's friend and ineffectual conscience, cannot reform the hero's behavior. But after Manon dies, his exhortations are also turned into an interior, abstract, and therefore more potent force: "I announced to him that the seeds of virtue which he had previously sown in my heart were beginning to produce fruit" (p. 188).

Before Manon's death, the couple repeats three times the same cycle of prostitution-theft-prison because they lack the internal mechanism to learn from their past behavior. Manon's death, because it installs the internal mechanism, ends that repetition and allows a leap to a new order. Now living in memory rather than solely in the present moment, des Grieux relates to the forces within him rather than to worldly gratification and tends toward a mentality which sees the "self" as an absolute, atomic entity rather than in relation to a community. Manon, that supreme feminine individual, never makes it into the individualist order.

Like Isolde, she is necessary to the formation of individualist consciousness and necessarily excluded from being one. This consciousness is the thought structure of urban capitalism that later in the eighteenth century develops an ideology in which the concept of loyalty to one's "true, inner essence" replaces the concept of loyalty to one's family, god, or king. A new relation to self and other characterizes not only the autonomous subject but also the capitalist subject who seeks to make the world into his own reflection. As Robert Mauzi says: "Man of this era [the eighteenth century] . . . is an *absolutist* man, that is to say that from now on everything depends on him, that he is to himself his only justification, that he feels himself the master of all things, and imposes his form on the universe."[24] While des Grieux is hardly the master of all things (although the end of the novel indicates that this is about to change), he certainly imposes his form on the universe.

For Kristeva, this absolute self is the subject of Western class societies who upholds the established order because it finds intolerable, or even inconceivable, any true difference or otherness in the world or even in itself. Difference is excluded through that process of the "cut," which forms consciousness as a homogeneous, unified structure informed by monological thinking. In repressing processes, the cut represses those forces which could intrude upon the monologic of consciousness, break it up, impose forces which differ from it, or that could introduce into it other forms of logic. At the same time the cut, stopping the immediate relation between subject and world, makes the subject live in the world through the mediation of his own self-reflection. He lives in the world as in a hall of mirrors, "foreclosing the other and putting himself in its place."[25] The end of *Manon Lescaut* brings into being this mirror self, which as in *René*, *Adolphe*, or *The Lily in the Valley* requires the ultimate sacrifice of the heroine. In *Manon Lescaut* the feminine individual must die for the masculine self to be born.

The formation of this mirror self at the end of the novel suggests another reason why Manon must be portrayed as a destructive force. During most of the novel, Manon is a true other, differing from des Grieux's desires. Although he projects onto her an image that corresponds to his desires, that projection is revealed as an extreme distortion. Prévost sets up the narration of their adventures in France so that des Grieux's attempt to see the world as a reflection of his personal desires fails miserably because Manon, although she recognizes his authority, obstinately refuses to conform to his image of her. Des Grieux's portrayal of her as perfidious and mysterious is also his failure to reduce her as the other to a reflection of the self.

As an autonomous feminine other, however, she is portrayed as a force of evil, a *femme fatale*. Only as her death approaches does she cease to spread evil. This is because at the moment of her supreme sacrifice, des Grieux can be absolutely sure for the first time that her expressions of love are totally sincere and that her devotion to him is genuine. In other words, she finally does become a mirror of his subjective fantasies, so that the objective world truly becomes what he desires it to be.

While Renoncourt's world vision represents reality as a reflection of general, eternal maxims, des Grieux's world vision represents it as a reflection of his personal desires. Manon, by dying for des Grieux and excluding herself from the world, gives validity to that representation and allows the personal, individual point of view to replace the general maxim as a valid basis for explaining reality. In *Manon Lescaut* the course of the narration gives rise to an ideology whose universal standard of value is this self.

Conflicting Logics: Patriarchal Ideology and History

This ideology and its literary code take shape through narrative techniques that turn the uncertainty and distortion of des Grieux's vision into certainty and truth. One of these techniques is the illusion of multiple interpretations of events to reinforce one single "truth." For instance, on the occasion of Manon's infidelity with M. de G——— M———, Sr., des Grieux tells us: "I gave time to Lescaut [Manon's unscrupulous brother] to converse with his sister and to inspire in her, during my absence, a horrible decision. He spoke to her about M. de G——— M———, an old lecher who paid generously for his pleasures" (p. 77). But later he offers a second interpretation of this event: "He

[Lescaut] told me that Manon, unable to bear the fear of poverty . . . had begged him to procure a meeting with M. de G—— M——
who was known as a generous man. He neglected to mention that the
advice had come from himself" (p. 80).

Or had it? The narration sets up an ambiguity as to which of these
conflicting accounts is true, and suggests two possible interpretations.
The first is that des Grieux's version, according to which Lescaut
inspired his sister to approach M. de G—— M——, is true. The second is that since des Grieux could know who convinced whom to do
what only by listening to Manon, and since he is blinded by his passion, Lescaut's version is true. This interpretation is consistent with
the views of his father, M. B——, and M. de G—— M——. But there
is a third interpretation, which operates on a different level from that
of the other two. Instead of asking which version of an event is "true,"
it reconstructs the same material of the text but outside the framework of the interpretations possible within the narrator's logic.

The narration of *Manon Lescaut* excludes a coherent set of perceptions which could explain Manon's seemingly incomprehensible actions. If the value system implied by her fragmented words and acts
were to find a coherent expression, there would be a fading away of
that mystique, which makes her appear Sphinxlike, duplicitous, or as
Deloffre says, a "character more and more mythical, who ends up by
being identified with the 'eternal feminine.'"[26] What is "hidden"
from us is not *in* Manon but in the text that surrounds her. However
much Manon's discourse is contained in des Grieux's discourse like
quotations in another writer's text, her own subtext is not totally repressed by his supertext.

Bringing it out needs an interpretation not based on a realistic
reading that asks: Who is the *real* Manon behind the paper? It needs
instead a symptomatic reading which seeks to find the "not said" in
what is both repressed and indirectly implied by the language of the
text. The relays between words and images work, like symbols in a
dream, to produce their own meanings which refer not to a presumed
preexisting event that the narrative copies, but to the text's unconscious processes and to the gaps left in it by repression.[27] In *Manon
Lescaut* the heroine is such a symbol whose disturbing presence points
to a multiple absence. This absence is not exterior to the text: it is the
very process underlying and producing the text's structure, and of

which all the speakers in the text (des Grieux, Renoncourt, Manon when she does speak) are unconscious.

One passage that lends itself to such a reading is des Grieux's account of their life together in their first Parisian apartment and of Manon's first infidelity.

> She softened her refusal [to visit his father] with such tender and passionate caresses that I, who lived only in her, and who had not the slightest distrust of her heart, applauded all her answers and all her decisions. I had left with her the arrangement of our finances and the care of paying our daily expenses. (P. 45)

While the aristocratic chevalier's complete unawareness of money guarantees his noble purity, it also indicates in this scene his unawareness and lack of concern for Manon in whose hands financial matters have by necessity been left, because she is more expert in matters of money and independent urban survival.

Her actions also imply that she realizes, unlike des Grieux, that if she accepts her lover's proposal to meet his father, the older man will merely chase her away, and that she understands her lover's naïveté. The novel here shows us a relation between two people in which she, the better equipped for life in the urban world, is actually taking care of des Grieux. Contrary to what he later says, and even more contrary to what eighteenth-century mores will increasingly dictate about the economic roles of men and women, he could not at this point survive without her.

Other passages suggest that as the stronger and more capable partner in this environment, she acts out of what from another perspective could be called generosity. When des Grieux runs away from his studies at St. Sulpice, and she leaves M. B——, she says: "'I want to leave him his furniture, . . . it belongs to him, but I shall take, as is only fair, my jewelry and the almost sixty thousand francs I pulled out of him in two years. I have not given him any power over me'" (p. 67). When she becomes the mistress of M. de G—— M——, she sends des Grieux a letter saying: "I adore you, count on that, but leave to me for a while the management of our fortune. Woe to anyone who falls into my net! I am working to make my chevalier rich and happy" (p. 78). Her dealings with M. B—— imply a strict business code which in

Manon's view is consistent and principled. The word "working" in her reference to M. de G—— M—— must be taken literally. Manon is speaking about practicing an activity of which des Grieux is incapable as a noble scion of a French aristocratic tradition that barred nobles from most kinds of work.[28]

But in the world represented in *Manon Lescaut* women are also being forbidden from performing this activity in an ever-growing number of domains. Left unsaid in the passages concerning her approach to M. de G—— M——, and excluded from the seemingly multiple interpretations of Manon's actions, is that few if any other courses are left open to her. Outside of service and prostitution, there are scant professions for middle-class women who want or need to be economically independent. "Economically," says historian Louise Tilly, "it was extremely difficult to be single and independent," as Manon tries and fails to be. "In the best of jobs," Tilly continues, "female wages were one half to one third of men's."[29]

Manon is the more able provider and protector of the couple in a society that, as the focus of the economy leaves the family, assigns more exclusively the economic role to the male. Therefore her actions seem inspired by "vulgarity" (p. 79). In an age when the family begins to lose its economic role, women are pushed more and more exclusively into adopting motherhood as a profession; and as economic opportunities expand outside the family, women are more and more excluded from extrafamilial professions and professional education.

By 1789, when we do hear a few women's voices, in the *Cahiers de doléances* and in a "Petition from the Women of the Third Estate to the King," they address exclusively this economic issue. Their description of what they consider the most serious problem for contemporary women sounds very like the unspoken story of Manon's life lying behind des Grieux's outline of it.

> Women of the Third Estate are almost all born without fortune: their education is very neglected or very defective: it consists in their being sent to schools at the house of a teacher who himself does not know the first word of the language he is teaching. They continue going there until they are able to read the service of the Mass in French and Vespers in Latin. Having fulfilled the first duties of religion, they are taught to work; having reached the age of fifteen or sixteen, they can make five or six *sous* a day.

If nature has refused them beauty, they get married without dowry to unfortunate artisans, lead aimless, difficult lives stuck away in the provinces, and give birth to children they are incapable of raising. If, on the contrary, they are born pretty, without culture, without principles, without any idea of morals, they become the prey of the first seducer, commit a first sin, come to Paris to bury their shame, end by losing it altogether, and die victims of licentious ways.[30]

The petitioners end by asking the king to prohibit men from exercising certain feminine professions, to provide good professional education for girls, and to take measures against prostitutes. These women, who speak from quite a different worldview than that of des Grieux, lay down in their petition almost the same chain of events that he narrates in *Manon Lescaut,* although he carefully shifts the blame for seduction.

In the course of the French Revolution, more feminine voices are heard, and their concerns broaden to include political rights and participation in all areas of social life. But the two-hundred-year-old historic process that had gradually excluded women from economic autonomy speeds up as it reaches its climax. By 1793, the masculine governors of the French state voice the now formulated decision that with the separation of the workplace from the home, women's place is in the home. The representative Chaumette, in an indictment unanimously adopted by the convention, condemns women for breaking "all the laws of nature" by appearing in the chambers, and says: "But [Nature] has said to women: 'Be a woman.' The tender cares owing to infancy, the details of the household, the sweet anxieties of maternity, these are your labors; but your attentive cares deserve a reward. Fine! You shall have it, and you will be the divinity of the domestic sanctuary."[31] But what if a woman is not in a position to receive this reward? She will be severely condemned. Manon is such a woman, who must earn a living in a world which offers fewer and fewer opportunities to do so. She appears "vulgar," "frivolous," "fickle," and treacherous because the text of the novel represses the historical process that produces her actions.

Although there emerge in *Manon Lescaut* many conventions of a realist code, the novel is not a fully realist text in the sense that the novels of Balzac and Stendhal are. While *Manon Lescaut* portrays details and surface phenomena of the existing contemporary society, it does not, as will novels of its quality a hundred years later, portray the internal social and historical processes that produce a society. The realist novels of Balzac and Stendhal translate into narrative structures the early-nineteenth-century awareness of historical movement and change. Such awareness would be an anachronism for Prévost and does not figure in des Grieux's interpretation of events.

The hero/narrator of *Manon Lescaut* continues to find Manon's character unfathomable because instead of seeing her as acting in a changing relation to a changing world, he attempts to *define* a static group of character traits as an entity unto itself lurking behind her appearance: "she is frivolous and imprudent, but she is forthright and sincere" (p. 144), he says.[32] It is only at the very end of the novel, just before she goes to her death, that Manon, as a mark of her repentance, adopts des Grieux's perception of her and therefore adopts this static, reified view of herself: "I was frivolous and fickle" (p. 176), she tells him when they are in America. Earlier, she accepted the authority of his view but not the view itself. When he confronts her at the home of M. de G—— M——, she is confused by his anger but saddened: " 'I must really be guilty then,' she said sadly, 'since I could cause so much grief and emotion' " (p. 150).

A narrative interpretation that does not embed Manon in this vision of fragmentary, static images and hidden, mysterious essences would see her as both product of and participant in a process of historic change. The historical process is the same one that brings disorder into Renoncourt's orderly worldview, and gives rise to the contradiction between two ideologies, aristocratic and bourgeois, and two literary codes, classical and realist, in *Manon Lescaut*. It both produces the multiple form of the text and is repressed from the text in the sense that, as we have seen, no character is conscious of how the inexplicable contradictions of their world have come about. As a formal element of the novel, the character Manon is the symbol of those historical contradictions.

A narrative which would take account of them would have to include Manon's own interpretation from her own perspective as well as des Grieux's. It would of course be a very different book. As it is, the seemingly multiple interpretations offered by the narrative, that of des Grieux, and that which is visible through his distortions, interact to exclude the kind of logically different form of interpretation that

Manon's would provide. Really two sides of the same interpretation, they function as a pair of symmetrically opposed alternatives which together make unthinkable any interpretation of a different order or level, which would question not the "facts" themselves but the framework which incorporates the facts. Since the alternatives of the same viewpoint in the novel present themselves as the totality of opposing viewpoints, they render invisible any viewpoint and value system which is radically other. While the explicit ideology of *Manon Lescaut* is aristocratic, the monological interplay of these two points of view pave the way for a bourgeois liberal ideology, whose individualist doctrine of "free choice" evolves by creating a frame that severely limits the possibility of choices and determines their nature.

The logic of liberalism evolves through a second narrative technique of *Manon Lescaut,* the first-person narrative of the romantic hero, which helps the individual vision of the world to replace the general maxim as the basis of a value system. Des Grieux's actions become more understandable and more deserving of sympathy the more we identify with his point of view and see the world through the filter of his emotions and values. Although first-person narrative is already a tradition at the time of *Manon Lescaut's* composition, when combined with the technique of multiple but unilevel interpretation, it makes individualist identification the basis of an unspoken value system in which very few people count as individuals. More successfully than the ideology of Renoncourt, the individualist ideology of des Grieux is structured to conceal its foundation in the privileged class position and sex of the viewer. The reader's identification with the first-person hero/narrator works together with the illusion of multiple interpretations within the novel to reinforce des Grieux's interpretation and exclude the possibility of Manon's.

Although des Grieux feels himself an outraged victim of Manon's infidelity, she can justify becoming the paid mistress of M. de G——— M——— because she perceives des Grieux's perception of her. Recounting to des Grieux her conversation with G——— M———, she says: "I answered him . . . that you were not . . . very well off, and that you might not regard my loss as a great misfortune, because it would relieve you of a burden that was weighing on your shoulders. I added . . . that you hadn't seemed extremely anxious when I left you" (p. 142). In fact des Grieux was not anxious as she left to carry out their mutually thought out plan to dupe M. de G——— M———, Jr. He was not anxious because he was willing to use Manon's sexual charms to their monetary advantage as long as the other man did not "possess" her. Only when Manon does not return to des Grieux with the money at the appointed time is he overcome with jealous rage. This incident can appear to us "so cruel" (p. 143) for him only if we are participating in that identification with des Grieux, analyzed by Wayne Booth, that implies a complicity with him and a shared community of values.

The combination of narrative techniques discussed here hides the irrationality underlying des Grieux's seemingly rational view of Manon, and also the discordance between his narrative interpretation and the events of the plot. For instance, des Grieux assumes that he sacrifices himself for this temptress: "Demand my life, what more do I have left to sacrifice for you?" (p. 42) and "I am going to lose my fortune and my reputation for you" (p. 61), he cries tragically. "What more can I do for her after all I have sacrificed for her?" (p. 79) he asks himself in an equally tragic mode. Yet the events of the plot show very little sacrifice on the part of des Grieux for Manon, while she sacrifices all for him. He can at any moment regain his fortune and his good reputation, which he does at the end of his adventures. Manon, on the other hand, after the first night spent with des Grieux, has irrevocably sacrificed all possibility of regaining her position in society. She moreover sacrifices her fortune three times for him. While this seems too obvious to mention, the narrative voice has apparently made it invisible to readers, and Manon's death prevents it from becoming a problem.

The ambiguity of Manon's character, stressed since Renoncourt first introduces her, is ultimately a pseudoambiguity, reducible to two quantitative variations of the same interpretation. One says that Manon is less deceptive than she appears, and the other that she is more deceptive than she appears. In both cases she appears as mysterious object and as other to the self. A true ambiguity between really different interpretations, for instance between that of Manon and that of des Grieux, is unthinkable in the context of the narrative. Instead of incorporating ambiguity, the text operates by an oppositional logic, whereby des Grieux and his father represent the "opposing sides" of an interpretation, while Renoncourt gives the illusion of objectivity that excludes a logic involving true difference. His apparent lack of opinion or evaluation concerning Manon's deception or sincerity conceals the way his dismissal of her as an illustration of "the incomprehensible character of women" (p. 37) provides a framework in which the view of des Grieux and that of his father seem to cover the totality of possible views. This illusionist framework, composed of oppositions that are really mirror reflections of each other, act to affirm the worldview of the mirror subject, and also conceal the subjectivism of his ideology under the appearance of neutrality and objectivity. While a framework is necessary for imposing any ideology, this one suits liberal ideology that proclaims its openness to all views.

It is no coincidence that the character who must be excluded from this framework in order to make it function is lower-class and female. The image in the novel of the two fathers, des Grieux *père* and G—— M—— *père,* joining forces to exclude Manon from France and save des Grieux, is an image of the formal work in the novel's text. In the text the conflicting masculine discourses work together to exclude Manon's. In addition to representing all those uncontrollable impulses which must be repressed if society is to function, she is also the symbol of that which contradicts the worldview of the dominant class. Her presence points indirectly to all that cannot be directly expressed and becomes the symbol of its absence.

It may seem strange that liberal individualism, which will enjoy a symbiotic interdependence with romantic love in the first half of the nineteenth century, should require the exclusion of feminine individuality to establish itself. But more explicit doctrines of traditional liberalism also establish themselves by excluding women. Justifying, in a speech in 1791, why women must be excluded from sociopolitical life, Talleyrand said:

> One half of the human race excluded by the other half from all participation in government; native born people by fact and foreigners by law in the land which nevertheless saw their birth. . . . We have here political phenomena, which in the abstract, in principle, seem impossible to explain.[33]

But, Talleyrand assures his colleagues, the answer is simple; it lies in liberal doctrine itself.

> But there exists an order of ideas in which the question changes and can be easily resolved. The goal of all institutions is the greatest happiness of the greatest number. . . . If the exclusion

from public employ pronounced against women is for both
sexes a way to increase the sum total of their mutual happiness,
it is thenceforth a law which all societies have to recognize and
consecrate.

Invoking Bentham's doctrine of the greatest good for the greatest
number, and doing in a heavy-handed way what the narrative of
Manon Lescaut does much more subtly, Talleyrand tells his audience
that they can be objective, look at both sides, the man's and the woman's, without even having to hear from the women: "and the women
will never have an interest in changing the assignment that they have
received."

Talleyrand's speech is familiarly, even banally, outrageous. Yet the
narrative of *Manon Lescaut* forges in a more subtle and seductive way
the ideological structures which made this exclusion, not only from
politics but from the status of being individual human subjects, seem
natural and even invisible, so that it does not have to be justified. The
novel expresses not the ideas but the framework of thought, the very
forms of logic by which we come to ideas. In this framework the
representation of a feminine character with economic, social, sexual,
and subjective autonomy like Manon stands as an example which
justifies the removal of women from public life and from an independent status, and all the more so in that her author makes her so
believable and so obsessively seductive for her readers. The way Manon's autonomy is presented as destructive paves the way to the passive
nineteenth-century romantic heroine; and the silence imposed on her
announces theirs.

Chapter 4

Stendhal's Bad Mothers

Stendhal's novels pose a problem for critical readings that focus on the relation between history and narrative. How can one talk about history in a text where it so insistently and obviously talks about itself, and where it seems to impose a single linear form of history which excludes all other forms? In *Tristan and Isolde, Manon Lescaut,* and romantic love narratives of later periods, history works in the text as what Fredric Jameson calls "an absent force,"[1] requiring a symptomatic reading of the gaps and silences it leaves. Reading the absent force of history in these texts can bring multiplicity to their apparently unified surface, and show the productive workings of the text in the language of the finished product. But in Stendhal's *The Red and the Black* history is so overwhelmingly present as an object of representation, framework of narrative structure, and determining force of the hero's character that a reading of history in the text would seem to involve little more than a summary of the plot and a complicity with its dominant ideology.[2]

Yet history in *The Red and the Black* does not work as unambiguously and self-evidently as it seems. Accepting the linear representation of history as an unquestioned given, as a background for the apparently more problematic issue of deciphering Julien's character and motivations, some critics have tended toward a psychologism that reinforces monolinear history.[3] This form of history in the novel centers around a single hero, follows strict cause and effect logic, and presents itself as free from gaps and holes. The mutual reinforcement between a certain type of psychological reading and a certain type of monological history renders invisible the multiple forms of history and of individuality that really do enter into play within the text. The following reading of *The Red and the Black* shifts this focus and examines how the narrative works to hide from the reader different historical processes of the early nineteenth century that are incorporated into the novel.

While in Balzac's novels history appears as class struggle, which moves as difference between the conflicting parties and has no center, Stendhal's novels incorporate a liberal vision of history. According to this vision, history moves forward through the acts of great energetic individuals, and so the novels revolve around the destiny of a single central hero. The other characters appear as mediators of his destiny within the single narrative line. So compelling is this central spine of the novel that it hides the way these other characters act as bearers of different historical processes and different potential narrative structures which are not realized in the text but lurk there as possibilities.

The central narrative structure of *The Red and the Black* concerns Julien's struggles in the Restoration period and, according to Peter Brooks, is inseparable "from the issue of authority and the theme of paternity, which provide not only the matter of the novel but its structuring force, the dynamic that shapes its plot."[4] While paternity shapes Julien's historicity, it is maternity and the nineteenth-century myths surrounding it that shape the very different historicities of Mme. de Rênal and Mathilde de La Mole. These other historicities, while perfectly visible in the text, seem to be repressed to a textual unconscious.

Historical Forms and Textual Forms

The dominant notion of history, not only in *The Red and the Black* but in Stendhal's other novels and in his autobiography *The Life of Henry Brulard*, could be called that of disillusioned liberalism. It sees the French Revolution as a rupture with the past that brought about undesirable effects but was nonetheless authentic and momentous as a transformation. One of its disillusioning effects is that victory turns the sublime, energetic revolutionaries into repressive, narrowly self-interested bourgeois. Thus the aftermath of the revolution can do nothing but constantly, albeit in less authentic modes, repeat that moment of rupture, which always leads to the same disillusionment as the original event when a new generation of energetic revolutionaries become bourgeois. As a minor character in *The Red and the Black* says,

Robespierre and Napoleon, who began as sublime heroes, ended by making "possible the reign of the de Rênals and the Chelans [the monarchist priests]."[5] But by the same token they also make possible "the return of Robespierre . . . because . . . these young men from the lower classes" (p. 94) will have to struggle against the de Rênals and will displace them to end up like them, oppressing other poor people. Julien, modeling himself on the sublime Napoleon, driven by his desires to rise from his lowly position and then finding disillusionment when he succeeds, provides the homologue of this historical pattern. But the whole pattern is already fully inscribed in miniature in the introductory paragraphs of the novel and already repeated on the second page.

In the first paragraph, the narrator, adopting the voice of a naive tourist, introduces us to the scenic town of Verrières as seen from afar. He can see its quaint houses, "the smallest bends" (p. 3) of its hills, the flowing Doubs, the fortifications "formerly built by the Spaniards and now ruined," and the rim of mountains in the background. He ties the whole scene together by describing a ribbon of river: "A torrent, which rushes down from the mountain, crosses Verrières before running into the Doubs" (p. 3). This scene is a daydream landscape, affording the viewer the combined ability to see the totality of the place as if from a distance and also to pick out tiny details as if from up close. Into that distant daydream the narrator projects his desires for idyllic tranquility, as Julien will project his desires for adventure, fame, and romantic passion into a distant future. The note of the ruined Spanish fort admits history into the scene as something that happened in a remote romantic past, but the introductory paragraphs do not admit the notion of a historical process that still goes on.

Therefore it is with a disillusioning shock that when one does enter the scene, one finds oneself "stunned" by a noisy din of new machines, and sees that the "antique Spanish" (p. 5) features of M. de Rênal are now embedded in capitalist jowls. For the narrator, as for his textual alter ego, M. Giraud, whose plaints of disillusionment with the post-Napoleonic French countryside begin the second part of the novel, history has had a bad ending, and one is living decidedly after the end. It is up to the naive like Julien to repeat it.

The second page projects the pattern of disillusionment back to an even more distant past. We find that the mercenary, hostile relation between M. de Rênal with his avaricious vanity and Père Sorel with his avaricious cunning simply replays the social relations of the romantic Hispanic times themselves, when the de Rênals were masters and the Sorels slaves. Julien's history will not only encapsulate contemporary social and political struggles but will also repeat that older struggle, in a world full of clues to its inevitable end. His own father is a slave turned cruel tyrant, and he begins his quest in the landscape that presents the development of history to all eyes which care to see: the ancient castle, the older handicraft forms of production, and the new machines.[6]

This linear form of history makes the narrative resemble in some ways the "bounded text" analyzed by Julia Kristeva. This is a textual structure which, "terminated in its beginning," announces its conclusion at the outset.[7] The "bounded text" also begins its narrative by posing pseudo-oppositions—good/evil, truth/falsehood, life/death, fidelity/betrayal—and then in the body of the text dissolves them into figures of ambiguity, which make possible psychological realism. Characters are not emblematic of good or evil, but ambiguous, capable of both, self-divided and also masked so that a deceptive exterior hides a contradictory interior. In a "bounded text" these ambiguities once again become oppositional forms at the end of the narrative in order to be resolved into unities. Yet while *The Red and the Black* is marked by these elements, it also in many ways goes beyond a "bounded text." Within the body of the novel the monolinear history gives way to a multiplicity of histories before reimposing itself at the end, and the ambiguity that temporarily dissolves dichotomies acts to subvert the moral, social, and ideological categories reigning in French society of the 1820s, and carries a scathing criticism of them.

The novel's introduction emphasizes in its description of Verrières the dichotomies that have divided the world, and treats them in an ironic, critical tone. The oppositions of masculine/feminine, business/home, ambition/love, authority/obedience, money/beauty, and also the division of the social structure into the separate spheres of masculine-economic and feminine-domestic, are embodied in M. and Mme. de Rênal, whom we see walking side by side, contrasted in every way. M. de Rênal has created in Verrières "its atmosphere fouled by the petty affairs of money" (p. 5) and decides everything according to the sole criterion of "bringing in revenue" (p. 8), while his wife has no interest in these matters. She is enraptured by a beautiful view while her husband thinks about the cost of the landscaping. Into this sexually and morally split world comes Julien, a sympathetic hypocrite, a misfit, a male who belongs in the feminine realm of love, deep emotion, and beauty.

He dissolves these oppositions, starting with the masculine/feminine.[8] When he first knocks at Mme. de Rênal's door, she does not realize that he is the new tutor for her sons but takes him for a "young girl in disguise" (p. 26). Categories of generational and class authority dissolve as a relieved Mme. de Rênal thinks that Julien will not be the tyrannical tutor she expected but a "comrade" for her sons, and Julien thinks that Mme. de Rênal is twenty years old. On the level of narrative form, subject/object categories dissolve as the hitherto stable point of view shifts between Mme. de Rênal and Julien as they contemplate each other. When the de Rênal family goes to Vergy, and Julien's education of the children includes their "butterfly hunts," work merges with pleasure, and the adult women who join the hunt merge with their children. The reader identifies with the "crime" of Julien's and Mme. de Rênal's joy, while M. de Rênal, staunchly defending the world of dichotomies, explains the meaning of this dissolution of categories: "Everything in this century tends to throw odium on *legitimate* authority. Poor France!" (p. 144, italics in text).

As the love between Mme. de Rênal and Julien develops, the authority/obedience dichotomy dissolves, and the authority vested in hierarchies of class, sex, and personal qualities shifts unstably between the lovers. The love/ambition dichotomy also dissolves as the two emotions, sometimes at war with each other, sometimes serving each other, mingle in Julien's soul. Moreover, in order for this love to develop, Mme. de Rênal has to change from a woman with an "abnegation of will . . . that was the pride M. de Rênal" (p. 36), and with "no experience of life" (p. 67), into a woman who is in the eyes of her society, and in her own eyes, a criminal, and who employs "a truly admirable craftiness in such a natural woman" (p. 99) to advance her criminality. In other words, she has to become an agent of history, and of a history which is in certain respects quite different from Julien's.

The passage at the beginning of the novel which introduces Mme. de Rênal presents her as the stereotypical bourgeoisified noblewoman of the 1820s and as an object without any subjective life beyond her total absorption in her maternal vocation.

While listening to her husband who spoke in grave tones, Mme. de Rênal's eye followed anxiously the movements of her three young sons. The eldest, who looked about eleven years old, approached the parapet too often and showed signs of climbing it. A sweet voice would then pronounce the name of Adolphe, and the child would give up his ambitious plan. Mme. de Rênal appeared to be a woman of thirty years, but still sufficiently pretty. (P. 9)

Where this stereotype is presented by other nineteenth-century authors, such as Balzac, Sand, Hugo, or Vigny, as a faithful copy of reality, this whole passage introducing Mme. de Rênal in *The Red and the Black* acts as an ironic sign of the stereotype that is imposed on women. It is like a shell that will be broken to release Mme. de Rênal from the prison of stereotypes and transform her into a figure who is both product and producer of history, a unique exception whose inner conflicts and actions raise to the highest degree the contradictions of her situation.[9]

A Hugo or a Vigny might present this mindless devotion to motherhood not as the historical effect of women's exclusion from society but as natural and eternal. But Stendhal first historicizes the stereotype, and then makes Mme. de Rênal the active producer of her own destiny. Her revolt does not deny the concept of domestic bliss, but rather transforms it, since when she enjoys it with Julien, domesticity changes from an arena of bourgeois ideology to an arena of her revolt. Stendhal effects such a transformation in a scene where M. de Rênal interrupts the joyful play of Julien, Mme. de Rênal, and the children: "Suddenly the door opened; it was M. de Rênal. His harsh, discontented face formed a strange contrast with the sweet joy his presence chased away" (p. 146).

While the "sweet joy" of domesticity was a stock image hypocritically celebrated by bourgeois morality, in *The Red and the Black* it signifies Julien's and Mme. de Rênal's violation of that morality, their "noble and romantic souls" (p. 154), their generosity, and their love of danger. All these Stendhalian qualities evade the reach of those characters consumed with amassing money and petty power over others. Transformed into a sign of revolt against bourgeois domesticity, the "sweet joy" they share at home makes Julien even more confirmed in his "vague hope of the most atrocious vengeance" (p. 56), while Mme.

de Rênal, to her own amazement, comes to join him in this feeling: "For the first time in her life Mme. de Rênal felt a sort of desire for vengeance against her husband" (p. 56).

As an agent of history, she has, as opposed to Manon Lescaut and to her contemporary Mme. de Mortsauf in Balzac's *The Lily in the Valley,* her own autonomous subjectivity and voice in the novel. The novel presents her as unknowable to Julien because he is too absorbed in his ego, in his ambition, and in his rigid preconceived ideas "for him to be in a state to observe anything outside of himself" (p. 150). But she is knowable to the readers because we are admitted to the fictional inner development of her thoughts and can see how they conflict with Julien's.

By presenting the conflicting subjectivities of his hero and heroine, Stendhal makes himself a rarity among nineteenth-century realists. Realism in early-nineteenth-century novels depends less on an objective and empirical portrayal of reality than on drawing the reader into an intimate, subjective identification with a hero as an individual whose psychological reality the reader does not question. The readers share the hero's consciousness of reality and self as if it were their own, even filling in the gaps to that consciousness with their own thoughts.

The Red and the Black, however, leads the reader to identify subjectively with both hero and heroine, and to share their often conflicting perceptions so that they are both opaque to each other, both transparent to us. Robert Alter notes the "innovative technical details"[10] of Stendhal's craft, which "bridged the gap between" first-person narrative and third-person narrative. This technical originality translates an original sexual politics of narration which represents reality as filtered through the conflicting consciousnesses of characters of different sexes and different classes.

The belief in a homogeneous and monolithic reality, which the narrative techniques of *Manon Lescaut* reinforce, becomes in *The Red and the Black* a target of irony, and is seen as a distortion of a multiple reality, lived differently by oppressed and oppressor. This distorted vision is presented through M. de Rênal. Tyrannic, bigoted, incapable of love, possessed of "blind hatred for every line of reasoning contrary to [his] own" (p. 37), and refusing any alternate vision of reality, he relentlessly strives to impose this vision on his social inferiors—his servants and his wife—by censoring their books and newspapers, isolating them physically, and indoctrinating them with a highly politicized form of religion.

As Mme. de Rênal becomes an agent of history and of her own destiny, she learns how to take advantage of M. de Rênal's blindness. At a crucial moment of the plot, when M. de Rênal's bourgeois rival, M. Valenod, sends her husband an anonymous letter revealing her love affair with Julien, she foils his plot with a daring, brilliant, and complex counterplot of her own. At this moment she directs the course of Stendhal's novel and even writes her own novel, which takes the form of a long letter to Julien, laying out her plot in detail and assigning Julien his role. In this letter she develops a strategy which can defeat the two more powerful men because it flows from an awareness that she is forced to live in her husband's vision of reality. It thus implies a further awareness of the vast chasms separating the different realities. With this double consciousness she can play upon the men's desires and prejudices, imitate Valenod's style in composing a forged anonymous letter to M. de Rênal, and manipulate M. de Rênal into a raging dismissal of her as the embodiment of all the feminine stereotypes: "'How much good sense can one expect from a woman? You never pay attention to what is reasonable . . . . feeble beings!'" (p. 129). In addition to reading the characters of these two men, Mme. de Rênal writes them as well.

In her letter to Julien, the passage outlining her most brilliant stratagem is followed by the despairing self-accusation: "Ah! what a bad mother! These are two vain words that I have just written, my dear Julien" (p. 122). If the sign of Mme. de Rênal's stereotypicality includes what is considered maternal devotion, the sign of her historicity is "bad" motherhood. She writes these words at the very height of her activity in directing the plot of the novel and in transforming the historical image of women. In order to be a subject of history, she has to live in a space where categories of good and bad dissolve, but she also has to be a bad mother as motherhood was then (and is now) defined.

Yet Mme. de Rênal's role as a historical agent stops here. The novel she writes places Julien at its center. She has told Julien to hide in the mountains around Vergy until she gives him the prearranged signal of victory. And when she goes out to signal him with a wave of her handkerchief, she looks *up* into the mountains. In both *The Red and the Black* and *The Charterhouse of Parma*, the mountaintop is the privileged place where the heroes situate themselves in the center of their world, and master the view of their destiny. Mme. de Rênal is never allowed to attain that summit. She herself remains down below and is unable even to see Julien. This is the end of her novel; she stops writing and in her next letter will let her confessor dictate to her what to write. When she next plays a major role in *The Red and the Black*, she will have merged into Julien's history as a mediator of his destiny.

In the interval, Julien, having gone to Paris as M. de La Mole's secretary, falls in love with his employer's daughter Mathilde, who is already a subject of history when he meets her. In a superficial symmetry to the way Julien takes for his model Napoleon, she takes for her model the sixteenth-century Marguerite de Navarre, mistress of her ancestor Boniface de la Mole. As Julien is impassioned by the idea of a lowly peasant rising to glory in Napoleon's army, so Mathilde is impassioned by the idea of heroic and decisive action by women of the high aristocracy in the sixteenth century. Both characters are driven by the desire to mold history by passionate action, and both are characters of infinite desire in a society which for the first time in history could evoke infinite personal aspirations and ideals but afford them only finite and predetermined realizations.

But here the symmetry ends. Mathilde's history follows a form completely different from that of Julien. This difference can be seen in the nature of the obstacles that prevent each of them from immersing themselves in passion the way Mme. de Rênal does. Julien is so prevented by his oppressed status. He must hide the passion which is always ready to burst out of the carefully constructed armor of his hypocrisy. Mathilde, because of her excessively privileged position, is incapable of experiencing passion and longs for a world in which she can.

While Julien's adventurous quest will inevitably end in his becoming a bourgeois, Mathilde does not even know where to begin her quest. Endowed with the same "strength of character" (p. 281) as Julien, and having the courage to live her ideal, even if it means imitating a model, Mathilde is even more pushed into a corner by history than Julien, and her ideal of heroism marks a qualitatively more drastic rupture with the past than his. Julien, in contemplating his Napoleonic ideal, often mourns the fact that instead of living in a world where men rose to fortune and power through direct action, he now inhabits a world where men can rise to fortune and power only by hypocrisy and self-repression. Mathilde's Renaissance ideal represents a world in which ruling-class women (of the stamp of Catherine de Medicis, Catherine of Aragon, Marguerite de Navarre, Marguerite d'Angoulème, Elizabeth of England, and Mary of Scotland) acted on their own to shape history, and marks a radical change from the bourgeois world where women are extensions of active men.

Whereas Julien sometimes intuits the disillusioning end of his adventure, Mathilde's "ending" happened three hundred years ago. Whereas Julien is always plunged into the unexpected, Mathilde sees her whole life, including her love life with the prudent young aristocrats of her circle, stretching before her in excruciatingly boring and predictable detail. But she does have one advantage that Julien lacks. His historicity, homologous to the bourgeois rise to power, will make him repeat the form of his Napoleonic model and the pattern according to which one segment of the bourgeoisie replaces another in the same power structure. Mathilde has chosen to act according to a model whose pattern cannot be repeated in the nineteenth century, and which makes her act outside the structure of history which dominates the novel. While she is herself a product of that history, an aristocrat looking for a role in the bourgeois liberal world, she does not reproduce the forms of that world but remains an anomaly.

However much her love affair with Julien begins as an inauthentic imitation of models, she seeks through it a way out of her historical dead end. After she becomes pregnant, she writes to her father: "I will not be a duchess, my father. . . . My fall is irremediable" (p. 432). Her "illegitimate" maternity is not, as it would have been generally considered in 1830, an end to her life or the way to ensnare a man. On the contrary, it marks her rupture with boring security, a going beyond the end of history that had blocked her, a leap into insecurity and into the necessity for historic practice, a denial of the laws of patriarchal society and a deliberate dare to it to bring its wrath down upon her. This same leap will characterize her public attempts to save Julien at the end of the novel.

From History to Myth

The interlude of Julien's love affair with Mathilde also has the effect of making us forget our readerly attachment to Mme. de Rênal. By the time that M. de La Mole receives from her the fatal letter denouncing Julien, we barely remember her. Earlier in the novel, in her own plot against M. Valenod, she directed Julien to cut and paste the words of a false anonymous letter she herself composed. This letter to M. de La Mole reverses the process: it is composed by her confessor who directs her to write it.

This letter cuts a rupture in the narrative, changing it from a form based on multiple realism to one based on a monolithic vision of reality, from a technique that develops several realist subjects with whose experience and interpretations we identify to a technique which lets us share the reality and subjectivity of a single realist subject—Julien. After Julien reads the letter, shoots Mme. de Rênal, and becomes a tragic hero, Mme. de Rênal will become nothing more than the mirror complement of Julien, and Mathilde will become an antipathetic character. These transformations of narrative structure also propel Julien out of historic process into mythic stasis.

Reading this letter, if as readers we have entered into complicity with the realist illusion of the novel and have been well manipulated to identify increasingly with Julien, we will feel, like him and for him, a flash of indignation at the words written therein. In spite of the undeniable "facts" in the letter—Julien does use hypocrisy, he did seduce both women in cold calculation, he has no principles of religion, and he knowingly left Mme. de Rênal to desolate unhappiness and regret—the letter does not communicate the truth.[11] Although the letter repeats the same events we have already read in the course of Stendhal's narration, it provides a competing and very different narration, omitting an essential aspect of the original recounting of events. It takes no account of Julien's subjective motivation and does not see his behavior as produced by his inner conflicts, but sees only the result of his actions in the world. One of the major themes of the novel revolves around the crucial difference between heroes of the past who can be judged by their acts and Julien who does not have this opportunity and so can only be judged by what he keeps hidden inside himself.

We have learned that Julien seduces women not, as the letter implies, because of a vulgar desire for money, but out of a private nobility of soul and out of the same pride that makes him desire to rise through the only channels and to the only status his bourgeois society provides. The vengeance that moved him to seduce both Mme. de Rênal and Mathilde forms part of his noble code of honor, but this code, as opposed to the chivalric codes of feudalism, is entirely subjective and idiosyncratic. It lacks a social base, a reference group, and a social outlet, but it is this code which impels Julien to shoot Mme. de Rênal out of vengeance. Julien lives in a period when he can no longer achieve recognition by noble deeds. He will have to be recognized for the subjective nobility of his inner character and his hidden motives, and this is what a reader implicitly agrees to do in sharing his indignation over the letter. These hidden conflicts at the source of Julien's split self are what we have come to identify as the "real" Julien, and what we have come to identify *with* in entering the novel's realist illusions.

Some critics have identified so strongly with his inner character that they have supplied Julien's "hidden" motives for shooting Mme. de Rênal, even though the text omits them and leaves a gap where one would expect to find them. This practice does not limit itself to critics of an older generation like Henri Martineau,[12] but is also found in insightful studies by contemporary critics like Elizabeth Tenenbaum. She begins by saying that in the scene of the shooting we are "deprived of our privileged view of Julien's hidden feelings,"[13] and then ferrets them out by extrapolating from the rest of the novel. But Julien is a fragmentary linguistic and literary construct who has no hidden feelings which the narrator does not describe. Stendhal has left here a gap, which Tenenbaum and others, in an effort that Barthes sees as defining psychological criticism, tries to fill in without questioning why the gap is there. The reasons for Julien's crime do not lie in psychological motives that are distinctly absent from the text, and critical attention to that absence neglects another absence in the text.

If Mme. de Rênal's letter to M. de La Mole fails to take into account Julien's subjective motivation, the narration surrounding the letter takes care to omit hers. We are not even told until later in the novel that its writing was imposed on Mme. de Rênal by her politically crafty confessor. Mme. de Rênal has ceased to be a realist subject. We not only identify with Julien's interpretation, but identify with it alone, from here to the end of the novel which now presents a monolithic vision of its reality. When later in the novel we again share Mme. de Rênal's inner life, it will have merged completely with Julien's. We find out she is innocent of the letter at the point when Julien's heroic glory demands an objective complement to mirror it, and she reenters the text in that role. Julien's sociohistoric struggle ends in the same moment as the textual struggles between conflicting visions held by different characters in the novel.

After the shooting, the novel represents one reality, and it revolves around Julien as its center. A hero in the eyes of all the people, especially "the hero of the young women of Besançon" (p. 505), Julien's glory is the creation of Mathilde's efforts. But now that Julien finally has the heroism, glory, and recognition he had always dreamt of, he is not only indifferent to it but unconscious of it. Feeling "tired of heroism" (p. 470), and living in the memory of his earlier love with Mme. de Rênal, Julien demands: "Leave me my ideal life. . . . What do I care about *other people*" (p. 475, italics in text), and spends his time in solitude "without suspecting that his appearance was awaited every day by all the telescopes of the city" (p. 475).

At the beginning of his quest, he had wished, when Mme. de Rênal first expressed her passion, to have "all those terribly proud nobles for witnesses." Now, after she arrives in his cell, and they do become witnesses of her romantic sacrifice, he would rather not know about it. When, at the beginning of his novel, he first made love with Mme. de Rênal, he could not enjoy it: "Instead of being attentive to the ecstasies he evoked . . . , he feared frightful remorse and eternal ridicule if he deviated from the ideal model he had set for himself to follow" (p. 86). Now in prison, Julien has become that ideal model in the eyes of other people, and "hopelessly in love," he wants nothing but to "give himself entirely to memories of the happy days of yore he had spent at Verrières" (p. 471). The narrative has closed its circle.

During the novel Julien's inner self was split from his external appearance, his ideal self was opposed to the lowly person he actually was, his dreams for the future were opposed to his present experience, and he was himself at odds with the world around him; but once he is in prison, dream and memory form a closed circle. Inner/outer, self/world, actual/ideal, past/present have all united in a single, nonconflictual identity. Julien, having both achieved his ultimate goal and scornfully rejected it, unites his split conflicting selves into a harmonious closed circle of a self.

While Mathilde, active in securing his acquittal, is "busy with real things, as it suits an aristocratic heart" (p. 475), Julien, plunged into his "ideal life" within the prison, "smoking excellent cigars," learns for the first time "the art of enjoying life," in an idealized form of what the bourgeois seeks in his leisure time away from his business, in the domestic half of the work/home dichotomy. Whereas during the novel Julien had dissolved the dichotomy between sociopolitical action and the pure realm of sentiment and enjoyment, he now idealizes that split. His ideal self-unity takes the place of his former attempt to forge a lived union between love and sociohistoric action. He erects a barrier between the "real things" of the sociopolitical world and the "ideal life" of the private realm.

Even his speech to the jury, which so spectacularly unites a political philosophy and an outpouring of deepest personal feeling, has the ultimate effect of splitting them apart. Uniting his inner and outer selves in action, he tells the jurors they "will want to punish in me and discourage forever that class of young people who, born into an inferior class and in some way oppressed by poverty, have the good fortune to obtain a good education and the audacity to mingle with what the pride of rich people calls society" (p. 480). His speech makes his most personal expression into his most political, but formed of a very strange kind of politics. Julien can speak this way because he has decided to die. He is free to be himself on the condition that his apparently political act has the effect of strengthening the power of the Valenods and de Rênals he attacked in his speech. He is recognized as a hero by the women who weep for him, as he leaves the world of masculine power intact and retreats to the world outside of it. The speech which unites his inner and outer selves fixes in static dichotomy the sociopolitical world of men and the feminine realm of sentiment.

The Bad Mother and the Mother Myth

Victor Brombert sees the Stendhalian prison as symbolic of the hero's return to the Mother,[14] and it can also be seen, especially in the case of Julien, as symbolic of the patriarchal *myth* of the return to the mother, which, as Luce Irigaray points out, underlies the ideology of "the desire of the same"[15] or the desire to return to an original, unitary self-identity. Julien finds that identity in prison, which symbolizes for him not only the return to the mother, but the return to the bourgeois home, with all the other myths its idealized image perpetuates. Prison also reestablishes for Julien the split spheres of masculine power and feminine sentiment, the rigid, dichotomized gender categories, and the "legitimate authority" he had opposed all his life.

When Mathilde comes to Julien's cell after his speech to insist that he appeal his case, the author has her behave in a particularly obnoxious way, calculated to win the antipathy of the reader. Julien, the former androgyne, rejects both her manner and her concern for affairs in the outside world on the grounds that they are unfeminine: "Heaven owed it to the glory of your race to have you born a man" (p. 488), he tells her sarcastically.

But the main reason he gives for choosing Mme. de Rênal and rejecting Mathilde is based on bourgeois patriarchal ideology in the narrowest sense of the word. Earlier in the novel, when Julien first heard that Mathilde was pregnant, he fell into a new obsession for his future son, and he never doubts that his child will be a son. In prison he tells Mathilde that he is rejecting her because she will be what Mme. de Rênal called a "bad mother": "He stopped all of a sudden and became dreamy. He found himself once again confronting this new idea which was so shocking for Mathilde: 'In fifteen years Mme. de Rênal will adore my son, and you will have forgotten him'" (p. 473). This passage is noteworthy not so much for what Julien says, but for the narrator's lack of irony in presenting it. Earlier in the novel, this same fatuous self-seriousness and self-righteous egotism on the part of Julien would have been treated with sharp irony. It is strange that we are meant to be moved by Julien's expression of the most banal bourgeois sentiment in an antibourgeois novel.

Mathilde's pregnancy signified for her not devotion to a patriarchal ideal of motherhood, but an act of heroism, a cutting herself adrift from the secure identity she had enjoyed. For Julien it becomes a means of perpetuating his own idealized self-image through a son. While Mathilde's act breaks what Julia Kristeva calls "the unifying enclosure of [her] self-identity,"[16] Julien uses it to reproduce his own self-identity through a son he will never meet, and whom he can therefore also idealize. Mme. de Rênal will be the vehicle of that reproduction. Like Mme de Rênal, Mathilde has to be a "bad mother" in order to act in history, but now that the novel has reestablished the traditional categories of good and bad, her efforts are condemned.

Mme. de Rênal had to be a "bad mother" so that she could become a "good Mother" for Julien in order to fulfill his "desire for the same." While at the beginning of the novel, the ironized sign of stereotypical motherhood was shattered to make Mme. de Rênal a historical figure, the signs of historicity are now absorbed into a new, all-encompassing, unconscious stereotype of motherhood. The reader accepted Mme. de Rênal as a "bad mother" earlier in the novel, because the narrative was structured to lead the reader into suspending bourgeois-patriarchal ideology. Now she must become a "good Mother" so that this ideology can reassert itself, allowing Julien to *possess* a static identity reflected in Mme. de Rênal. And he reflects to the readers their imaginary identity which they find through their identification with him.

Identity and Identification

In many cases, critics who have shared Julien's final feelings toward the two heroines also share the novel's final mode of thinking in fixed dichotomies. With a few notable exceptions, critical studies have seen the heroines as the symbolic poles of an opposition, which represents the opposing poles of masculine desire, and where Mme. de Rênal occupies the positive pole and Mathilde the negative.[17] Gérard Genette, following Gilbert Durand, notes the "recurring themes of feminine duality and symbolic opposition between two types, the Amazon . . . and the tender woman."[18] For him "the abandon to feminine tenderness as a return to the mother" constitutes the positive pole, because the "typically maternal function of the triumphatory heroine is found at the basis of what is essential to Stendhalian novelistic creation" (p. 179).

Hans Böll-Johansen sees the two heroines as "classical stereotypes of woman" coupled in "hyperbolic idealization." In the opposition Mathilde "has nothing positive to give [Julien]. Cold and insensitive, she feeds herself, like a vampire, on his feelings. The opposition is almost absolute between the idealized woman, capable of generous passion, and the woman of evil omen, entirely devoted to her egotism."[19] For Martha N. Moss, "Mathilde de La Mole functions . . . as the antithesis of Mme. de Rênal,"[20] and Robert Alter sees Mme. de Rênal as "a woman of hidden liveliness and feminine charm shyly subjected to the male-dominated bourgeois order, and in her natural unreflective grace the antithesis of the self-conscious Julien as well as the histrionic Mathilde de La Mole."[21]

René Girard, carrying this mode of thought the furthest, sees in Mathilde and Mme. de Rênal "not so much a question of opposition between two types of women as two antinomic functions exercised by the feminine element in the existence and creation of the novelist."[22] Not coincidentally, his antipathy for Mathilde is most intense. He defines Mathilde as a type by saying: "Mathilde is succeeded by the venal Mme. Dambreuse" (p. 135).

This group of critics includes Stendhal himself. *The Red and the Black* treats the heroines in an ambiguous way, sometimes setting them in a binary opposition but also setting each into the text as a whole. But a critical article, which Stendhal wrote on his own novel under the pseudonym Don Gruffot Papera, describes the two heroines in terms of a hierarchized opposition. He says that Mathilde's love represents Parisian love, which "makes a fine contrast with Mme. de Rênal's simple and true love, which does not reflect upon itself. We have here love of the head compared to love of the heart."[23] In the novel itself, at the beginning of the Mathilde/Julien love affair, Stendhal compares Mathilde's "love of the head" to Mme. de Rênal's "true love" (p. 356). Yet the novel as a whole does not treat the two heroines in terms of this comparison.

One critic, Michel Guérin, reverses the opposition. Noting that readers usually "take the side of Mme. de Rênal against Mathilde de La Mole," he says: "I had always been the advocate of Mathilde."[24] The point, however, is not to take the side of one heroine over the other, but to go beyond seeing them in terms of a moral opposition between good and bad to see them in terms of a complex text that harbors many potential narrative structures. In the text Mme. de Rênal ultimately functions as the necessary complement to the hero's narrative structure while Mathilde functions according to her own potential narrative structure in the same novel. If the heroines are seen in this way, certain questions arise: Why do readers react with sympathy and approval to the heroine who complements the hero and with antipathy and opprobrium to the heroine who strays into an independent textual structure? And how does enclosing these heroines in a polarized opposition help to reinforce these readerly reactions?

One difference between critics who react against Mathilde and those who do not is that critics who see her as hateful tend to treat the characters psychologically (even if they are structuralist critics), while the critics in the second group treat her as a textual construct and also analyze the text in a historical perspective. Where one critic, seeing her only as complement to Julien, finds her "utterly . . . cold-hearted,"[25] Lukács, seeing her in terms of the text as a whole, finds her "passionately devoted to romantic monarchist ideals."[26] And Christopher Prendergast finds that the way she "countervenes the generic and social codes that inform our established models of vraisemblance marks the strength and vitality of Mathilde as a literary creation."[27]

Psychological criticism, as Roland Barthes points out, has a "horror of empty spaces"[28] and tenaciously hangs on to a belief in codes of verisimilitude according to which characters' personalities and motivations must be consistent, logical, and full, so that they can be treated like "real people." There is a mutual interdependence between the code of psychologism demanding the full, logically consistent character readers believe Julien to be, and the codes of realism, which depend on reader identification with this kind of unified, stable character and its ideology. Mathilde, as Prendergast points out, threatens that identification, and so she receives reader antipathy, and is made unthreatening by being reduced to a polar opposition with Mme. de Rênal.

This opposition functions to center Julien, just as Julien often opposes in his own mind the two heroines precisely at those moments of the text when he feels his own identity dangerously disintegrating, and needs to anchor it in a secure center. In like manner D. Gruffot Papera (alias Stendhal) makes of the two heroines a symmetrical opposition in an article that attempts to give to *The Red and the Black* the aura of a finished aesthetic object. For the author in the act of writing, the novel is a process of textual production, but as critic of the finished book Stendhal presents it as a product awaiting unproblematic readerly consumption. The character of Mathilde, unless neutralized in such a symmetrical structure, does not lend itself to such consumption.

Critical antipathy focuses itself on Mathilde because far from centering Julien's identity, she threatens it, and so also threatens reader identification with it. René Girard's comments show an intimate relation among the "horror of empty spaces," an identification with Julien, and antipathy for Mathilde: "The personality of Julien Sorel remains an unbroken unity, but this unity is threatened at the time of that temporary aberration which is his love for Mathilde" (p. 91).

A Different Logic of History

In their disapproval of Mathilde, these critics do correctly perceive one thing about her: she does disrupt Julien's stable identity and the ideology which protects it. What readers don't "like" about Mathilde is that she takes Julien out of that ideology and makes him what Julia Kristeva calls a "subject in process."[29] But according to Kristeva, only this form of a subject is capable of producing historic change. As a textual construct Mathilde invites the reader to enter a different logic of history and a different insertion of the subject within it than that of classical realism and the linear history which seems to dominate the text. But she also asks the readers to give up their seductive identification with Julien.

Julien loves Mme. de Rênal rather than Mathilde at the end of the novel not only because Mathilde is still concerned with the "real things" that no longer affect him, but also because she forces him to come out of his self-absorption and involve himself with other realities. By contrast with Mathilde, Mme. de Rênal, when she is in Julien's presence, gives him no need to disturb the fixed boundaries of his self: "I speak to you as I speak to myself" (p. 492), he tells her. Mme. de Rênal maintains Julien's ideal unity of self by dissolving herself into him: "From the moment I see you," she tells him, "all my duties disappear; I am nothing but love for you" (p. 491).

If she is the "tender mistress who thinks no more of her own existence from the moment she has brought happiness to her lover" (p. 345), Mathilde, earlier in the novel, caused Julien to dissolve *his* ego: "Julien had no idea of such an intensity of unhappiness; he was on the brink of crying out; *this firmest of souls had finally been overturned from top to bottom*" (p. 353, emphasis added). While the love with Mme. de Rênal requires from her a permanent loss of self, the love with Mathilde requires of Julien a temporary loss or overturning of self, from which he will come back changed and stronger.

This temporary loss of self is, according to Kristeva, the necessary condition for any practice that brings about productive change, be it historic, scientific, artistic, or erotic and interpersonal. In becoming a "subject in process," the ego enclosed in fixed boundaries, product of culture, ideology, and theology, "dissolves its compactness and its presence to self" (p. 179) in a moment of practice. Kristeva defines practice as an "activity of socio-historic transformation," and any practice requires that the subject also be transformed. Through an "annihilation of consciousness, of its presence and of its metaphysical unity" (p. 175), the subject comes into "relation with, thus in negation to, objects and other subjects of the social milieu, with which he enters into contradiction, be it antagonistic or not" (p. 179).

The polarization of the two heroines, effected by both critics and Julien himself at certain points in the novel, is metaphysical in the sense that Kristeva gives it here, in that it functions to deny historic process and to take Julien out of that process. Julien nostalgically contrasts Mme. de Rênal to Mathilde in moments where he not only feels his identity waver but when he wants an escape from the battle in which he has staked his life, when he wants to cease being a subject in struggle and makes himself, even momentarily, into a subject in repose.

Without the self-shattering negativity described by Kristeva, there is no practice, no self-transformation, no real reciprocal relations in love and no historic change. This is the process Julien goes through when he is "overturned" by Mathilde, when he comes to understand the need to struggle against her arrogance and when he fights his battle to arouse her passion, before he comes back to himself knowing that he has transformed himself, her, their relation, and the social balance of his place in the world. The very fact that he has to "master" her indicates that the process of their love is not ended and would submit to negativity many times more. Julien goes through this negative process in a more intense form when he goes into a trance, shoots Mme. de Rênal, and then comes back to himself at a different level of identity.

This return to a different self, after the contradiction which negates the self, is, according to Kristeva, the second moment of productive practice. In the first instant, "the subject breaks his unifying enclosure and with a leap . . . passes into the process of social transformation which also passes through him" (p. 181). In the second instant the force of such negativity "favors the discovery, by the reconstituted subject, of this new object" (p. 181). This discovery is double: the subject has actually produced the new object, as for instance Julien actually produces Mathilde's passion, and by shooting Mme. de Rênal he produces his own transcendent heroism; and he is also able to "symbolize" that subject or to formulate it in language.

This alternation between self-identity and self-negation-in-struggle describes Julien's development throughout the novel, and explains the gaps in his psychological unity. They are dissolutions of his self-identity without which he could not engage in his great love affairs or in the social processes of his times, nor could he grow in self-knowledge and gain victory over the world around him. Yet for Julien this alternation ends in static self-identity, which becomes its dominant and positive term. In Kristeva's theory, on the other hand, the alternation and its process of negativity are infinite, since any belief in the essential reality of a permanent self-identity is mythic and ideological. But if at the end of the novel Julien refuses practice and contradictory, transforming relations with others, the text of the novel does not deny them. Mathilde is still desperately, and perhaps fruitlessly, given the bias of the narrator, searching for both.

Mme. de Rênal's love allows Julien to live outside society, outside history, and outside of any human involvements which "overturn from top to bottom" the subject in productive struggle. In his love for Mathilde, Julien is neither so stable and unchanging in his self-identity, nor so able to close himself off from involvement in historic struggle. Julien's love with Mme. de Rênal may seem more "authentic,"[30] but throughout their love affair he can easily forget her when not in her presence. This love allows his consciousness to maintain the stability demanded by bourgeois-patriarchal ideology, and also the fragmented and compartmentalized bourgeois-masculine structure that Stendhal described in *De l'amour*. According to Stendhal historical forces have brought about this fragmented consciousness and also a different feminine-domestic mentality, characterized by intense and total emotional involvement with a single, small part of the whole social world.[31] At the end of the novel Julien accepts this domestic form of emotion and rejects the love that Mathilde seeks, a love which refuses both domestic partiality and capitalist fragmentation, and that effaces the dichotomy between sexual love and historic practice in society.

Love and History

While Julien at the end of the novel tells Mme. de Rênal, "Know that I have always loved you, that I have loved no one but you" (p. 491), these claims are belied by many events in the novel as a whole. Whatever Julien may feel for Mme. de Rênal, "ambition or even simple successes of vanity would distract him from the feelings that Mme. de Rênal had inspired in him, but Mathilde had absorbed everything; he found her everywhere in his future" (p. 390). While Julien's love for Mathilde may be inspired by what Girard calls "triangular" or mimetic desire,[32] he is also attracted to her by a powerful erotic passion: "he felt penetrated by love even into the most intimate folds of his heart. Never had he adored her to this extent. He was almost as mad as Mathilde" (p. 420). His love for Mme. de Rênal is not described in such superlative terms until the novel's conclusion.

Although when Julien is in the presence of Mme. de Rênal he is able to lose himself in passion momentarily, he has no trouble putting her out of his mind when he leaves her in order to focus on his ambitions. With Mathilde this fragmentation is effaced for two reasons: she yearns to participate in those social matters that absorb Julien, and when she ceases to love Julien, he is unable to think about his ambitions for months: "Every thought foreign to Mlle. de La Mole had become hateful to him; he was incapable of writing the most simple letters" (p. 391). His feelings for her leave him indifferent to his success when he finally does start to realize his ambitions; his adventurous mission to England, and even the prospect of a bishopric leave him cold.

In *Deceit, Desire and the Novel* René Girard integrates to his theory of mimetic desire Stendhal's theory of the difference between "*amour-passion*" and "*amour-vanité*" put forth in *De l'amour*.[33] Like mimetic desire, *amour-vanité* consists in copying or imitating the desires of a prestigious rival (p. 10). Girard distinguishes between mediocre novels which simply reflect mediated desire in a passive and unconscious way, and great novels like Stendhal's which actively reveal it (p. 16). But Girard neglects a third, more problematic way of treating mediated desire which much more aptly describes Stendhal's proceedings: this is to *conceal* the workings of mediated desire which the text evokes and exploits in the reader. Girard thus imitates a very ideological model of desire when he says: "The real Mme. de Rênal is the one desired by Julien; the real Mathilde is not" (p. 19), and when he defines the first desire as passion and the second as vanity. The "real" object of desire is thus the one who completes rather than challenges Julien's idealized, fixed identity and the reader's secure identification with it.

But the distribution of passion and vanity in *The Red and the Black* is not so simple. It would not be the great novel it is if the heroines simply illustrated the abstract categories of *De l'amour*. Like the categories masculine/feminine, political/domestic, and public/private, the categories of love erected in *De l'amour* are dissolved in *The Red and the Black*. While Mathilde's love for Julien and his for her conform in certain instances to "*amour-vanité*," their love also soars to the heights of "amour-passion" as described in *De l'amour*: "I have given a woefully poor idea of true love, of that love which takes up the whole soul, fills it with images which are sometimes the most happy, sometimes make us despair, but which are always sublime and which make our soul completely insensitive to all the rest of what exists" (p. 102). "Insensitive to all the rest of what exists" certainly describes Julien's soul while he is in love with Mathilde.

The love between Mme. de Rênal and Julien can seem to be the sole "spontaneous," "immediate," "natural," "authentic" passion only if a reader identifies with Julien, accepts the codes which make him realistic, and so does not notice that he and Mme. de Rênal are fictive constructs imitating culturally determined models of which they are unconscious and whose function in the text is hidden from the reader and kept under silence. The reader's own attachment to Mme. de Rênal as object of desire and to Julien as subject to identity with are mediated by powerful culturally determined models. Julien conforms perfectly to the model of the individualist romantic hero, and Mme. de Rênal to the self-sacrificing romantic heroine. Her love for Julien mediates the reader's desire to identify with him and with the model he represents. Since Mme. de Rênal effaces herself and declares that she feels for Julien "what I should feel only for God" (p. 491), one wonders which of the two loves in the novel is more based on vanity, especially given strong reader identification with Julien.

Since Mathilde does not have the onerous responsibility of completing the hero's identity, she is both at an advantage and at a disadvantage. She becomes the despised antiheroine, the sign of all that must be excluded from Julien's life if he is to be the model individualist hero, identical to himself. But from a certain perspective her position can appear privileged, yielding possibilities for action outside of the linear history that dominates the narrative structure. Since the reader does not have to identify with Mathilde, she is freer, as the embodiment of values the novel finally rejects, to act outside of the reader's ideology.

A Different Textual Logic

While Mathilde and Mme. de Rênal can be and are contrasted, they are not abstract logical types-in-opposition even at the end of the novel. In spite of the narrator's often heavy-handed contrasts, *The Red and the Black* for the most part presents and develops the two heroines not as two poles of masculine desire but as two different figures responding to sociohistoric processes of their world. Both are exceptions to their sex and their class, both act out to the most intense degree the historical contradiction of their social situation, both are members of the Stendhalian "Happy Few," both struggle to go beyond the different social determinisms that repress them, and together they show that the historic process incorporated into the text is too multilinear for one feminine figure to represent its course.

To the extent that at a certain level of the text they are in part also opposed stereotypes, they function according to one of the several different ideologies that structure the narration, the subjectivity of the characters, and the notions of history that combine in the text. Even if the narrator at one point contrasts Mathilde's "love of the head" to Mme. de Rênal's "true love" (p. 356), this bias does not apply to the novel as a whole. If it did, all of Mathilde's qualities would necessarily fall into the fixed model of "love of the head," while all of Mme. de Rênal's qualities would necessarily fall into the fixed model of "true love." Mathilde's courage, her love of heroic action and social struggle, her piercing consciousness and intelligence would be inextricably united with her coldness and egotism. Mme. de Rênal's warmth, passion, and generosity would be inextricably united with her oppressed status, her ignorance, and her lack of consciousness. The logic of opposed types would necessarily lead to the conclusion of advocating feminine oppression as the necessary condition for "true love," and the novel as a whole is more ambiguous on this score.

Moreover, the novel hardly presents Mathilde as a unified model of anything. Even more than Julien, she is a fragmentary and contradictory character. At times the narrator speaks of her "great coldness of soul" or her "dry prudence," at other times he says: "Courage was the primary quality of her character" (p. 345). Even more than in the case of Julien, her negative qualities are imposed by her social situation: her wealth, her Parisian upbringing, her coming of age during the Restoration. And even more than Julien she "scorns" her situation, is subject to change, and even becomes capable of "real love" at the end of the novel.

Even as logical-types-in-opposition the two heroines do not function to center the text but rather to pull it in different directions and to introduce difference into it. One heroine works to center the hero and focus the reader's attention on a presumably unified text, while the other works to decenter the hero while creating contradiction in Julien and multiple narrations in the novel text as a whole.

After Julien's "novel is finished," Mathilde begins what Mme. de Rênal calls her own "strange novel" (p. 481). It is understandable that readers prefer Mme. de Rênal to Mathilde since one completes the hero we are supposed to be seduced into identifying with, while the other brings the love between her and Julien into her own history. Mathilde could be imagined as the heroine of her own novel, whereas Mme. de Rênal could not. It is when Julien begins to reestablish the bourgeois categories he had disrupted that Mathilde, refusing to think in such categories, starts her own "novel." Impassioned both for Julien and for her ideal of heroic action, disguised as a peasant, arousing enthusiasm for Julien, producing the dramatically charged situation in which his trial will take place, Mathilde is still imitating models, but unlike Julien, she begins her process of transformation just when he stops his. Critics have seen Mathilde in terms of a static coldness and dryness, but in this last section of the novel she displaces Julien to become the character undergoing the type of transforming development usually reserved for the hero of a novel. The conclusion to *The Red and the Black* would in fact fall into sentimental and boring stasis without her countervailing practice.

Although in the body of the novel Mme. de Rênal is the agent of a different form of history, in the end her history is but a completing mirror of Julien's. While her history reflects Julien's, Mathilde's exceeds it. Because Mathilde's desires are based on models which are either unlivable in her world or on an unlivable combination of parts of disparate models, she cannot repeat history nor can she, like Julien, be directed toward an end already inscribed in her beginning. While the other characters, having completed their destiny, die, her "strange," unrepresentable novel is left unfinished.

The final scene of the novel, in which she kisses Julien's severed head, has been seen as her final inauthentic act of imitation.[34] But what concerns her here is not the head as fetish, just as in her act of becoming pregnant she did not share Julien's concern with the baby as fetish. Instead she is concerned with the act itself, as a search on a blind path for a meaningful form of romantic heroism. Julien tried to transform the act of her pregnancy from a sign of heroism and self-creation through loss of identity into a sign of bourgeois possession. Her final act marks another attempt to go beyond this model and models of the past, to enter the course of history, and to write her own novel. It remains to be written.

Chapter 5

Feminine Romantic Desire
Charlotte Brontë's *Shirley*

Charlotte Brontë's *Shirley* provides a more striking and complex comparison to *The Red and the Black* than any of the novels by French women authors writing at the time of Stendhal.[1] Like *The Red and the Black*, *Shirley* is a historical novel of the mid-nineteenth century which links sexual love and historic process. But in Brontë's novel the textual struggle between the disruptive forces of feminine desire and the rationalizing forms of linear narrative are not only more intense than in *The Red and the Black* but also take a significantly different form.

That *Shirley* does not simply reverse the traditional masculine romantic love narrative, making the heroine the self-seeking subject and the hero her object, but instead subverts romantic ideology, is to be expected, given the many differences separating the inner and outer worlds of women from those of men in the nineteenth century. Even if Brontë treats the same romantic themes, writes in the same genres of romanticism and historic realism, and unfolds the same narrative structure of the quest for self-fulfillment, her work does not symmetrically mirror the masculine versions of these themes, genres, and structures. Subjected as she might be to write within their dominant framework, she also carries them into different forms and at the same time implicitly challenges their underlying values and assumptions.

Sandra Gilbert and Susan Gubar, writing on the anxiety of influence among women writers, say: "Just as in Freud's theories of male and female psychosexual development there is not symmetry between a boy's growth and a girl's . . . , so Bloom's male oriented theory of the 'anxiety of influence' cannot be simply reversed or inverted in order

to account for the situation of the woman writer."[2] The same is true
of a woman writer's relation to romanticism. In addition to differences in psychosexual structure (on which this chapter will focus),
men and women writers also relate in sharply divergent ways to their
social world, as Elaine Showalter has extensively documented. Analyzing the reasons for differences between men's and women's literature
in the nineteenth century, she finds the following: that women shared
a subculture within the dominant masculine culture; that they were
deprived of certain forms of language and consciousness; that many
arenas of social experience excluded them; that role expectations
concerning domestic duty and feminine modesty were serious obstacles; and finally that the double standard of literary criticism itself
hampered them. Brontë's treatment of passion in *Jane Eyre* was considered immoral once the public discovered the novel's author to be a
woman.[3]

   Shirley, written when Brontë was more famous, was criticized for
different reasons. Weaving a feminist vision of personal relations into
a fictionalized account of the Luddite revolt of 1812, *Shirley* is one of
the very few historical novels which focuses on the relation between
feminine subjectivity and sociohistorical process, and in which a feminine discourse threatens to explode a traditional historic narrative.
For this reason some critics have seen it as being amorphous, incoherent, and fragmented.[4] Although it has exerted a strong attraction for sociocritics, they have had wide-ranging disagreement as to
what exactly the politics of the novel are, and how well it integrates a
social vision into an aesthetic form.[5] Such differences among critics
affirm Gubar's point concerning the real difficulty of solving the questions Brontë raises about gender oppression, sexuality, and history,
even in an imaginary world (p. 373). They also suggest that the very
structures of conventional language and narrative exclude the possibility for a woman writer to speak coherently and directly the desire
to integrate feminine sexuality and love into history.

   Thus while the novel explicitly expresses a feminist vision, this is
more deeply and strongly expressed by the "not-said" of the text, in
the spatial and temporal configurations underlying the characters'
relations, in the symbolic networks, and in the workings of language.
(For working definitions of the terms "feminine" and "feminist," see
chap. 1.) By the actions of its discourse, *Shirley* undermines what Luce
Irigaray calls a phallocentric system of representation.[6] Through this

discursive action, images that may have little meaning in themselves are linked together throughout the text to form a network that gives them a meaning not overtly expressed in the narrative.

Yet this symbolic network is not completely subversive of phallocentric representations; it instead expresses both aspects of the contradiction between Brontë's power to undermine and transform the dominant ideological structures of romantic and historic narrative, and her necessary immersion within them. It therefore gives us insights not into one side or other of the critical debate surrounding *Shirley*, but into what the contradiction itself can tell us about feminine textual practice in a sociohistoric structure ordered by patriarchal power.

Like any historical novel, *Shirley* has a double nature as both a mimetic representation of a social world and as an autonomous textual practice which produces new meanings. And when this female author uses the form of historic narrative to treat questions of feminine oppression, she reveals that the sources of oppression are located not solely in social experience nor solely in invisible logics that shape subjectivity, language, and relations between self and other, but in the interplay between the two. The novel reveals the movement of this interplay between empirical experience and underlying logic both in its undermining of patriarchal values and in its succumbing to them.

Theories of Feminine Subjectivity

Feminist psychoanalytic concepts from both American and French traditions help explain why the romantic heroines in *Shirley* cannot simply reverse the traditional romantic gender roles so that the hero would be for the heroine the Other who completes for her a static and closed identity. Unlike Tristan, des Grieux in *Manon Lescaut*, or nineteenth-century heroes like Julien Sorel, René, or Felix de Vandenesse, the heroines of *Shirley* seek fulfillment not in the solitary splendor of the absolute self, nor in self-completion and transcendence of social relations, but within relations to other people. These fulfilling relations would be similar to those familial and friendship ties that already claimed the emotional energies of women of the time, but they would have an essential difference: the whole system of social relations in which these ties were inserted would change so that they would liberate rather than martyr the heroines.

This difference between masculine fulfillment in transcendence and feminine fulfillment in relations recalls Nancy Chodorow's theory about how boys and girls develop differently as they go through the Oedipal complex and the castration crisis.

> From the retention of preoedipal attachments to their mother, growing girls come to define and experience themselves as continuous with others; their experience of self contains more flexible or permeable ego boundaries. Boys come to define themselves as more separate and distinct, with a greater sense of rigid ego boundaries and differentiation. The basic feminine sense of self is connected to the world, the basic masculine sense of self is separate.[7]

Feminine self-definition has a "relational complexity" not found in masculine self-definition (p. 93).

Both Chodorow and Irigaray point out that this specificity of feminine development and feminine subjectivity goes unnoticed in the Freudian tradition whose theories of development revolve around the castration crisis and center on the phallus. Witnn the framework of this theory, women, seen as already castrated, are defined, according to Irigaray, as a "lack," a "nothing to be seen" (p. 53). But when an analysis shifts its focus away from phallocentrism, as in the writings of Brontë, it no longer centers on the object of vision (the imaginary phallus) but instead revolves round relations as dynamic movement between self and other. In this relational perspective, woman no longer appears as a lack.

Yet trying to write within this perspective poses a double problem for a feminine writer: since Western language and culture have a phallocentric structure, geared toward representation and the visible, how can a feminine writer construct a discourse that expresses this invisible focus; and how can women transform the social world so that women's self-definition in relationships rather than in transcendent isolation can become a source of power and fulfillment instead of appearing as a feminine lack, deficiency, or inferiority? These two questions will be explored in this study of *Shirley*, not to test whether or to what extent Brontë succeeded or failed in solving them, but to learn more about the practice that surrounds them.

Since *Shirley* combines historical representation and a search for feminine forms of writing, it interweaves even more complexly than *The Red and the Black* the personal/subjective sphere with the social/political sphere, and in fact dissolves the illusion of their separateness. As mimetic representation it presents the mad and wasteful contradictions of the world of developing industrial capitalism, which instills in women the vocation for love, assigns them in life the almost exclusive task of loving, and then makes love, or any tender human emotion, impossible. But the representation of this contradiction presents difficulties since, as Irigaray points out, "women's sexuality is foreign to history in general" (p. 75). As Brontë weaves her web of sexual relations and historical struggle, the writing of historical narrative itself has to find new forms.

A Critique of Social Reification

Shirley differs from a traditional romantic-historic narrative like *The Red and the Black* in two ways, which can be described with reference to Bakhtin's "historical poetics."[8] According to Bakhtin, the "process of assimilating real historical time and space in literature" (p. 84) can be analyzed through the concept of the "chronotope" or the "intrinsic connectedness of temporal and spatial relations artistically expressed in literature" (p. 84). Each different chronotope or time-space defines a different genre, but all the chronotopes and all the narrative genres defined by Bakhtin have one thing in common: they are all modeled on the single, linear development of the central hero.

Even in this respect *Shirley* differs from the traditional narrative along the lines suggested by Chodorow's definition of gender difference, for in *Shirley* the narrative line multiplies into several connected threads in order to trace not the quest of one central heroine, but the quests of two heroines—Caroline Helstone, the shy, lonely orphan, and Shirley Keeldar, the bold heiress—who are strengthened in their quest for love by their intimate relation to each other. In a second difference from a traditional masculine narrative, *Shirley* places its heroines in a different chronotope from its heroes, and even in different chronotopes from each other. While a novel like *The Red and the Black* models history on the chronotope of the hero and tries to exclude a heterogeneous feminine historic process from the narration, in *Shirley* Caroline and Shirley live a different historic process than the heroes, Robert and Louis Moore.

In fact much of the heroines' anguish comes from the fact that this difference is also an unequal power relation, since the women are forcefully excluded from the men's historical sphere, which dominates, determines, degrades, limits, and distorts theirs. *Shirley* thus introduces multilinearity and multitemporality into historical representation on a much more explicit level than *The Red and the Black* or *Manon Lescaut*. Because of women's social subjection to the men's sociohistoric sphere, the novel has to situate Caroline's and Shirley's history in relation to the socially dominant and officially recognized chronotope of Robert Moore, the cloth manufacturer. By so relating a submerged feminine historicity and an official masculine historicity, the novel dissolves the illusory separation between the personal relations of the women's sphere and the socioeconomic struggles of the men's to reveal the "relational complexity" (Chodorow, p. 92) between the two spheres.

The relation between love and political struggle emerges very early on in the novel. Robert cannot afford the "weakness"[9] of loving Caroline because he feels compelled to regain the reputation and fortune his family had lost in the transition from mercantile capitalism to the much more competitive and impersonal industrial capitalism. The Napoleonic wars between England and France have deepened the pressures on Robert, intensifying his grim obsession, especially since the English parliament has responded to Napoleon's cutoff of trade between Germany and England with Orders of Council imposing controls and taxation on English trade with Europe. In order to save money in the present and raise profits in the future, Robert has lowered the wages of his workers and is replacing many of them with machines. As a result, his starving mill hands, modeled in the novel after the Luddites of 1812, are conspiring to attack and destroy his machines and his mill if he does nothing to improve their situation. Robert cannot indulge in feelings of love for Caroline if he is to fight effectively against his workers. He decides instead on a calculated move to marry Shirley for her money. But Shirley is in love with Robert's brother Louis, her girlhood tutor, who is not interested in capitalist ambition, and appears as the Byronically romantic counterpart of his pragmatic brother Robert.

Robert's feeling of separateness stems, the novel shows, from the inner logic of industrial capital itself. This logic of illusory fragmentation veils not only the connections between the men's sphere and the women's sphere but between all parts of its world. Robert's mill is one element of a larger system ruled by an international market. The decisive feature of this system for the characters of *Shirley* is that while its different productive and exchange units are all interdependent on each other, they have no perceived organic relation to each other. Robert can raise his productivity, but he can neither exert any control over the other fragments of the system, nor be sure that by his labor he will fulfill his basic needs, nor do any other labor. His position is as absurdly paradoxical as that of Caroline, who has been taught to live by love in a world that makes loving impossible. Compelled by invisible forces to continue trying to make a living this way by any means possible, Robert is forced into a harsh struggle against his mill hands, his middle-class neighbors, and his own repressed feelings for Caroline.

Brontë emphasizes this historical process of separation by contrasting to it the old "organic" economic system surviving on Shirley's rural estate, portrayed as an idyllic place of "sweet herbage and clear waters of bonnie Airedale" (*Shirley*, p. 345), where Shirley is presented as fostering a harmonious network between herself and her cottagers, honoring the "custom" of providing "their supplies of milk and butter from the dairy of the Manor House." While she shows concern for her cottagers, stepping "in amongst the gossiping groups," and bidding "them good morning with a certain frank, tranquil ease" (p. 345), Moore, we are told, "did not sufficiently care when the new inventions threw the old work people out of employ: he never asked himself where those to whom he no longer paid weekly wages found daily bread" (p. 61).

Having "a tendency to isolate his individual person from any community amidst which his lot might temporarily happen to be thrown" and feeling himself "disconnected" from "philanthropic consideration" (p. 60), Robert Moore's historical space-time is one of isolation, of disconnection, but also of illusion, since the real connections between things and people are invisible in this world.

But Shirley and Caroline, although intimate friends, also live in different space-times. While Shirley continues to maintain the old "organic world" in an idealized form, Caroline, plunged into the world of early capitalism, wanders through a desolate wasteland questing fulfillment in a social reality which seems bereft of the dynamic interactions and interconnections that give a world life. All of the characters, even Shirley, are engulfed in what Lukács calls the "reification"[10] of capitalist society, where relations fragment into atomized objects. In this respect, too, *Shirley* reveals the hidden connections of the social world by critically representing reification not only in socioeconomic relations but in sexual relations.

Systems of Vision and Actions of Discourse

Shirley presents love in the masculine world as a reified love, which contrasts to a very different form of love in the feminine world. In reified love, the lover sees his beloved and her personal qualities as objects to be admired and possessed for the enhancement of his disconnected self, and as a mirror which reflects to him his own idealized and static image, which he can also believe he possesses as an object. With respect to this sexuality, the Byronic romantic hero Louis is really not very different from his capitalist counterpart Robert.

The romantic Louis Moore loves Shirley in an idealized, but structurally identical, version of his brother Robert's desire for Shirley. Both brothers see Shirley in terms of what Irigaray calls a phallic "economy of representation" (p. 20). That is to say that her beauty and prestige represent for them the capital in which they can invest their privilege and reap the profits of self-affirmation. She becomes a mirror which reflects them to themselves in what Irigaray calls "a process of specula[riza]tion of the masculine subject" (p. 20). While Louis's passion takes an exalted form, it goes further than Robert's calculation in making Shirley an object of speculation and a mirror of his superiority.

Louis is most in love with Shirley not when they are together but when he can wander around her house in her absence, literally replacing her with a collection of disparate objects, fetishes which he can invest with erotic charm. Describing his solitary wanderings, Louis records in his diary his fascination with these objects: "A bag, a small satin bag hangs on a chairback. The desk is open, the keys are in the lock; a pretty seal, a silver pen, a crimson berry or two of ripe fruit on a green leaf, a small, clean, delicate glove—these trifles at once decorate and disarrange the stand they strew" (p. 486). With Victorian hypocrisy, he regards with more passion than Shirley herself this collection of objects that are very visible symbols of sexual intercourse. They are also fetishes in the strict Freudian sense of imaginary substitutes for the "lost" feminine phallus. Robert's possessive gaze resembles what Irigaray calls the "phallic look" which defines sex by organs that can be seen, and which translates the fear that woman, with her lack of a phallus, "would expose a *nothing* to be seen" (p. 53, italics in text).

Only in the absence of that "nothing to be seen," when he can substitute something for it, does Louis take pleasure in his sexual desire. It signifies for him not a relation between two different people, but a seductive memory of how Shirley's virginal purity reflected back to him his own masculine glory. He tells his diary: "As she passed to the window, after tacitly but gracefully recognizing me, I could call her nothing in my own mind save 'stainless virgin': to my perception a delicate splendor robed her, and the modesty of girlhood was her halo" (p. 487).

This scene, recounted not in the narrator's voice, but in Louis's voice, has a disturbing ambiguity. Disturbing because Louis's voice really is seductive, while the language of the text sends up many danger flags to warn us against that very seduction. In confiding his erotic fascination, Louis obliterates Shirley and replaces her with a "phantom," a frozen image which lives "in [his] own mind," and has little to do with the bold, independent, elusive heroine of the novel. In Louis's image of Shirley, moreover, the value-laden social model of "stainless virgin" provides the capital which makes the "recognition" that he takes from her all the more profitable to himself. While this passage may be seductive by itself, the symbolic network of which it is a part acts as a silent reminder of how destructive this seductive visualization really is.

Suppressed as an independent other, immobilized by her robe of delicate splendor and her halo of girlhood modesty, Shirley becomes so much a thing to be possessed that she can promise Louis self-fulfillment only so long as she remains unattained. As if in recognition of this dialectic, she remains after her engagement to Louis aloof and distant, and puts off their marriage, telling him: "You don't know how happy you are!—any change will be for the worse!" (p. 586).

As an imaginary object of love, Shirley mirrors to Louis an imaginary glorified image of himself. As if to underline this, the novel contains one scene in which Louis says: " 'The fire shines on you and me, and shows us clearly in the glass, Miss Keeldar; and I have been gazing on the picture the whole time I have been talking' " (p. 483).

Even when Shirley and Louis are physically together, he obliterates that threatening presence and enhances his erotic sense by substituting for the real relation between them a mirror image, a distant "picture" with which he can at the same time identify himself and distance the relationship.

Louis's narcissism might be passed off with the remark that psychoanalysts since Freud have seen primary narcissism as the precondition of every subject's human love relations.[11] But Brontë's treatment of love suggests that it does not have to be their dominant structuring force—except under certain historical circumstances. The novel suggests that in other circumstances narcissism could be incorporated into other forms of love as a subordinate force.

While Louis, appearing as the romantic outsider and objectifying Shirley in an erotic way, seems to express a timeless form of love outside of and uninfluenced by historical forces, Robert's pursuit of her links more directly the historic forces of capitalism and narcissistic sexual relations. Robert reveals, as he describes his feelings toward Shirley, the same underlying structure of relationship, dominated by the same kind of representation as that of Louis. Toward the end of *Shirley*, the repentant Robert criticizes his feelings with a great deal of bitter self-deprecation, and more consciously, clearly, and directly than Louis, he analyzes the relation between him and Shirley as a problem of phallocentric vision.

> I *looked* at her, Yorke: I *saw* in her youth and a species of beauty. I *saw* power in her. Her wealth offered me the redemption of my honor and standing. . . . Could I believe she loved me? Could I hear wisdom urge me to marry her, and disregard every dear advantage, disbelieve every flattering suggestion . . . ? Young, graceful, gracious—my benefactress, attached to me, enamoured of me,—I used to say to myself . . . with an admiration dedicated entirely to myself, and unimpaired even by esteem for her. (P. 497)

While Louis's idealized passion ultimately sees in Shirley a metaphoric capital to be invested in psychic self-affirmation, Robert's frank perception of Shirley as the source of literal capital ultimately meets a personal need, fulfilling in Irigaray's words his deep psychological "desire for . . . the self" that "dominates the economy of representation" (p. 26).

Dissolving the Phallic Economy of Representation

Robert's speech criticizes this system of representation, not only by its overt message but by the action of its discourse. As part of the text's own feminine production of meaning, this passage participates in producing a silent network of symbols that act to criticize patriarchal relations. They also act to create feminine forms of discourse and sexuality that go even deeper than the overt feminist ideas expressed in the novel. Robert criticizes himself by saying simply: "I looked at her," and in Brontë's novel not only mirrors and pictures, but the very act of *seeing* often symbolize destructive error and illusion about the nature of human relations.

But while Brontë symbolizes phallic relations by seeing, she symbolizes feminine sexual love by talking and by blindness—most notably at the end of *Jane Eyre*. Jane develops this symbolism as she describes her married life to Rochester: "To be together is for us to be at once as free as in solitude, as gay as in company. We *talk*, I believe, all day long: to talk to each other is but a more animated and an audible thinking."[12] Rochester is able to engage in such talk only because he first loses the power to see, and while seeing symbolizes narcissistic objectification, "talking to each other" (that activity which, in misogynist jokes, women are frequently doing) will symbolize a very different economy of meaning, one that can represent the movement of reciprocal sexuality.

In the same passage of *Jane Eyre*, Jane goes on to explain the happiness of their marriage: "Mr. Rochester continued blind the first two years of our union: perhaps it was that circumstance that drew us so very near—that knit us so very close! for I was then his vision, as I am still his right hand" (p. 553). Elaine Showalter has shown that works of feminist critics "revise views like those of Richard Chase who describes Rochester as castrated thus implying that Jane's neurosis is penis envy."[13] Far from symbolizing castration, Rochester's blindness takes the couple outside of a structure of representation and sexuality dominated by symbolic castration, the phallus, and penis envy into another structure, another discourse, where the woman is not compelled to assure by her penis envy "a remedy . . . against man's anguish over castration" (Irigaray, p. 59). Through blindness Rochester exits his economy of representation (and also of sexual desire) to enter Jane's economy, marked by a different process of production and reproduction of meaning, not dominated by the phallus, its presence or absence, and the need to *see* whether or not it is there. Such a different production of meaning is suggested by Jane when she says that she became Rochester's "vision." She thus changes the meaning of the word *vision* to signify not an object of sight for Rochester, but a faculty which brings him to a new relation to the world and to Jane by translating objects of sight into the sounds of conversation, as Jane "impress[es] by sound on his ear what light could no longer stamp in his eye."

Like Rochester, Louis undergoes a type of blindness at the moment he finally does become engaged to Shirley: " 'I hardly *saw* her for a moment but I *heard* her *voice* ' " (p. 579, emphasis added). In contrast now to his brother Robert, he says: "Once I only *saw* her beauty, now I feel it" (p. 568, italics in text). It is this ambiguous nature of the Louis-Shirley love relation that makes Caroline say: "it *is* romantic, but it is also right" (p. 563). And if Louis must undergo blindness in order to love Shirley, Robert must be, at least temporarily, completely crippled in order to love Caroline.

In *Shirley* sexual relations develop not so much through images as through the conversations between the two sets of lovers, and this forging of love between men and women models itself on the feminine bonds women forge with each other. The novel records more conversations between the two heroines than between the two lovers. These conversations do not so much represent an image of their friendship, as present the very matter of their intimacy.

Two qualities of feminine heterosexual love—that it is based on a feminine way of loving women, and that it cannot be represented in visual images as easily as masculine love—are suggested in a chance remark made by Shirley. This remark conveys its meaning not through its overt message or through the conventional meanings of its words, but like the symbolic network in the text, through the action of its discourse. This is because it refers to relations, movements between people, rather than to people-as-things which can be represented in images. In one of her intimate and absorbing conversations with Caroline, Shirley, trying to describe her ideal husband, includes among the qualities she lists:

> He likes them [women] not only for vain and selfish reasons, but as *we* like him—because we like him. (P. 224)

Shirley and Caroline, too modest to talk about love, refer to a relation between a man and a woman based on the way women "like" men, but the nonrepresentative language of her phrase signifies a very different economy of desire.

One among many notable qualities of Shirley's apparently simple but really complex statement is that she will love a man not for any objectifiable quality he may possess but for the way he returns an emotion. The actions of her discourse also transform objectified qualities into reciprocal processes because it expresses meaning not through direct referential language but by acting out this new reciprocal relation in a variety of ways. One way is in its contrast to the love characterized, as Shirley says, by vanity and selfishness, which is easily described by referring to distinct, recognizable qualities— "vain," "selfish." Such love is easily and neatly captured in words with commonly recognized meanings, and its description can stand on its own. This is not so for the feminine way of liking. It can be described only by cross-reference to the masculine way of liking, and defined by what it is not. Its language does not capture a definite image, but dramatizes the movement of relations by the infinite interplay of cross-reference. Moreover, its language is awkward, hesitant, vague, and ambiguous, as if to point out two problems: one, the lack of a ready-made language to express feminine sexual desire; and two, the need for a different *form* of language in which to express it.

The vain and selfish form of liking, so neatly defined with reference to static personality traits and whose formulation seems to stand on its own, uses a language whose form resembles the form of narcissistic love, in which the lover reduces his beloved and his own ego to images, while he also lives in the illusion that his love stands alone as the only possible form of love. By contrast, the feminine form of liking, described not by adjectives but by the indirect words, "as we like him—because we like him," dramatize the hesitant, suppressed feminine lover, who attempts to state the claim that there do indeed exist different forms of love relations, and different forms of desire within a love relation. The love she is seeking does not have a recognized, preestablished model, and therefore it needs to be invented, in language, in literature, and in society.

Shirley's statement implies that a love relation between a man and a woman based on feminine liking cannot be captured in a single descriptive image. Both because it has been excluded from linguistic formulation, and because it refuses to objectify the people in the relations, it can only be understood as a process, as a never-ending history. As a historical novel, which is both a representation of social history and an autonomous textual production of meaning, *Shirley* gives a place to genuine sexual difference and heterogeneity in the workings of its discourse, in its integration of history, and in its narration of sexual desire. In love as in history, and in love *as* history, the single phallocentric view give way to multiplicity.

Love as History and Love in History

Critics have often puzzled over why Caroline marries Robert, and Shirley marries Louis, since in terms of objectifiable and visible qualities, Caroline matches with Louis while Shirley matches with Robert. Thus Burkhart explains the seeming mismatches by saying that "opposites mate,"[14] and Eagleton says that what would seem "the 'right' relations . . . are inverted."[15] But the novel is outside of this ideology that matches people according to reified qualities like physical beauty and wealth. Characters fall in love with each other not because they "possess" the same qualities, but because they share a long history together. Caroline has shared such a history with her cousin Robert, and Shirley with her girlhood tutor Louis. This seemingly trivial difference from traditional literary love indicates a transformation in the whole structure of literary romantic love.

Even in Louis's love for Shirley, the history of their shared crises makes Louis finally renounce his image of Shirley as a "stainless virgin" who "asked for [his] protection—appealed to [his] strength," and so provided him with "recognition" (p. 487). After they confront Shirley's hostile uncle, Louis tells his diary: "I thought I would have to support her . . . , and it is she who has made me strong" (p. 522). Louis here at least begins to question the idea that a couple have fixed gender roles and gives some support to the conflicting notion that a relation is by definition movement.

The development of the Caroline-Robert love is more complex. If Robert's chronotope provides the framework for the narration, Caroline's history provides its main developmental line. Her history traces her journey from accepting the mirror world of phallic love and her role in it to creating the space for the movement of feminine heterosexual love. At the beginning of the novel, she is seduced by the double illusion that Robert will propose marriage and that her own image in the mirror contains that promise: "She recommenced combing her hair, long as a mermaid's; turning her head, as she arranged it, she *saw* her own face and form in the *glass* . . . . Caroline *saw* a shape, a head, that *daguerrotyped* in that attitude . . . would have been lovely; she could not choose but derive from the *spectacle* confirmation of her hopes" (p. 123, emphasis added). Reducing herself to a frozen image seen in the symbolically significant mirror, situated in the specular system of representation, Caroline sees herself as the reflection of Robert's desire. Ominous in their symbolism, the mirror reflections foreshadow the bitter disappointment into which she is plunged the very next day by Robert's coldness. Her hopes unconfirmed, she realizes that she must begin to face the barren life of a spinster.

In coming to terms with her heartbreak, Caroline enters a different system of representation. In another conversation with Shirley, the heroines discuss how women, being powerless outsiders of the social world, are by the same token powerless in love. Caroline seeks answers to their questions not in the "spectacle" of visible objects but in invisible, elusive, and shifting relations between her, Robert, and the world they live in.

> "Shirley," [she says] "men and women are so different: they are in such a different position. Women have so few things to think about—men so many: you may have a friendship for a man while he is almost indifferent to you. Much of what cheers your life may be dependent on him, while not a feeling or interest of moment in his eyes may have reference to you." (P. 235)

Noting how this difference in social "position" makes the relations between men and women asymmetrical, truly heterogeneous, Caroline goes on to describe this relation, but she must stray from conventional modes of discourse and representation, and suggests this unrepresentability by mentioning "a strange certainty of conviction I cannot describe" (p. 235). She then relates a "vision" she had one lonely night when Robert was in London.

> "If a magician or a genius had, at that moment, offered me prince Ali's tube. . . , and if with its aid, I had been able to take a *view* of Robert—to *see* where he was, how occupied—I should have learned, in a startling manner, the width of the *chasm* which gaped *between* such as he and such as I. I knew that, however my thoughts might adhere to him, his were effectually sundered from me." (P. 235, emphasis added)

Caroline's protest against women's one-sided emotional dependence on men uses a language which subverts the traditional phallic form of representation. Her imaginary "view" of Robert is not a view at all in the usual sense, because it does not *see* an image or an object. Caroline's *view* of Robert is the very opposite of Louis's *relation* with Shirley, since for Louis the movement between himself and his beloved *freezes* into a picture of his beloved and a mirror image of himself, while Caroline's view *dissolves* into a relation, into what is happening "between" her and Robert. And this relation is a multiple, heterogeneous one, a "chasm," a sundering on his part, and an adherence on hers. Having given up the illusion of a relation between two people as a mirror reflection identifying one with the other, Caroline recognizes that Robert's consciousness is not contained by hers and does not reflect hers, but exceeds hers into realms she does not know. As Jerre Collins, Mary Lydon, and others say:

> Indeed, in any relationship the only escape from the hall of mirrors is through a constant attempt to make contact with that in the other which is in excess of the transferences [identification of the other with one's own fantasms], even though the unknown quantity in the other . . . cannot be known. Knowledge beyond the transferences is a knowledge of difference, a knowl-

edge that there is something in the other . . . that escapes one's grasp.[16]

But, as Caroline's anguish suggests, "knowledge of difference" in a relation is not necessarily fulfilling if it is one-sided. If only the powerless, oppressed member of the relation has that knowledge because she is forced to have it by her position, the more privileged, powerful member of the relation can afford to remain in blissful ignorance. This is what Shirley implies when she responds to Caroline not by talking about love, but about the socioeconomic world: "Caroline," demanded Miss Keeldar abruptly, "don't you wish you had a profession—a trade?" (p. 235). The unanswered crucial questions are whether and how Caroline's more advanced vision of sexual relations, born of powerlessness and rejection, can become the foundation for a love between social equals.

In *Shirley* the need to change sexual relations between men and women implies the need for historical change in the larger social system. While Shirley makes this connection in the above-quoted conversation with Caroline, Robert makes the same connection in the conversation with Hiram Yorke toward the end of the novel where he criticizes his behavior toward Shirley. Robert has completed his search for the workers who destroyed his machinery and attacked his mill, and through his search has come to a deeper understanding of the class struggle he is engaged in. Now viewing his own class and its activities with distaste and the working class with much more understanding and compassion, he explains that this political struggle has brought about personal emotional changes in him. In this context, he contrasts his treatment of Shirley to his feelings for Caroline.

In terms of the symbolic network of the text, Robert's description of his feelings for Shirley are wholly enclosed in a phallic economy of vision while the description of his feelings for Caroline combine in a strange way that economy, here concealed in sentimental Victorian domestic ideology, with the feminine sexual economy based on shared history and the symbolic act of talking.

"supposing she [Yorke's former beloved] had *possessed* a thoughtful, original mind, a love of knowledge, a wish for information, which she took an artless delight in receiving from your lips . . . ; supposing her *conversation*—when she sat by your side—was fertile, varied, imbued with a picturesque grace and genial interest . . . ; supposing that when you stood near her . . . , comfort at once became your *atmosphere,* and content your element; supposing that whenever her face was under your *gaze* . . . , you gradually ceased to be hard and anxious, and pure affection, love of home, thirst for sweet discourse, unselfish longing to protect and cherish, replaced the sordid, cankering calculations of your trade. . . . Would you have left her to court another woman for her wealth?" (Pp. 503–4, emphasis added)

In this passage two different systems of representation interpenetrate: the overt message expresses the domestic ideology of patriarchal capitalism, while the form of its discourse produces a new meaning that contradicts that ideology. As ideology, Robert's opposition between selfish commerce and the "pure affection" of domesticity, unlike Shirley's contrast between vain, selfish love and feminine love, is a false opposition, since in the nineteenth century the feminine domestic morality did not oppose but bolstered the world of the market economy. It is significant that Robert *sees* this domesticity when he holds Caroline's face under his gaze, and that in this domestic scene he can see her mind as a thing she possesses, almost as an object, and as a mirror which reflects the contents of his mind, which she has gratefully received from him.

But just as Caroline succumbed to the lure of phallic self-identification just before she fell from grace and was rejected by Robert, so now Robert indulges in what is left of his smug masculine vanity just before he is, as he himself will tell Caroline, "unmanned." Just as he finishes this speech, Robert is shot by a vengeful worker and forced to lie for several months in a condition of extreme weakness, in the Yorke home. Now Caroline will be the strong, cherishing protector, battling the elements of the outside world to bring Robert comfort, but she will make him question his imaginary ego rather than reflect it in a flattering way. This changed relation, however, is not an exchange of sex roles, but a dissolution of fixed roles and of the preconceived model of the heterosexual relation as the static linking of traditional roles Robert sees. Before discussing this relation more fully, we need to go back to the passage in which Robert describes his feelings for Caroline in order to trace the other, feminine thread woven into its discourse.

Victorian domestic ideology sees marriage as the perfect union between husband and wife, where the two merge into one, and where the husband is the One. Although Robert's description of Caroline is patronizing, the form of discourse that expresses it does not see her as merged into him, but as an independent and separate subject, who talks to him, and whose conversation changes him. This is in sharp contrast to his vision of Shirley who for him existed solely as an extension of himself.

Robert's language refers on the surface to a conventional Victorian relation, but implicitly refers to that unconventional and unformulatable relation intimated by Caroline and Shirley. Instead of saying that Caroline would bring him comfort and contentment, two emotions of middle-class family life, Robert says that if you stood near her, "comfort became at once your atmosphere and content your element." Using the words *atmosphere* and *element* to describe the sphere in which two people unite, Robert suggests a union which is not a merger of two into one but an "atmosphere" that they build precisely by remaining different and distinct from each other.

This unrepresentable form of love is again symbolized by the contrast between *seeing* which suppresses the woman as difference and *talking* which, over a long period of time, enables the two people, by remaining different, to construct their intimacy. In fact the talk of conversation in the course of the novel symbolizes the love between Caroline and Robert as development in time or as history, since their love develops through a series of conversations where the very structure of communication changes. At the beginning of the novel, they can converse only indirectly about their feelings by discussing Shakespeare's *Coriolanus,* a ready-made discourse, having a common meaning for a large number of people in England. By the time they have their conversation in Robert's sickroom, their common discourse is almost a private language they have invented between them. This discourse, where words are charged with emotional connotations shared only by the two of them, could have been constructed only through a long process of shared crises and a store of shared memories.

The form of their conversation now resembles the form of Shirley's description of her ideal husband. Robert tells Caroline that "the state of [his] mind [that imaginary place formerly inhabited by imaginary people who sent him a very flattering image of himself] is inexpressible—dark, barren, impotent" (p. 542). But Caroline makes it more expressible, not by language that refers to external, fixed images but by relating it to her own feelings in an infinite interplay of cross-reference. She answers him: "I understand your feelings: I experienced something like it." She then tells of her own recent, almost fatal illness from loneliness and heartbreak, to which Robert replies: "You speak my experience," and then tells her: "I am too feeble to say what I feel; but while you speak I *do* feel." Robert now begins to join Caroline in an atmosphere of intimate conversation, and that atmosphere now competes with the mirror relation.

Joined in their atmosphere, the lovers enter an erotic structure that differs from phallic eroticism localized around the genital act. Brontë's novels express an intense sexuality but one that is diffused into the overall relation between the lovers. In the conversations between Caroline and Robert, Shirley and Louis, as well as Caroline and Shirley, what Robert Heilman calls "erotic energy"[17] forms that "atmosphere" in which words are suspended. Whereas our culture bases eroticism on seeing (as for instance in *Playboy* magazine) and on visual description, in Brontë's novels erotic feeling emanates from talking, and is communicated along with the dialogue. Visual elements, although not absent, are like narcissism subordinated into new structures. In this feminine erotic economy the lovers do not desire to possess the other as mirror of self, but to produce the relation as movement and difference in time.

As a sexuality which is both diffuse and productive of difference, this eroticism lies outside already formulated categories of sexuality. It is neither a regression to pre-Oedipal fusion, nor the post-Oedipal sexuality centered on the isolated phallic act of penetration, but can be described in the words that Carol Gilligan uses to express that not-yet-existing, more historically advanced form of "connection" between two people, where "the self is neither stranded in isolation nor lost in fusion."[18]

The novel shows that this sexuality cannot come into being without a more general process of social change. The space of Robert and Caroline's personal history is not closed off and separated from the larger social process, but very much enmeshed in it—for good and for ill. Robert, recognizing the double need for change in sexual and class relations, can love Caroline because, as he tells her, he is no longer obsessed with financial gain, and not only wishes to reform conditions of the working class, but has also ceased to fear becoming a worker himself. Since the fulfillment of love necessitates social changes, these changes happen—but only in a superficial and mawkishly utopian way. And it is the abstract, utopian quality of social change, required by the change in love, which causes the love itself to appear abstract in the end, and which causes the economy of representation based on vision to reassert itself not in the dialogue of particular characters but in the narrator's discourse and in the textual structure.

Historical Process and Mythic Structure

The notion that the lack of any concrete and deep social change spells doom for the possibility of sexual love is brushed over in the overt plot of *Shirley*, but more strongly expressed in the implicit language of the novel's underlying symbolic network. This fragmentary "submerged" plot,[19] read through the gaps of the dominant linear plot, unfolds as the tragic, dark negative of the novel's course toward a happy ending. Unlike the main plot, which shows paternalistic reforms in capitalism bringing happiness to its domestic heroines, this submerged plot has any possibility of feminine love crushed by the system of capitalist social relations. The story told by this symbolic network concerns mainly the Yorke family, a set of characters in the novel which critics have seen as extraneous.[20]

In this mythic world caught in the gaps of the novel's realistic world, Hiram Yorke's teenage son Martin functions as Robert's symbolic double and sees Caroline with a fascination that exaggerates the reified sexuality practiced by Robert and Louis. He sees Caroline not only as an image or a picture, but as the copy of a picture representing the image of a dead woman, who even during her life was a fixed image, a "girl of living marble," and who, the novel takes care to note, was never heard to talk! This character, Mary Cave, was killed years ago by the coldness of her husband, Caroline's own uncle and guardian Mathew Helstone, and has no connection with the plot of *Shirley*. She functions as Caroline's symbolic double. Martin Yorke, seeing Caroline as the projection of his own fantasies for power, tells himself: "I have power over her" (p. 537), and thinks: "I made her sob, shudder, almost faint; I'll see her smile before I've done with her" (p. 536). Martin makes much more bold and direct the interconnections between sexual objectification and patriarchal political power Robert and Louis had made in more subtle ways before.

As the symbolic double of Robert, Martin makes his bid for sexual and political dominance at the same time that the wounded Robert begins to renounce these privileges. He agrees to arrange a secret visit between Caroline and Robert while Robert is convalescing in his father's house, but only, he decides, for a price—a kiss from the unwilling Caroline. He tells himself: "She is not coming for me. But I have power over her, and I want her to come that I may use that power" (p. 537). When Caroline does visit Robert, her lover uses a striking similarity of language, saying to her: "Unmanned as I am, I have not the power to cope with such a topic" (p. 542).

It is as if Robert's patriarchal "power" has been symbolically transferred from him to Martin, so that now Robert, "unmanned," can give up his obsession with family name and wealth to become, like a woman, more open and vulnerable to love. There is also a symbolic transfer from Robert to Martin of the craving for economic power, for at the same time that Robert renounces his obsession with monetary gain, Martin says, in reference to the kiss from Caroline: "Whatever I do, I'll be paid for, and in coin of my own choosing" (p. 533).

Joining in a more exaggerated yet harmless and purely metaphoric way those acts of economic and sexual oppression that Robert had committed in a really destructive fashion, Martin functions like a ritualistic scapegoat in an underlying mythic structure of *Shirley*. In René Girard's words, the scapegoat acts as the receptacle for "all the dissentions . . . within the community that the sacrifices are designed to suppress. The purpose of the sacrifice is to restore harmony to the community, to reinforce the social fabric."[21] Martin's act, in accepting the transference of all those negative and violent qualities of the novel's world, cements the union of Caroline and Robert and also permits the harmony of the novel to establish itself. He gives Caroline to Robert and receives from Robert those qualities that prevented the older man from loving her.

But Martin is an inverted scapegoat in the sense that instead of acting as what Girard calls the "surrogate victim," he is the surrogate oppressor, who by assuming the functions of the real oppressor puts an end to sexual and class conflict and so allows the novel to close happily as a traditional novel should. This inversion might indicate some difference between feminine myth and patriarchal myth that could be pursued elsewhere.[22] For here suffice it to say that the inverted myth reflects both the revolutionary implications of Brontë's feminism and also their historic limitations. In order for the novel to close harmoniously, Robert must change personally, and he must also inaugurate a transformation of the social class system. That transformation takes place, but only on an abstract level.

The figure of Martin embodies this contradiction in the novel. As a symbolic, mythic character, he helps bring about a change in social and sexual power relations, but as a realistic character, he represents their continuance by the next generation. Martin is harmless because he is young, but as a foreshadowing of the future he provides a harsh commentary on the utopian nature of Robert's transformation and acts as a reminder that no real social change does occur in the novel. His generation will perpetuate capitalist relations and brutal sexual relations in an even more crass and reified way.

Sexual Power and Class Power

Because of this inner contradiction, the novel's treatment of social conflict has been evaluated by critics in widely divergent ways. As Möglen says, the novel expresses sympathy for the exploited and starving mill hands, recognizes similarities in the position of women and of workers, and pleads for social reform. As Eagleton says, the reforms are couched in terms of condescending paternalism.[23] And Gubar points out the "ambiguity" (p. 387) in Shirley's attitude toward the working class. My argument lies closer to Gubar's. It focuses not so much on the class struggle itself as on the narrative language used to represent it. This language expresses the very same economy of representation based on objectifying visualization and self-affirming "specula[riza]tion" which the text vigorously criticized and discarded in the narration of sexual relations.

Even when Robert Moore's opinions about the working class are treated ironically or critically by the narrator, he, as well as Yorke and Helstone, are seen from the inside as subjects, while the workers are seen only from without, as stereotyped objects, boxed into uniform categories. Whether they are good, like the meek William Farren, who deserves help from starvation, because after all he has endured, he is "still patient" (p. 158), or bad, like the ferocious drunkard Moses Barraclough, without whom, we are led to believe, the workers would not be misled to such violent revolt, they serve the same ideological function in the novel. They send back to the middle-class characters (and readers) an affirming reflection of their own values and social organization.

But the text really mimics a masculine discursive system, at the point where the social chronicle comes to a climax in the great battle scene at Moore's mill. This scene is narrated not from the perspective of the participants, but from the viewpoint of Caroline and Shirley as excluded, marginal observers, i.e., as people who do not participate in the battle but who *see* it as a set of images. At this crisis they identify with the men of their class, accept their economic organization, and so enter their "economy of representation," producing a picture of the battle which affirms the men's ideology. Adopting the symbolic language of the text, Shirley says: "We shall see what transpires with our own eyes" (p. 334). But according to the novel's own system of meaning, "seeing with one's eyes" leads to destructive illusion.

Not only the characters Caroline and Shirley, but also the narrator of the battle adopt a language of reifying vision. Seeing only external details rather than internal relations and seeing them from a fixed position, the narrator makes coherent sense out of them by fitting them into a framework of preestablished models against which the participants of the battle are measured.

A yell followed this demonstration—a rioters' yell—a North-of-England—a Yorkshire—a West-Riding—A West-Riding-clothing-district-of-Yorkshire rioters' yell. You never heard that sound, perhaps, reader? So much the better for your ears—perhaps for your heart: since, if it rends the air in hate to yourself, or to the men or principles you approve, the interests to which you wish well, Wrath wakens to the cry of Hate: the Lion shakes his mane, and rises to the howl of the Hyena: Caste stands up ireful against Caste; and the indignant wronged spirit of the Middle Rank bears down in zeal and scorn on the famished and furious mass of the Operative Class. It is difficult to be tolerant—difficult to be just—in such moments. (P. 335)

In this passage the rhetoric of an enlightened attempt to overcome bias veils a deeper bias embedded in the connotations of the figurative language. To refer to the middle class as a "Wrathful Lion" and the working class as a "Hate-filled Hyena" is to rely on a long-established tradition of literary associations in which one image has noble connotations, the other despicable connotations. To put the scene squarely in the phallocentric logic of the mind/body split, the passage associates the middle class with a "spirit," the working class with a "mass."

Upon the foundation of these preconceptions, the attempt to be "just" and "tolerant" is made in a context which sees the workers as objectified other and represses them as subjects. The message of the passage is that *we* lofty, spiritual beings must try to be just and tolerant to *those* irrational beings. In this system of representation the mill hands are represented in a way that makes it inconceivable for *them* to represent *us* in turn. They can only act as mirrors whose essential deficiency serves to reflect our essential rightness. A power relation is expressed by language that denies the working class the right to language. They are reduced to nameable objects and assigned to categories controlled by the group in power.

And so when the novel comes to its "happy ending," the heroines have not totally rejected what Irigaray calls "a speculary, and speculative, economy which leaves [their] drives without signs, symbols, emblems, and even graphisms, capable of representing them" (p. 155). The last scene, in which the two married couples dedicate their bright new mill and progressive workers' village, is recounted not by the narrator but to the narrator by a servant several years after the events of the story. This apparently utopian account of patriarchal marriage and paternalistic capitalism is strikingly marked by that symbolism of *seeing* which throughout the novel has suggested masculine power, injustice, and illusion.

"Ay!" said she, "this world has queer changes. I can remember the old mill being built—the very first it was in all the district; and then, I can remember it being pulled down, and going with my lake lasses [companions] to see the foundation stone of the new one laid: the two Mr. Moores made a great stir about it; they were there, and a deal of fine folk beside, and both their ladies; very bonnie and grand they looked; but Mrs. Louis was the grandest, she always wore such handsome dresses: Mrs. Robert was quieter like. Mrs. Louis smiled when she talked; she had a real happy glad, good-natured look; but she had een that could pierce a body through: there is no such ladies now-a-days." (P. 599)

As opposed to the principal narrator of *Shirley*, who "sees" the action from the interior as a dynamic process, the narrator of this scene *sees* it from the outside and as filtered through her idealized preconceptions of the upper class. Throughout the novel, this outside, idealized view signals illusion and untruth, and the signs of exteriority in this passage are even more exaggerated than in other similar passages.

Now the system of objectifying vision which the novel had struggled against encompasses it. In this passage we can see nothing but the beginning (when the mill was first built) and the end (when the new mill was built). All that has happened between, all the inner development of self and relations that form the inside of the novel, and the history that the love relations have gone through, have suddenly disappeared, as if they never happened, behind the outer walls of this passage's closure. The only remnant of opposition to visual objectification is Shirley's eyes—"een that could pierce a body through"—but the passage suggests that they are not to be found "now-a-days."

Given the contrast between seeing and talking around which the symbolic network of the text turns, what is especially troubling in this exterior view of Caroline and Shirley is the double silence surrounding Caroline. First, while the narrator describes what Shirley wore and how she looked, there is no such detailed description of Caroline. Secondly, the passage says that Shirley "talked," but suggests that Caroline was quiet. The emphasis on Caroline's powers of conversation throughout the novel, along with the symbolic role of conversation in general, make its absence here very pointed.

In the novel's conclusion, as in the rest of the text, the underlying symbolism speaks more eloquently than the overt message of the interdependence between sexual power relations and class relations. But the conclusion gives more cause for alarm than the rest of the novel, since here the unconscious symbolism of the text expresses a darkly tragic message that enters into contradiction with the overt representation of happiness on the level of plot. It is as if Brontë, faced with the larger power system into which an author sends her finished work, had to hide the feminist conclusion behind the patriarchal discourse and ideology of the overt conclusion. Yet if we consider some of the qualities of the fragmentary and silent feminine discourse she produced in the body of the text, we can remember that it gives a lesser importance to the linear plot, and we might conclude that the last word does not come at the end.

Chapter 6

Romantic Love without Hero or Heroine

Alain-Fournier's *Big Meaulnes*

After the great wave of romantic novels in the 1830s and 1840s, romanticism came to be regarded as a myth to be dismantled. One could expect that Flaubert's *Madame Bovary* and *L'Education sentimentale* would signal a final disillusionment with romantic love and a final dissection of its mythology. But in the early years of the twentieth century *Big Meaulnes* with its naive nostalgia, its innocent narrator, and its tale of pure, inaccessible love contributed to a renaissance of romantic enthusiasm for a whole generation of adolescent intellectuals. While it may not be as well known today as *Tristan and Isolde* or *Manon Lescaut*, Simone de Beauvoir claims *Big Meaulnes* among the most influential novels of her youth.[1] But even she sees in it primarily "magic" and "fantasy."[2]

The novel also enjoyed wide popularity as well as academic acclaim later in the century. Like the other classics studied in this book, it has been translated into different media: it has been made into a film, a popular BBC radio play, and a ballet at the Royal Ballet Company of Sadler Wells.[3] Translated into thirty-three languages, *Big Meaulnes* has had at least two translations into English. In 1928, translated as *The Wanderer,* it had an introduction by Havelock Ellis. The same translation was republished in 1958 with an introduction by Henri Peyre. Another translation, under the title *Meaulnes: The Lost Domaine,* appeared in 1966 in England.[4] The amplitude of the novel's popularity caused critic Marcel Schneider, in 1964, to say in exasperation that while "we assert the immense success of this book for the past twenty years," critical claims about it have gone too far: "It is a habit today to compare to *Big Meaulnes* any book that talks about the magic of childhood and the enchantment contained in daily experience, as if Alain-Fournier had invented the genre of the marvelous, as if he had bestowed upon it its model and held a monopoly on it. *Big Meaulnes* is cited as the sole source of contemporary enchantment."[5] Schneider may here be referring to such critics as Henri Clouard, who praises Alain-Fournier for having "remained as inimitable as he is imitated." According to him: "If there exists today a new novel theme, that of deep, poetic adventure in the direction of the impossible, Alain-Fournier is its creator, and his novel is its great example."[6]

Even though the novel is quite a bit more dreamlike and other-worldly than the other novels studied here, it also goes further than these other novels to rationalize threatening passions and to recuperate them into an ideological order. In *Big Meaulnes* the disruptive forces of sexual desire are almost stilled; autonomous feminine voices conflicting with the dominant narrative voice are more brutally silenced; and struggles between masculine and feminine historicity are almost repressed. But while the forces of a unifying, rationalizing power work efficiently in this text, they also work invisibly, hiding behind the pure, apparently timeless delicacy and nostalgia of the writing.

The very purity of this novel's form means that in *Big Meaulnes* complexities of form and language dominate its by now very traditional themes. It also means that in this novel the historic forces that make romantic love so central to culture, and which *The Red and the Black, Shirley,* and *Sentimental Education* express explicitly, have become very implicit and deeply embedded in the complexities of form and language. But while historic forces work silently, they do explain the formalism of the novel. Given the complexities of form in *Big Meaulnes,* its interpretation calls for formal and linguistic analyses which can reveal how the novel produces the language or discourse of its own narration. Such analyses can also show how this very production of discourse in *Big Meaulnes* encloses sexual relations and social history in a rationalizing ideology. But these analyses need to be based on a preliminary look at how the thematic material of the novel both repeats and radically changes the romantic tradition.

The Romantic Tradition: Change and Repetition

Big Meaulnes is both very much the same as the traditional romantic narrative and quite different. It is different precisely because it places itself with a higher degree of self-consciousness in the tradition of medieval courtly love and nineteenth-century romantic love literature. It also combines this tradition with the early-twentieth-century movement of the "Roman du terroir"[7] since in addition to being a romance, *Big Meaulnes* is also a regional novel set in Alain-Fournier's native Cher during the Third Republic.

As a literary construct combining turn-of-the-century regionalism and several centuries of national tradition, the hero Augustin Meaulnes begins his novelistic quest at the age of fifteen. Like *Manon Lescaut*, Balzac's *The Lily in the Valley*, or other novels which follow the classical form of the genre, *Big Meaulnes* has a circular form and begins with the first-person narrator explaining how he came to write this tragic tale. But one difference that will turn out to have decisive significance distinguishes *Big Meaulnes* from those earlier romantic narratives: the first-person narrator, François Seurel, is not the hero; he is the hero's best friend. He begins by telling the reader how he met Augustin Meaulnes when the hero came to attend the rural school run by François's father. A boarder in the Seurel home, Meaulnes runs away with a borrowed horse and buggy, loses his way, and disappears for three days on a journey that takes him symbolically through the history of nineteenth-century and medieval romance to the source of romantic love.

When Meaulnes returns from his adventure, François discovers him wearing secretly under his coarse, peasant, schoolboy clothing "a strange silken waistcoat . . . from the 1830's."[8] In explaining this relic of the Romantic Generation of 1830, Meaulnes tells François of his strange voyage in the countryside, which in apparently naive and unconscious ways alludes constantly to voyages of chevaliers in Chretien de Troyes romances, to the Arthurian "Autre Monde," and to the imagery of nineteenth-century Romantic and post-Romantic poetry. Like heroes from Tristan to Julien Sorel, Meaulnes "felt growing in him the ever more impatient desire to arrive at something in spite of all obstacles" (p. 59). He stumbles upon an old *"Domaine"* in ruins, where a mysterious *fête*, attended mostly by children and old people, has been organized to celebrate the marriage of the *Domaine's* young master Frantz de Galaïs to a poor weaver's daughter, Valentine. Meaulnes's "strange adventure" (p. 74) leads him to meet Frantz's sister Yvonne.

> She was without a doubt more beautiful than all the other girls of the country, more beautiful than Jeanne whom you saw in the nuns' garden by peeking through the key hole, or than Madeleine, the baker's daughter, all blond and rosy, or than Jenny, the daughter of the chateau people, who was lovely but crazy and locked up. It was certainly about a young girl that he thought at night, *like a hero in a novel.* (P. 33, emphasis added)

Even more phantomlike than the nineteenth-century heroines like Balzac's Mme. de Mortsauf, Nerval's Sylvie, or Chateaubriand's Amélie, Yvonne is placed here into a new, more extreme dimension of their tradition. Not only more beautiful than any other girl, she exists in another, spiritual order, completely outside of lived reality. She is introduced in a way that makes her triply distanced, imagined by a narrator who has never seen her, imagined as existing in the thoughts of a romanticized hero, and imagined as always/already existing in a novel.

Through the mediation of Yvonne, Meaulnes pursues the real goal of his quest which is to arrive, in the manner of Hegel's Spirit, Balzac's Felix de Vandenesse, or Stendhal's Julien Sorel, at possession of his own self-identity. While exploring the *Domaine*, Meaulnes comes to the central core of his adventure.

> Once he was in the garden, Meaulnes leaned upon the wooden barrier of the fish pond. . . . He saw himself reflected in the water, as if leaning upon the sky, in his romantic student's costume; and he saw another Meaulnes; no longer the pupil who had run away in a peasant's cart, but a charming figure of romance, in the middle of a beautiful prize book. (P. 93)

At the farthest reaches of the strange "Autre Monde" is the "Autre Meaulnes," the identical but idealized reflection of the hero's self.

The *fête* ends tragically as the bride fails to arrive, and Frantz attempts suicide. After Meaulnes's return to the Seurel school, he and François try to find the way back to the *Domaine*, which they believe to be "very far from here" (p. 54). While the largest, coarsest, and most prosaic of their comrades, Jasmin Delouche, makes fun of this attempt, a mysterious new pupil arrives at M. Seurel's school, a bohemian boy traveling with a band of roving actors. He vows to help them. At the end of the boy's short stay, Meaulnes recognizes him as Frantz de Galais, and soon after, leaves the school himself to continue his quest for the elusive Yvonne.

After several years of Meaulnes's absence, Jasmin finds the *Domaine*, a ruined estate called Sablonnières, not "far away," but very close to their town. In his prosaic, peasant way, Jasmin tells François: "The young girl? Meaulnes will marry her after he's done his year in the service" (p. 198). François, by now a schoolteacher himself, takes up the quest for Yvonne, but in a way that transforms the strange and mysterious into the familiar and rational. The nearby locality of Sablonnières turns out to be inhabited by "M. Seurel's whole family."

It seems that Meaulnes's romantic search will end in conventional middle-class marriage, but on his wedding night, Frantz de Galais returns and calls him away. The next day Meaulnes abandons his new wife for further mysterious adventures. François cements "a friendship more moving than a great love" (p. 208) with Yvonne, who, true romantic heroine that she is, dies in childbirth nine months after Meaulnes's departure. François thus inherits the guardianship of the old *Domaine*, and of Meaulnes's daughter. He finds at Sablonnières the journal in which Meaulnes had written of his sordid love affair with Valentine, and of the violent remorse it caused. A year later Meaulnes returns, bringing back Frantz and Valentine as a married couple, and takes away his little girl on further adventures.

Love as Exchange Value

Contrary to appearances, this dreamlike and otherworldly novel does, in fact, have active connections to the mundane historic processes of Third Republic society, and those connections are both similar to and different from the connections that *Tristan and Isolde* has to historical change during the late twelfth century. While the French state had been centralizing its power over rural France since the sixteenth century, isolated rural communities had retained their own local economy and customs. During the Third Republic, institutions of the French state and of large-scale capitalism integrated more tightly under a standardized bureaucratic control large sections of rural France. Up till then the relation of many communities to national political and economic institutions had been limited to matters outside of daily life like taxation, conscription, and some trade.[9] A decisive political role in this new integration is played by the rural middle-class intelligentsia, especially rural schoolteachers like François Seurel and his father. This group rises to a new prominence in "organizing the hegemony,"[10] as Nicos Poulantzas says, not of its own class, but of the urban bourgeoisie.[11] As centralization and a money economy lay new claims upon the world of the peasant village, socioeconomic forces similar to those which worked to create *Tristan and Isolde* in the twelfth century now create a middle-class, rural version of their love in the early twentieth.

Big Meaulnes is also similar to *Tristan and Isolde* in that it transforms oral folklore, this time that of rural France, into written, personalized romance. It contributes to a literary movement which parallels the work of scholars in this "golden age"[12] of folklore studies, who "rued the loss of olden ways and sought to record and preserve their memory"[13] in the journals, collections, and great folk museums that were established in this period. *Big Meaulnes* is a kind of textual folk museum, which serves to integrate indigenous rural culture into a centralized Parisian culture.

Both Eugen Weber in *Peasants into Frenchmen* and Julia Kristeva in *The Revolution of Poetic Language* discuss how economic, political, and cultural centralization in this period all reinforce each other. One finds, as in the eras of *Tristan and Isolde,* of *The Princess of Clèves,* and of *The Red and the Black,* an increased rationalization of daily life, to which romanticism is a reaction. *Big Meaulnes* idealizes changes in which immediate relations of rural people to the community, to its members, and to the physical world are replaced with a passive, distanced relation mediated by a stronger, more bureaucratic state.

Economically, Weber sees this "watershed of change" (p. 41) happening differently in different parts of rural France during the Third Republic. Detailing "the passage from relative isolation and a relatively closed economy to union with the outside world through roads, railroads and a money economy" (p. x), he says that even toward the end of the nineteenth century, peasants of many localities "close[d] in on themselves to live off their own products instead of obeying the great law of exchange."[14] Living in the realm of use value, they did not treat products as if they "had a cost" (p. 212), so that, for instance, "in Var figs were fed to local pigs" (p. 207). Although peasants had paid taxes and engaged in trade, and although "money—or rather the lack of it, reigned over the countryside" (p. 37), it was not until the period of 1870 to 1905 that certain rural communities experience "the shift to a money economy" (p. 40), bringing with it the general tendency toward abstract, quantifiable, standardized models for many daily activities. A self-sufficient community revolving around use value turns into one part of a larger society regulated by exchange value.

Previously, peasants had not used uniform, standard measures of land, but often measured it according to "the amount of land a man could work in a day" (p. 30). Nor was time a uniformly "measurable quantity." Weber says: "As with watches, so with the calendar. The calendar year meant nothing, the rhythm of the seasons, everything" (p. 483). But the new ways meant that "Labor, no longer diffuse, turned into a commodity that could be . . . quantified in terms of time. . . . Time made sense only when money made sense" (p. 483).

Although the "standardization of organization in the bureaucratic expansion of the last century" (C. Tilly, p. 62) occurred at diverse times in different parts of France, Alain-Fournier's early-twentieth-century regional novel unmistakably traces on the level of form the same process that Weber describes on the historical level. The passage from the "old forms of intuition" (Weber, p. 483) in the world of use value to "the practices of rationality" in the world of exchange value goes on in *Big Meaulnes*. At the same time, the novel idealizes the old form of labor as it describes the disappearing community workshop.

> No one said anything. . . . From time to time, the peaceful, reg-
> ular work of the shop would be interrupted for a minute. . . .
>   The worker would remain with his hand in the air at the chain
> of the bellows, put his hand on his hip and look at us laughing.
>   Thus the muted noise of work would begin again. (P. 27)

This workshop is not only preexchange but prediscursive. Even the speech of the workers serves more to establish a rhythm than to communicate ideas. This "was a place full of sparks and noise" (p. 28) rather than a place of language; a place of direct, immediate interaction between the workers and physical reality as between the workers themselves. In the novel, the hero Meaulnes, like Tristan and *Manon Lescaut*'s hero des Grieux, symbolically brings about the rupture between the old world with its immediate relations and the new world with its mediated relations. Augustin Meaulnes, coming to "overthrow everything" (p. 27), symbolizes a cataclysmic rupture with these old ways. He will import a mediating language and a more self-conscious form of human relation—romantic love.

But *Big Meaulnes* differs from *Tristan and Isolde* in that it does not, as did the twelfth-century romance, help to create a new form of culture. It serves to infuse a by now very traditional French romanticism into rural culture, and so contributes to absorbing the concrete diversity of regional culture into the homogeneous "transcendent unity" (Weber, p. 97) of an already existing national culture. Although before 1870, France had enjoyed relative cultural homogeneity, Parisian life, according to Weber, had been "leagues apart" (p. 8) from many regional cultures of which the state of the Third Republic was increasingly "suspicious" (Weber, p. 82). This effacement of local particularities is an integral part of political and economic standardization. "With production no longer regulated by custom," says Weber, "a mass of popular traditions and feasts were either abandoned altogether or became hollow rituals" (p. 125). Such a feast is, in *Big Meaulnes,* the mysterious *fête* at the *Domaine.* Through his nostalgia and his quest for purity, Alain-Fournier removes the *fête* to a dreamlike world divorced from its socioeconomic roots.

Weber finds that in political terms

> the popular tradition in songs and other old forms was hurt by the marriage of politics and folklore, which led the government to move against them. What we call folklore always reflected local politics. When local politics became national, the government began to meddle; the agents of authority turned against songsters, farandoles, Carnivals, and the like. (P. 437)

Big Meaulnes, by removing customs of concrete rural life to an idealized realm of nostalgia, by making them the backdrop of a romantic love scene, and by cutting off this realm from any organic ties to political life, repeats and contributes to the larger historic process.

Language and Exchange Value

The scene in *Big Meaulnes* describing noise and work in the old community workshop suggests that historic changes in rural life include a change in the relation between speakers and language. The emergence of rational discourse out of rhythmic, immediate communication has some connection to the emergence of exchange value out of use value. As Saussure and Lévi-Strauss have shown, systems of language are really systems of exchange value; and Marx has shown the converse: the capitalist system of exchange is structured like a language: "the language of commodities."[15]

Lévi-Strauss maintains that culture originates and organizes itself through symbolic exchange: exchange of signs, of symbolic objects, and, for him, of women, who function as signs.[16] But Anthony Wilden proposes several modifications to Lévi-Strauss's theory, one of which is immediately relevant to the way *Big Meaulnes* reproduces romantic traditions in its own particular historic situation: Wilden distinguishes two forms of cultural exchange, one regulated by "symbolic exchange value" and the other by "imaginary exchange value."[17] Symbolic exchange value organizes relations such as those in the old village workshop, in the *fêtes* when they were still an integral part of village life, and in the whole village life itself when its economy was based on use value. "Imaginary exchange value" organizes societies regulated by commodity exchange. Wilden gives as an example of a "symbolic exchange value" a shell or a bracelet that one person in a clanic society gives to another. While it signifies the dynamic relations between the two people, an "imaginary exchange value," like money or gold, signifies a thing or a commodity. Production of narrative discourse in *Big Meaulnes* will very much concern this distinction.

It also concerns certain similarities between Saussure's notion of language as a system of pure values and Marx's "language of commodities." For Saussure, signs have no necessary relation to their referents, but "are purely differential, defined not by their content, but by their relationships with the other terms of the system."[18] Likewise, for Marx, exchange value has no logical relation to use value but merely expresses a relationship between differential terms in the exchange system; it "is the expression of equivalence between different forms of commodities."[19] Use values are purely individual, qualitative, and heterogeneous. They cannot be measured by any abstract scale, nor can they systematically relate to each other or to exchange values, which are quantitative, homogeneous, and "characterized," as Marx says, "by a total abstraction from use value" (p. 37). To produce a narrative discourse structured by "imaginary exchange values" but to make it seem to express use value is the task of François Seurel as narrator of *Big Meaulnes.*

Rules of Textual Production

Throughout the novel, underlying the narration of Meaulnes's story, is another implicit story, expressed through symbols and images, of the author's quest for a system of narrative language or discourse which will make it possible for him to write the novel. This underlying narration is, like the narration of Meaulnes's quest, circular, since it tells of the search for the very system of discourse in which the story is being told. The basic elements of this system are already present and expressed through the imagery of the opening pages. The narrator begins his double narration by saying: "He arrived at our house on a Sunday in November, 189. . . I continue to say 'our house,' although the house doesn't belong to us any longer. We have been gone from the country for what will soon be fifteen years, and we will certainly never go back there" (p. 11). These opening paragraphs emphasize two basic rules of the novel's textual structure. First, the text will form itself through the transformation of a something-somewhere into a nothing, a "no-longer," a spatial and temporal emptiness, which forms the center of the text. It is the necessary precondition for the fulfillment of romantic love and for the language of the novel.

This center, here in the guise of the no-longer existing "chez nous," is "that dwelling place through which passed the most tormented and the most precious days of my life—dwelling place which formed for our adventures the point of departure and the point of return, where they came to break like waves against a desert rock" (p. 12). That precious center, then, is the place where, by contrast to adventures, nothing happens, and which furthermore transforms the adventures into nothing, like waves destroyed by a rock. In the course of the novel, this empty center, this cozy linguistic home untouched by lived experience will come into being.

A second element of the structure is that this center is protected by impenetrable but always shifting boundaries. The importance of boundaries is emphasized by one image in which Meaulnes's arrival at the Seurel school actually cuts a boundary between the remembering narrator who stands on this side and the thing he remembers, which lies on the other side: "The whole peaceful landscape . . . is forever in my memory agitated, transformed by the presence of he who overturned our whole adolescence and whose flight itself did not even leave us any rest" (p. 13). The overwhelming force, which makes representation possible by creating the boundary between representer and the thing he represents, has long "fled." Like the empty center, it is "no more," but leaves the absolute barrier between the two sides. Throughout the novel the act of remembering, of talking about, and therefore of language, discourse, and narration, will be separated by an impenetrable barrier from what is being remembered or talked about or represented. In other words the signs are separated from the referent or object of representation. Experience can never be represented as it was lived but only as "agitated, transformed," and distorted through the hazy screen of the changes that made it disappear.

The scene that recounts Meaulnes's arrival at the Seurel school in this first chapter of the novel is marked by a great proliferation of boundaries. In this scene, François's mother is located inside the innermost boundary: "and my mother, who had retired until nightfall to her dim room, was mending her humble wardrobe" (p. 14). The mother's room is inside the house, which is in turn inside a court, itself separated from the "bourg" by "a small iron gate." At the moment of Meaulnes's arrival, François, returning home, sees the scene from outside the iron gate and recounts it in a way to call attention to all the boundaries between actors and observers: "In fact, at the dining room *door*—the closest of the five *doors opening on to the court*—a woman with gray hair, bent forward, was trying to see *through the curtains*. . . . I don't know what apprehension at the sight of her made me stop on the first step of the *stairs* in front of the *iron gate*" (p. 15, emphasis added). Although he is standing outside the court and is separated from his mother inside her room by the whole series of boundaries, young François clearly "sees" her in her "dim room" inside the house and the details of her activities there, as if the boundaries later set up by the adult narrator mean nothing to the little boy: "No one came to open the door for the strange visitor. Millie had, without a doubt, received her hat from the Station, and not hearing anything, in front of a bed strewn with old ribbons and unravelled feathers, was sewing, unsewing and rebuilding her mediocre headpiece" (p. 15).

At the end of the chapter, Meaulnes erects the first of those boundaries that eventually will form the structure of discourse for his reproduction of romanticism. Ignoring completely the maternal authority of which little François is so aware, Meaulnes invites him to go outside and set off leftover fuses of an abandoned and forbidden Fourteenth of July firecracker he found in the attic. The momentary blaze of the firecracker forges a barrier between the realm of childhood and the realm of manhood: "A moment later, my mother, who was coming out to stand in the doorway, . . . saw . . . two sheaves of red and white stars burst forth: and she could see me, during the space of an instant, outlined against the magic light, holding the hand of the newly arrived big boy and not flinching" (p. 19). This scene marks an exception to the recurrent structure of representation in which the observer placed on this side of the barrier is irreversibly separated from what he represents, which lies on the other side. It also marks a difference from the previously quoted scene in which all boundaries are permeable for the little François. Here the narrator, in recounting his rapid passage from one order to another, is on *both* sides. While standing on the side of Meaulnes, he shares the perception of his mother as he passes to a new place from which he will no longer be able to know "without a doubt" what is happening in her innermost chamber, and will no longer be able to act as if boundaries do not exist. Similar to des Grieux in *Manon Lescaut* and to Felix de Vandenesse in *The Lily in the Valley*, François is passing from immediate relationships, as represented by the mother-child bond, to more mediated, more sexually repressed, and more conscious forms in which both homosexual and romantic love play a major role. But again, between François and these earlier hero/narrators there are big differences.

For François, "the arrival of Augustin Meaulnes . . . was the beginning of a new life" (p. 20). It seems to signal his entrance into the symbolic order with its emphasis on linguistic structure, but François had already lived in a realm of language. Before Meaulnes's arrival, he had spent his free time after school "in the depths of the town-hall, ensconced in the archive room . . . , and I would read" (p. 21). Meaulnes's arrival takes François from the order of symbolic exchange into what Wilden calls "imaginary exchange." This "new life" is also the emergence of adolescence out of childhood, and the historical emergence of the new order of exchange value out of the old order of use value. The new order is governed not by symbolic exchange but by imaginary exchange where language attempts to capture objects rather than to express relations.

François's entry into this imaginary order of language is connected to a third element of discursive structure in *Big Meaulnes:* its apparent used or secondhand quality. Although the novel does produce a very original narrative, it presents its narrator as someone who "rebuilds," "repairs," or "mends" (p. 14) a used discourse. One metaphor of the narrator's work is the "mending" of the mother, who "sewed, unsewed, and rebuilt" used hat trimmings. This secondhand quality touches many of the text's self-images. Not only Millie's finery, but the firecracker whose blaze ushers François into the new order is a used leftover, as is, finally, the self-consciously copied, secondhand romantic quest itself. While not completely organized around the traditional romantic narrative structure, *Big Meaulnes* patches, rebuilds, and rearranges that used structure in its own organization.

Its narrative form depends for both its originality and its use of secondhand materials on those boundaries that separate the realm of discourse from the inaccessible realm of seemingly lost objects they signify. But these objects and the "mysterious country" for which the narrator and Meaulnes have so much nostalgia are not really lost at all. They are in fact newly created by the very barrier which puts them beyond the reach of the two young men. When François and Meaulnes see from afar the "humble hut" of the bohemian actors, it "appeared to be the mysterious passageway, the antechamber of the Country to which we had lost the way" (p. 149). But were they to refind the path, enter the antechamber, and live in the country, its reality would be experienced simply as a sordid masquerade. While the world of Meaulnes's adventure appears in a magic light from within the point of view of the boy's daily, mundane life, this same daily boyhood experience appears in a magic light from the point of view of their adult life.

Both the lost world of the de Galais's old *Domaine* and the lost world of childhood belong to the past of immediate relationships in communities regulated by use value. But the narrator can be conscious of them as such and represent them in a system of writing only from within the realm of exchange value. What makes the other side of the barrier an object of idealized nostalgic discourse is precisely the impossibility of being there. In this novel, a scene of romance, in order to become a scene of romance, must lose its particularity as lived experience to become, like the center of the textual structure, an empty space.

Four Partial Discourses and the Discourse of the Novel

In order to understand how and why *Big Meaulnes* reproduces the romantic tradition and at the same time radically changes it, it is necessary to examine in some detail the peculiarities of its narrative discourse. The story of the novel's own quest, told through a network of symbols to produce a language form that expresses lost use value, parallels and underlies the narration of Meaulnes's quest to refind his lost love. In this underlying linguistic quest, the text makes four attempts to produce a language system, all of which fail but leave in the text images of partial discourses. The failures themselves tell us a great deal about why this novel's heroine and hero are so familiar to the romantic tradition and yet so strange.

In the first of these partial discourses, the principal sign is the "strange waistcoat" ("étrange gilet") that Meaulnes wears home from the *fête*. The *gilet* is transformed from a use value into a sign by traveling out of a historical, cultural, and physical context in which its users interacted with it as an organic part of their lived experience, into a new context, where it does not fit and has no organic use. Its only use is to point to that other world, but as *other*, as a faraway, "no longer" accessible world with reference to this world. By changing from a useful element of daily life into a sign, the waistcoat transforms its "lost" world from a possible lived experience into the alienated object of representation with which the observer has only a distant and passive relation. Somewhat like a commodity, the *gilet* cancels out its use value to become the equivalent form of something else. It thus becomes a potential language that marks the distinction between This World and a disappeared Other World.

The *gilet*, so starkly out of context in the boys' garret, signifies not only the romantic past but the ineffable mystery and adventurousness of Meaulnes's mysterious adventure. This ability to signify the elusively undefinable and inaccessible is what the words of the novel aspire to capture. But the *gilet* fails to form a discourse, because it does not form or enter into a system of differential values. It is a single sign which refers to its concrete referent.

The second partial discourse seems to compensate for the failure of the first. It is formed out of a series of objects rather than a single object. These are the mysterious and fascinating objects that Frantz de Galais brings to the Seurel school.

> I can still remember that curious fellow and all the strange treasures he brought in that satchel attached to his back. First there were "magic lantern" pen-holders which he took out to use in writing his dictation. Through an eye-hole in the handle, you could see by closing one eye, the basilica of Lourdes or some other exotic monument appearing dim and distorted. . . . Then there was a Chinese pen-box filled with compasses and amusing instruments which started on the left hand bench, going from hand to hand, sliding silently, furtively, under the notebooks, so that M. Seurel couldn't see them.
>
> In the same direction passed brand new books, whose titles I had read with envy among the sparse books in our library. . . . Who knew where they came from, or whether, maybe, they had been stolen. (Pp. 131–32)

Like the *gilet,* these objects point to and signify a wondrous, unknown world, a "who knows where" outside the familiar school, where rare coveted books are plentiful. Taken out of their context and brought into the barren, routine context of the schoolroom, they become signs of that outside world of adventure. But while they set up a relation which seems to resemble that between the *gilet* and Meaulnes's adventure, they bring "anxiety" (p. 132), rather than wondrous longing, into the schoolroom, and cause the narrator to describe their circulation with words like "sneaky" and "furtive." They are somehow sordid.

While Frantz's objects signify unknown adventures, they point to a world that is, after all, accessible. These objects are not, like the *gilet,* relics from a more authentic time, which can be won only through heroic feats, but commodities, which can be purchased in stores. This second partial discourse seems in every way a degraded version of the *gilet* discourse. When taken out of its context, the *gilet* brings to This World the aura of a purer and higher order, while Frantz's objects bring disorder and confusion to their new context.

It seems that the single sign, when multiplied, must, through that process, fall into degradation. In fact, as the objects do come together, each loses by the union. Each cancels out its particular, individual quality to form, like the objects which enter Marx's "language of commodities," a set of abstract quantitative relations.

> The objects which were "made to pass" one by one, finally arrived each in its turn in the hands of Big Meaulnes who, without looking at them, indifferently put them down beside him. There was soon a pile, mathematical and multicolored, as if at the feet of the woman who represents Science in allegorical compositions. (Pp. 132–33)

Whereas the *gilet* shows that Meaulnes has been a participant in romance, this set of objects makes one an observer of science. Whereas the *gilet* retains the concrete, qualitative uniqueness of its former use value, Frantz's objects resemble the abstracted signifiers of "allegory." Whereas the *gilet* signifies the ineffable mystery that infinitely surpasses its own boundaries as signifier, allegorical signs reduce qualities to the boundaries of the signifier.

The disturbing, anxious aura these objects create in the mind of the narrator stems not only from the threat they bring to his orderly schoolroom life, but also from the threat they pose for the writing of the novel. The anxiety suggests despair about the very nature of language itself as a vehicle for expressing romantic relations. It seems that when language tries to signify elusive, ineffable, infinite mystery and adventure, it must degenerate, by its very organization, into a reductionist expression of abstraction.

The third attempt to form a discourse again suggests the possibility of expressing the authentic essence of Meaulnes's adventure, and this time in words, or rather in the lack of them. This is the discourse of Meaulnes himself, who most often acts "without saying a word" (p. 54), and appears in the novel as the quintessential strong, silent man: "As before and as always, a man slow to begin speaking, as are hermits, hunters, and men of adventure, he had made a decision without worrying about the words he would need to explain it" (p. 220). Meaulnes's silence adds to the infinite, mysterious quality of his love. He gives Yvonne a private, secret, unspoken name, and always refers to her family estate Sablonnières as the "*domaine* without a name."

The fourth partial discourse, the speech of Jasmin Delouche, holds the same relation to Meaulnes's "discourse" as the discourse of Frantz's objects holds to the *gilet* discourse. It threatens to rationalize and to reduce Meaulnes's adventure to the banal boundaries of rural daily life. Jasmin finds the "lost path" to Sablonnières "as clear and as easy as a familiar road" (p. 197), gives the *Domaine* a name, identifies its inhabitants, and reduces Meaulnes's great love to a country marriage. Like Frantz's objects, which discourage the possibility that signs like the *gilet* can be organized into a system without losing their special quality, Jasmin's speech discourages the possibility that Meaulnes's silence can be rendered into speech without losing its quality of romantic mystery.

In the course of the narration, this possibility of a sign system that signifies the ineffable does suggest itself, but the narrator does not at the time see it as a possible model for his narrative discourse. At the end of the scene of the mysterious *fête*, its pure, exotic ambience is shattered by the sound of bawdy drinking songs: "Meaulnes heard their cabaret songs float into the park which for the past two days had held so many graces and marvels. And this was the beginning of its disarray and devastation" (p. 107). At this point the songs cut a boundary between the Other World of romance and This World of vulgarity.

Several years later, at a picnic reuniting Meaulnes and Yvonne in This World, Meaulnes appears to François miserably unhappy. Then they hear the same drinking song, but this time it is a "far off . . . voice," singing "a rhythmic air like a dance melody, . . . which the singer drew out and saddened like an old melancholy ballad" (p. 237). The singing produces a dramatic change in the attitude of Meaulnes, fascinated by this "*Nothing* but a memory—the most wretched—of those lovely days that would *no longer* return" (p. 237, emphasis added).

The song now evokes the "no longer" existing romantic adventure in the same nostalgic mode that the textual discourse at the beginning of the novel evokes the "no longer" existing childhood home of François. The song thus provides a prototype for the novelistic discourse. At the same time, it shows that this discourse does not form itself through the *coming together* of wondrous *gilet*-type signifiers, but through the *repetition* of ordinary signifiers from vulgar language. When repeated in a certain distorted way, they collectively act as a single sign, which, like the *gilet,* signifies the mysterious adventure.

This prototype is not a silence translated into words, but a speech which, by being repeated in different contexts, becomes a "nothing," *empties* itself of its original meaning to become the sign of its disappeared context.

The scene in which the song is repeated takes place right in the middle of the novel. But the narrator does not recognize the significance of this repetition as a model for his narration. At the same time, each of the four partial discourses now reveals itself as even more inadequate than it had seemed. When the inaccessible *Domaine* becomes the familiar Sablonnières, we find that the *gilet* does not, after all, belong to another order from that of the commodities bought (or stolen) by Frantz. It too had been purchased, along with all the other costumes, to stage the *fête*. François's uncle tells him: "They had bought or rented a great quantity of marvelous clothes, games, horses, boats. Always to entertain Frantz de Galais" (p. 202). The mysterious *fête* appears here as a simple theatrical scene, faked by Frantz. The discourse of the *gilet* appears as nothing but the discourse of Frantz's consumer objects, and the other order as nothing but this order before it becomes familiar.

Even Meaulnes's silences, after Jasmin discovers Sablonnières, ring with a bad-faith innocence. To continue to speak of the *Domaine sans nom* when everyone knows its name, betrays a transparently futile attempt to avoid reducing the ineffable to the identifiably familiar. Perhaps more discouraging is what Jasmin ultimately represents. If the *gilet,* which promised to signify authentic use values, turns out to be an exchange value, Jasmin's prosaic life conforms most closely to the old rural life governed by use value, rather than by the exchange system and the centralized state. Jasmin's discourse, spoken from within that life, expresses use values not as alienated objects of nostalgic representation, but as immediately lived experience, where they appear, of course, as coarse and vulgar banalities.

Jasmin's speech, while it threatens the discourse that aspires to the quality of the *gilet* sign and of Meaulnes's silence, also reveals the real goal of that discourse. And it is in the goal of its narrative discourse that *Big Meaulnes* differs from romantic love novels of the 1830s and 1840s. *The Red and the Black* and *Shirley* sought, although unsuccessfully, to heal the split between the realm of domesticity, femininity, sentiment, and beauty to which use values had been relegated and the realm of economics and politics regulated by exchange values, and to create new, as yet unknown, connections between them. By contrast, *Big Meaulnes* does not seek connections between the world of use and the world of exchange, nor does its language really seek to signify use values. Rather it seeks to repress use values as lived experience and to replace them with idealized objectifications.

The text carries out this repression not by getting rid of Jasmin, but by killing off Yvonne. Because of the particular way she, as an element of the novel's structure, combines the *gilet* partial discourse and Jasmin's partial discourse, she poses the most serious threat to the novel's discourse. Until that moment in the novel when François actually meets her, she functions as a sign just like the *gilet*. Her person, instead of interrelating as an autonomous subject with the other characters, is simply a material form that signifies or refers to the infinite mystery of the other order.

But when she steps out of that other order into this order, she not only acts as an autonomous subject, but as one who assumes the anti-romantic, apparently reductive discourse of Jasmin, which betokens the world of use values as lived experience. Her speech throws into question the whole *gilet* discourse, not because she insistently tells Meaulnes and François that the wonders of the *Domaine* no longer exist, but because this creature, who is supposed to be herself the central wonder, speaks with the peasant common sense of Jasmin. Telling François she would like to be a teacher, she says:

> "And then I would teach the boys to be good, with a good behavior that I know. I would not give them the desire to go running all over the world. . . . I would teach them to find the happiness which is right in their own back yard, and which they cannot see. . . .
>
> "For instance," she said, "maybe there is some big crazy young man who is looking for me at the ends of the world, while I am right here in Mme. Florentin's shop." (P. 206)

The discourse of Meaulnes's silence requires the complicity of Yvonne's silence. By speaking she betrays the worth of the infinite quest that Meaulnes's silence claims to signify, and in addition calls into question the very existence and nature of the other order. It requires, to hold out its promise of mysterious authenticity, Yvonne's presence, but as an objectified sign of its ambience, or as the ideal woman Alain-Fournier describes in a letter: "Woman has never been for me anything but a landscape, the reminder of hours, of lands, and of landscapes."[20]

In order for Yvonne to fill that role, her autonomy must end, and more important, empty space must replace the old order of immediately lived use values she speaks for. As François says when she dies: "Everything is bitter because she is dead. The world is *empty*, vacation is ended. Ended are the lost long carriage trips; ended the mysterious fête" (p. 281, emphasis added). Here is produced finally that spatial and temporal emptiness that had not yet been created in the scene of the repeated song; that, as we saw, begins the novel; and that even makes possible the novel: "But now that everything is ended, . . . I can narrate his strange adventure" (p. 56).

The Reproduction of History

Through Yvonne's death, the novel's combination of turn-of-the-century regionalism and national tradition of romanticism forms a coherent literary structure. Her death serves both the specific needs of narrative structure in *Big Meaulnes* and also more general needs of romantic narrative as a genre. It resembles the death (or symbolic death) of other heroines in earlier novels of romantic love, in whose tradition *Big Meaulnes* consciously places itself. In *Manon Lescaut,* for example, the heroine's death establishes a barrier for the hero/narrator between active passion and restrained speech. The hero passes from a life of immediate experience, in which he is immersed in sexual desire and disruptive emotion, into a life of discourse in which desire is deferred, so that he may turn into the narrator who articulates in speech his past experience and emotions.

But the death of Yvonne signals two modifications of this romantic tradition, one concerning the nature of the hero, and the other concerning the nature of the heroine. The first-person hero/narrators of *Manon Lescaut, René, Adolphe,* and *The Lily in the Valley,* expressing the values of a rising bourgeoisie from the mid-eighteenth to the mid-nineteenth century, are subjects of both desire and discourse. In *Big Meaulnes,* this same character structure, historically the bourgeois-individualist form of consciousness,[21] is reproduced but in a fragmented and distorted way, so that Meaulnes is the subject of desire who cannot speak, while François is the subject of discourse who cannot desire.

The death of Yvonne marks a boundary between the quest for love by the silent hero Meaulnes, and the quest to narrate that love by the narrator François, who can dispose of language only if he displaces his desires onto the silent hero: "She was the wife of my companion, and I loved her with that deep and secret friendship which is never spoken. I would look at her and be happy, like a little child" (p. 282). François's all too obvious secret is that he can master language only so long as he does not have to recognize himself as a self—as the subject of discourse and of his own desire.

Along with this split of the hero/narrator into two characters, we find an increased distance between the heroes and the heroine, so that love is destroyed not only by an overt sexual relation but by any relation beyond "looking at" the heroine. The reasons for these two new elements can be found in the section of the novel after Yvonne's death. In this section, François seeks to reconstruct Meaulnes's adventures, and finally finds a model for his narrative discourse. After the death of Yvonne, François comes to live at Sablonnières, where he can search for information about Meaulnes "during the long silence of the past years" (p. 286). He finds not what he seeks, but "a large quantity" of objects like the *gilet:* old abandoned use values that signify the ambience of the past: "Those boxes emitted a certain indefinable faded scent, and a faint perfume, which suddenly awakened in me for an entire day memories and nostalgia, and which interrupted my research" (p. 286).

Meaulnes's *search* (la recherche) has been replaced by François's *research* (les recherches); the adventure has been replaced by the rational and intellectual reconstruction of it; and Yvonne's death has created the empty space and time in which "research" can be carried out. But for the purposes of research these *gilet*-type objects are defective, because they cannot signify the adventure in the form of a systematic, organized, articulated discourse.

Finally, François comes upon one of these old souvenirs which goes beyond the limitation of the others: Meaulnes's old "Notebook of Monthly Homework Assignments," which the hero had used as a private diary. Like Yvonne, the notebook (*cahier*) joins in itself the qualities of the *gilet* sign and of Jasmin's speech, but joins them in an inverted way, so that it does not, as she does, pose a threat to the novel's discourse. Unlike Yvonne, it does not speak autonomously. It seems to present exactly the combination of discourses the novel needs. Its material body refers to a disappeared time, while the writing on its pages speaks in an organized language. It tells of the sordid love affair between Meaulnes and Valentine, but effaces that sordidness behind a distancing veil of vague and obscure language. Furthermore, the diary is "drafted in such a chopped up, ill-formed way" that it contains the quality of Meaulnes's silence, so much so that François has to "take it myself and reconstruct this entire part of his story" (p. 297).

Conflicting Models of Textual Production

The text now presents conflicting images of its own formation. One image, the repeated drinking song, is more than an image and actually participates in producing the text through a repetition of the same signifiers in different contexts, thus forming what Saussure calls a system of differential values. The other image, which shows us François actually writing the text of the novel, is this reconstitution of fragments that someone else has written.

As he reads Meaulnes's diary, François discovers that he had in fact seen Meaulnes writing it when he had visited his friend at his family home in an old "town-hall."

> I hurriedly climbed the stairs, opened the door on the right where the "City Hall" plaque had been left, and found myself in a large room with four windows, . . . its walls adorned with yellowed portraits of Presidents Grévy and Carnot. On a long dais which took up the entire far end of the room, there was still a table covered in green baize and the chairs of the city councilmen. In the middle, seated on the old mayor's chair, Meaulnes was writing. (P. 220)

While writing the journal, Meaulnes assumes the symbolic position of a state official in a central site of state power. François does not inherit that power, but he does inherit the fragmented, incoherent discourse produced by it, a discourse that he will have to "reconstitute" and "rebuild." Meaulnes ends his journal by saying: "The manuscript, which I had begun as a secret diary, and which has become my confession, will be, if I do not return, the property of my friend François Seurel" (p. 310). Whereas the hero/narrators of love novels like *Manon Lescaut* or *The Lily in the Valley* inherited what is called "real property" which confers real economic and social power, François the schoolteacher inherits as "property" words and writing. He also becomes, after the death of M. de Galais, "by testament his sole legatee until the return of Meaulnes, to whom I had to account for everything" (p. 285), as well as the guardian of Meaulnes's daughter. Instead of inheriting name, property, and power, he inherits the guardianship of these for the absent master. But it is through guarding someone else's power that François becomes a subject of discourse.

The relation that the *cahier* creates between François and the absent Meaulnes corresponds to a relation between the bourgeois state and the petty bourgeoisie described by Nicos Poulantzas. According to him the capitalist state is not "derived" from the "logic of capital" but "incarnates intellectual labor as separate from manual labor."[22] From 1789 on, he says, it needs "a corps of *organic intellectuals*" who are "formally distinct from the bourgeoisie but play a role in organizing its hegemony" (p. 61, italics in text). Precisely such an intellectual labor is performed by François. In writing his narrative, he presents himself not as a manual worker who produces, but as a clerk who reorganizes Meaulnes's state discourse in order to transform it, making it coherent, while at the same time romanticizing it and idealizing it.

By 1914, when *Big Meaulnes* was finished, "the petite bourgeoisie—teachers [like François], tax-collectors, communal employees, shopkeepers, and artisans"[23] had become, according to Madeleine Rebérioux, the backbone "of a profound movement which permitted new social strata to have a voice in public life" (p. 42). These middle classes take on greater importance as a new social group in terms of their numerical growth, their prosperity, the growth of institutions that serve them, and their new key role as "support" of the Republic (p. 219).

Yet in spite of the historic rise of this middle class, in *Big Meaulnes* the middle-class narrator reproduces bourgeois consciousness not only in a fragmented and distorted way but as an empty form. In those earlier novels whose tradition *Big Meaulnes* inherits, the hero/narrator learns to defer immediate pleasure in order to prepare for future power, but in *Big Meaulnes* the narrative "subject" neither enjoys immediate pleasure nor prepares for future power. He simply mimes in imagination the whole process as an empty form.

In one chapter of *Big Meaulnes*, little François repeats the structure of Meaulnes's quest when he goes for the first time alone to the woods: "Here I am, I *imagine*, close to this mysterious happiness which Meaulnes had glimpsed one day. I have the whole morning in which to explore the border of the wood while my big brother has also gone off in search of discoveries" (p. 168, emphasis added).

Even to François's own mind, Meaulnes's experience has more reality than his own; and, unlike that of Meaulnes, his is a *conscious* imitation of the tradition of romance, accompanied by a conscious knowledge that it is a simulacrum and a game: "For the first time, here I am as well on the road to adventure. . . . I'm seeking something even more mysterious: that passageway you always hear about in books, the old obstructed road, whose entrance even the prince, exhausted from searching, couldn't find" (p. 168).

Whereas Meaulnes's adventure cannot become the matter of a book until after it is "ended," François's mini-adventure appears as simply the miming of an already written book. And whereas Meaulnes's adventure, because it is "real," must go through the entire process of expectation and disillusionment, François's mime short-circuits that whole process. It goes through all the motions, to arrive at the inevitable end even before the adventure of Meaulnes does the same many years later.

> But while I am thus growing intoxicated with hope, I suddenly come out into a kind of clearing, which turns out to be nothing but an old meadow. I have arrived without thinking about it at the far end of the Commune, which I had always imagined to be infinitely far away. . . . Never had we walked all the way there. We had sometimes heard of it as if about an extraordinary expedition: "he has been all the way to the guard's house! . . ."
>
> This time, I went all the way to Baladier's house, and I found nothing. (Pp. 168–69)

The banal "nothing" François finds at the end of his "adventure" is an empty foreshadowing of the cataclysmic nothing produced by the death of Yvonne. Unlike the death of Yvonne, this nothing is not produced, but is simply there, to mark that all François can do is repeat a form without its substance.

This discovery that the strange and distant paths of childhood are really close and familiar, that instead of leading to mysterious places, they lead back to home, and that disillusionment must accompany discovery, cannot fail to evoke Meaulnes's more famous contemporary Marcel in *In Search of Times Past.* Both novels, in the consciousness of preserving a disappearing world, express the ties between history and text as a will to cut those ties. But whereas *In Search of Times Past,* in addition to incorporating historical events into the text, discusses in its pages the necessity of cutting those ties, *Big Meaulnes* simply attempts to foreclose the historical and social context as if it did not exist.

This stronger will to shut literature off from history seems strange, since Proust tells the story of a social class whose role and way of life really are disappearing, while Alain-Fournier's narrator François comes from a class that is just rising to prominence. Yet he symbolizes that rise through forms of loss and emptiness. François even refers to his completion of the whole structure of the romantic quest as "my debacle" and "a great day of defeat" (p. 171).

While in the eighteenth and early nineteenth centuries "middle-class" culture expresses the bourgeoisie's real efforts to produce a new world and to wrest power and hegemony from the aristocracy, "middle-class" culture of the twentieth century expresses the aspirations of a class which never builds a new sociopolitical world, but acts to preserve the given world for another class, and to protect its hegemony. This "middle class" retires from history, even shuts out history, because it plays no active, shaping, creative role in historical production. Few of its members have real adventures, because their role is not to forge a new society, but to organize and preserve existing society.

This difference separating the two heroes of *Big Meaulnes* from the heroes of earlier romantic love novels concerns one of the major problems dealt with in this study: the way in which a sexual relation is enmeshed in the network of social relations and interacts with larger historic processes. As in other novels at other periods, the question of the role of women in love, in literature, and in society is a decisive one for this whole set of interconnections.

According to Jean-Paul Aron, the "institution of petty bourgeois life-styles" during the Third Republic required that women interiorize their identification with the home.[24] At the same time community *fêtes* and rites, presided over by rural women, disappear. These women thus lose an important, and perhaps their only, source of power.[25] In *Big Meaulnes* Alain-Fournier replaces the women presiding over powerful *fêtes* with the idealized image of the domestic housewife, guardian of order and limited horizons. These images include not only the mother Millie, but the idealized Yvonne herself, who is first presented as a figure in a domestic tableau. When Meaulnes first sees her, she is caring for children in a secluded room of the *Domaine* while the mysterious *fête* goes on outside.

All the images of Millie and Yvonne in this novel conform to what Anne Martin-Fuguier calls "a normative model of the woman as homebody," which developed between 1880 and 1914, and which proliferated in handbooks, magazines, and social science studies. Her primary duties, epitomized by Millie and Yvonne, are the propagation of order and domestic virtue.[26]

To understand why intimacy with such a heroine would kill romantic desire, one need only compare her to Balzac's Mme. de Mortsauf in his archetypal romantic love novel *The Lily in the Valley*. Although Mme. de Mortsauf's consciousness is nothing but the reflection of the hero's, she is presented as supremely intelligent, and as repressing with great effort powerful sexual desires. She remains, even through intimate conversations with the hero Felix, the symbol of all the mysterious infinitude he desires. This is because her mystery is her own repressed erotic desires, and it remains both concealed and revealed by the moral virtue superficially expressed in her words. She has to be intelligent and full of depth because from the confines of her domestic seclusion she is the invisible power that pushes Felix to participate in shaping society and in influencing the course of history. Alain-Fournier makes Yvonne the symbol of François's and Meaulnes's desires, and then has her encourage them to lead an orderly life, to stay at home, to be content with what they can find close by, not to run off to engage in any historic practice. Much less would she do so herself. The narrator's own fears and limits prevent him from imagining any other sort of heroine, and the moment he has Yvonne, his dream woman, speak, he wipes away all her infinite mystery. She is revealed as the perfect middle-class housewife, with her words of silly moralism, which conceal not the slightest repressed desire.

While sexual contact with Mme. de Mortsauf would have destroyed her in the mind of Felix as symbol of infinite spiritual desire, even conversation with Yvonne reveals that she is not "the bride of my soul"[27] that Mme. de Mortsauf was for Felix, but a facade without depth. The nineteenth-century romantic ideal of womanhood was unreal as the fantasm projected by a masculine ego to mirror itself. But the early-twentieth-century romantic ideal of womanhood as presented in *Big Meaulnes* is doubly unreal. Yvonne is the fantasy projection of a masculine ego, but, in addition, that ego has itself become an empty fantasm. As a result, the ideal she embodies is a pseudoideal. Antiheroines like Lady Dudley and Natalie de Manerville in *The Lily in the Valley* or Mathilde de La Mole in *The Red and the Black* are rejected by the heroes because they do not conform to the feminine romantic model. In *Big Meaulnes,* Yvonne is rejected by Meaulnes because she does. The model itself, as a reflection of the hero's ego ideal, can only show him an empty form.

In *The Lily in the Valley* Felix can love Mme. de Mortsauf only so long as their relation is not overtly sexual. Meaulnes can love Yvonne only so long as she remains a distant object of vision separated from him by an impenetrable barrier. Meaulnes first sees Yvonne, after he has arrived at the *Domaine* during the *fête* and has penetrated into the *Domaine*'s house through layers of corridors and rooms that lead him ever further away from daily experience. He finally arrives at a "silent room," a dining room filled with small children looking at "pictures." From this room, he is able to see into another, even more obscure and distant room.

> It was a sort of parlor; a woman or young girl with a brown cape thrown over her shoulders sat with her back to him, softly playing old dance melodies and songs. On a couch right beside her, six or seven well-behaved little boys and girls sitting in a row, as if they were in a picture . . . listened. From time to time one of them . . . would pass into the dining room: one of those who had finished looking at pictures would come and take his place.
>
> After that fête where . . . he himself had so crazily followed the big Pierrot, Meaulnes found himself plunged into the calmest happiness in the world. . . . It seemed a dream like his dream of earlier times. He could imagine to his heart's content that he was in his own home, married, enjoying a lovely evening, and

that his charming unknown figure playing the piano close to him was his wife. (Pp. 90–91)

Meaulnes is here plunged into the middle-class ideal of "calm happiness," firmly sheltered from the "crazy agitation" of the pseudo-*fête*. The goal of his quest turns out to be not the fulfillment of infinite desire, but a social conformism, keeping to the norms of limited middle-class domesticity—except in the form of a dream. The children who pass back and forth in the scene from looking at images in the nearer room to becoming part of an image in the further room symbolize François's and Meaulnes's desire to cross to the *other side* of the barrier but yet to experience that *other side* not as it is lived in experience but as it is seen from *this side*. This is of course impossible. Without the possibility of lived historic practice, this kind of love between the sexes can only be an alienated object of representation, something to look at from a safe distance, nothing to risk living.

When Meaulnes and Yvonne do make the mistake of trying to transform this image into a lived experience, their married life reveals to François the reality underlying the tranquil middle-class ideal. Seeing Yvonne run out to find Meaulnes when he goes to answer Frantz on their wedding night, François is "made to think of" the violence and chaos that always threatened to disrupt the fragile order of this tranquility: "I have seen in Paris in poor quarters a couple believed by their neighbors to be happy, united, honest, suddenly descend into the street, separated by policemen who had to intervene in the battle. The scandal had broken out unexpectedly" (p. 258). The scene of Yvonne and Meaulnes on their wedding night reminds François of this urban, lower-class sordidness, except that the scandal of domestic disintegration is no longer safely outside the middle class. It lies coiled in the very heart of Meaulnes's dream of "the calmest happiness in the world." Meaulnes escapes with Frantz, leaving Yvonne, who blames herself, to die so that the pseudoideal is protected.

The novel's narrative structure, in presenting itself as a reconstruction of secondhand materials, in replacing historic practice with emptiness, in setting irreversible barriers between language and the scenes it represents, is connected to another related historic development of the Third Republic. It is during this period that consumerism begins to play its modern role in the economy and in shaping people's consciousness. And it also plays a role in the novel. The narrator makes Meaulnes's adventures, romantic love, and Yvonne herself appear as objects of consumption, i.e., as labels emptied of lived substance.

The *gilet* sign once again provides a model for revealing how practice is transformed into consumerism.[28] François tells us: "It was a waistcoat of whimsical charm, such as the young men who danced with our grandmothers must have worn at the balls of 1830" (p. 49). But a few pages earlier in the narration, he had already described his grandparents in such a way as to leave no doubt that the men who danced with his grandmother in 1830 could never have worn such a garment: "My old grandfather, looking like a big, bushy Gascon shepherd, his feet heavily planted in front of him, his stick against his legs . . . was there. He was approving . . . what my grandmother was saying about her trip and her chickens and her neighbors and the peasants who hadn't paid their rent. But I was no longer with them" (p. 37). François here sees the old peasant world represented by his grandparents not with nostalgia, but with impatience, as a coarse obstacle blocking a more idealized version of the past. "This marquis' waistcoat" (p. 50) which Frantz had bought, and which functions as a sign, erases that image of the peasant past and substitutes a freshly created object of nostalgia, like the nostalgia objects one can buy in stores today. It thus provides a prototype for those models of discourse appearing in *Big Meaulnes*, which, we have seen, are neither produced nor derived from the logic of the total system of exchange. They express the ideals of a class which neither produces use values nor controls and masters the system of exchange, but which supports those practices through commercial consumption.

Yet *Big Meaulnes* as a text is not itself an object of consumption, for how then could it have so inspired Simone de Beauvoir and many of her friends, made them reflect more deeply upon themselves, and even provided the model for de Beauvoir's first novel-writing practice?[29] As opposed to commercially produced or second-rate novels, *Big Meaulnes* truly produces the original and self-reflecting textual tissue that has been analyzed earlier in this chapter. There are in the novel two conflicting models of narrative discourse: one the reconstruction of something secondhand; the other original and productive. It is in the context of this productive aspect that the secondhand, consumerist aspect becomes so disturbing.

The coexistence of two conflicting models of narrative discourse in *Big Meaulnes* reflects the structure of a modern middle-class ideology which insists that there should be "between school time [or work time] and recreation time that hard demarcation" (p. 139). While the middle class does produce culture, its mind erects a strong barrier between aesthetic culture on the one hand and production, exchange, politics, and social power on the other. Yet culture and socioeconomic power work in and through each other. Earlier narratives like *Tristan and Isolde, The Red and the Black,* and *Shirley* show that romantic love originated and grew in a search to connect these fragments. In *Big Meaulnes* the attempt to erect a barrier between economics-politics-history-production on the one hand and love-art-culture on the other becomes the attempt to erect a barrier between the aesthetic text and the social history which produces it and works in it. As a result history appears in the text as a barrier internal to the text itself between a secondhand discourse imitating a dead tradition, and a potently original and productive discourse that incorporates the romantic tradition into a living culture.

Chapter 7

Sex and the Working Woman in the Age of Electronics

Harlequin Romances

Big Meaulnes, written when consumer culture was first coming into its own, turns romantic love into a product of consumption, but its text still maintains a productive literary density. Harlequin Enterprises and its imitators in the romance industry went much further in this respect, transforming romantic love literature itself into a consumer product. Yet in spite of this, the contradiction traditionally found in romantic narrative between the disruptive passions of feminine desire and the rationalizing forms that repress them is in Harlequin Romances just as intense, if not more intense, than in *Tristan and Isolde, Manon Lescaut, The Red and the Black, Shirley,* or *Big Meaulnes;* but it now works at a different level of the narrative. In the earlier narratives it appeared as a struggle between different discourses and partial discourses in the text. In Harlequin Romances it appears as a struggle between the form of the romances and the raw material on which that form works.

While in *Big Meaulnes* this contradiction seemed resolved with the victory of rationalist form over disruptive desire, Harlequin Romances once again pit desires for revolt against an order that represses an autonomous feminine voice. Yet at the same time the romances recuperate that revolt so that it serves the interests of corporate consumerism. In fact, romance narrative has been in every way absorbed into corporate marketing so that like any consumer product it is an international phenomenon. One can no longer speak of French romances, or English romances, or American romances, but simply of mass-market romances which are translated and reproduced to sell all over the world.[1]

Harlequin advertises itself as the "world's no. 1 publisher of romance fiction!" Like its imitators and rivals, Simon and Shuster's Silhouette series (recently bought out by Harlequin), Dell's Candlelight Ecstasy, Berkley's Second Chance at Love, and Bantam's Loveswept, it turns out on its giant, computerized printing presses several series of uniformly jacketed and uniformly written romantic narratives per month. Formerly a moderately successful Canadian publishing house, in 1971 it hired Lawrence Heisley, a Proctor and Gamble marketing man, as its new president. He turned feminine romantic love into superprofits for his then all-male board of directors by transferring to the sale of books the techniques used to sell detergent to housewives. By turning love into a consumer product, Harlequin increased its net earnings from $110,000 in 1970 to over $21 million by 1980.

But packaging alone cannot account for the loyalty of fourteen million readers. The novels' flyleaf assures readers that "no one touches the heart of a woman quite like Harlequin," and marketing statistics—188 million books sold in 1980—support this claim.[2] What exactly is the secret to a woman's heart that Harlequin has learned, and how has it turned this knowledge into profits for itself?

Secrets of a Woman's Heart

The central conflict of the endlessly repeated Harlequin plot arises from the ever-changing, unresolved crux of many contemporary women's lives. Focusing on the juncture between their sexual, emotional needs on the one hand and their needs concerning work relations on the other, it involves both their deepest, most private, most intimate feelings, and at the same time their very broad relations to the process of social history. Impressive analyses by Ann Snitow, Tania Modleski, and Janice Radway[3] have explained the popularity of mass-market romance by examining how they respond to women's changed values or by analyzing technological and marketing changes in the book industry. But they have not talked about how these two changes have acted for the last ten or fifteen years as interdependent and contradictory elements of a single but complex social process.

Moreover, in the past couple of years, since Snitow and Modleski wrote their studies, the romance industry has been undergoing an increasingly accelerated process of change. Given the fact that their heroines' stories increasingly join the personal, sexual relations of private life to the work relations of the market place, we might ask what in the Harlequin formula responds to new needs of women as a result of recent profound changes in both their domestic and paid labor situations, and how that formula might change in the future.

As Harlequin Romances have become more popular, more and more of their heroines have jobs. Yet these rebellious working heroines have more subversive desires than simply to join the labor force: they are reacting to the limits of a sterile, harsh, alienating, fragmented work world itself. In spite of some fairly glamorous jobs, the working Harlequin heroines, melodramatically engaged in defiant struggles with their heroes, who are usually their bosses, demand from them and their world two additional changes in their situation. First, the heroine's struggle against her hero is, by the very fact that she struggles so intensely because she finds the power he represents so irresistible, also a struggle *for* something, which she calls "love," but beyond that does not define any further. What she wants from the hero is recognition of herself as a unique, exceptional individual. She demands that *in addition* to admiring her accomplishments and admitting his strong sexual need for her, he must also recognize her as a subject, or recognize her from her own point of view. Only from someone representing the power of the hero could such recognition serve its purpose.

In order for that to happen, a second change must occur in the romances. What the heroines seek is not simply to succeed in the man's world but to change that world. An analysis of the romances will show that on an implicit level they seek not so much an improved life within the possibilities of this social structure, as a different social structure. The very facts that in an increasing number of romances from 1981 to 1984 the hero is both boss and lover, that the world of work and business is romanticized and eroticized, and that in it love flourishes suggest that the Harlequin heroines seek an end to the division between the domestic world of love and sentiment and the public world of work and business.

Since in Harlequin the struggle to gain recognition for a deep feminine self merges with a struggle, however implicit or utopian, to create a new, more integrated world, a reading of these romances uncovers a certain power possessed by even formulaic narratives. Because they cannot help but recount a woman's life all of a piece, they may be able to reveal certain insights about women's lives and women's desires that escape empirical science. These romance narratives show us that an individual woman's need to be recognized in her own sense of self and the need to change a more global social structure are interdependent.

In *Loving with a Vengeance: Mass-Produced Fantasies for Women,* Tania Modleski says: "In Harlequin Romances, the need of women to find meaning and pleasure in activities which are not wholly male-centered such as work or artistic creation is generally scoffed at" (p. 113). But in the past few years that has changed. While in the mid-seventies the average Harlequin heroine was either just emerging from home, or was a secretary or nurse who quit her unrewarding job at marriage, by the late seventies many Harlequin heroines had unusual and interesting, if not bizarre, careers. More and more frequently both hero and heroine started taking the heroine's job or creative activity seriously.

Almost never images of passive femininity, the heroines of the late seventies are active, intelligent, and capable of at least economic independence. Nicole, in *Across the Great Divide*, is a dedicated and competent swimming coach; Anna in *Battle with Desire* is an internationally known violinist at the age of twenty-two; Kerry in *The Dividing Line*, also twenty-two, is on the board of directors of a prestigious department store. Furthermore, the hero often gives moral support to the heroine in her career, and intends to continue supporting her career aspirations after their marriage.[4]

By the early eighties, the heroines' careers go beyond the wildest dreams of the most ambitious contemporary career woman and often become the selling point that distinguishes one romance from another. As one example, Danni in *Race for Revenge* is about to "succeed triumphantly in the male dominated world of motor racing,"[5] and Karla Mortley in Candlelight Romance's *Game Plan* "joins the rugged New York Flyers as a ballet trainer" only to find that "the womanizing quarterback MacGregor proves hard to tackle."[6] In 1984 Harlequin added to its line a new, more sophisticated series, *Harlequin Temptation*, where the hero worries that the heroine will place her career before him. In the romances of the mid-eighties the careers range from the banal, like movie actresses and famous pop singers, to the unique, like engineering Ph.D. Frankie Warburton in *Love Circuits*, who falls in love with the electronics heir who contracts for her services as a computer consultant. More than one heroine is an advertising executive who falls in love with her client. University editorial assistant Liza Manchester in *Public Affair* is an "outspoken member of Graham University's feminist community" who falls in love with Professor Scott Harburton. And—inevitably—Garbriella Constant in *By Any Other Name* is a best-selling romance writer who falls in love with her publisher.[7]

While the hero of these romances is not always the heroine's boss, he most often either is the boss or holds a position of economic or professional power over the heroine. More important, as the advertising brochure for the new *Harlequin Temptation* series demonstrates, the boss figure remains the prototype for the Harlequin hero. Promising to let us experience "the passionate torment of a woman torn between two loves . . . the siren call of a career . . . the magnetic advances of an impetuous employer," it advertises its flagship novel of the new series, *First Impressions,* by saying: "Tracy Dexter couldn't deny her attraction to her new boss."[8]

Since in Harlequin Romances plot, characters, style, and erotic scenes are determined by formula, freedom to vary the heroine's job gives an author one of the few avenues for bringing originality, individuality, and creative freedom into a romance. An unusual job offers compositional opportunities for an unusual setting and unusual conflicts between the hero and the heroine. But the job situation also serves a deeper purpose. Beyond showing the uncanny ability of mass culture to ingest any kind of social, economic, or cultural historic change in women's lives, these heroines with their fabulous jobs might help to explain why women respond to romance so much more massively than to other mass-market reading. New Right how-to books exhort their readers to be "real" women by staying home to protect the family; liberal how-to books, such as *The Cinderella Complex,* exhort women to cease waiting to "be *part* of somebody else" and "to get into the driver's seat" of "the man's world";[9] and women's magazines claim to show readers how to excel in each separate segment—sex, work, family, emotion—of their madly disarticulated, schizophrenic lives. Supermarket romances, alone among mass-market literature, focus on the conflictual relations among the segments.

Women's Work/Women's Culture

The same socioeconomic changes of the 1960s and 1970s that created a new kind of working woman also created the conditions for Harlequin's commercial success. These are, according to Harry Braverman in *Labor and Monopoly Capital,* the restructuring of business into huge international conglomerates; the "extraordinary growth of commercial concerns" (like Harlequin) in comparison with production; and along with this the extraordinary explosion of bureaucracy and office work with its systems management, computerization, and assembly-line processing of paper.[10] These conditions include new categories of work, and, occurring around 1960, "the creation of a new class of workers," low-paid clerical workers, overwhelmingly female. According to Roslyn L. Feldberg and Evelyn Nakano Glenn, between 1960 and 1980, employment in clerical and kindred occupations doubled. They cite dramatic growth in work categories created by the new technology, and also by the business expansion that Braverman describes.[11]

The women who work for these huge conglomerates and bureaucracies in clerical positions, in service positions, and as assemblers of the new electronic machinery, as well as the women whose shopping, banking, education, medical care, and welfare payments have been changed by these new developments, constitute a large part of the readership of Harlequin Romances. And the musician, painter, poet, coach, car racer, Olympic athlete, photographer, executive heroines of the romances, with their glamorous jobs, are these readers' idealized alter egos. Although readers are well aware that the romances are unreal fantasies, their passionate attachment to the genre could not be explained without an intense identification with the heroine on the level of ego ideal.

Between 40 and 60 percent of the mass-market romance readership works outside the home.[12] The assumption has been that these romances contain housewifely fantasies, but if that is so then why do so many of them revolve around work situations, however glamorized? Among the many possible reasons for this the most obvious is that countless statistics show that almost all of these readers can expect to work sometime in their lives, moving in and out of the labor market. Moreover, a good number of them can expect to be single mothers for at least part of their lives. But these fantasies involving work situations might call into question a common categorization of women into working women on the one hand and housewives on the other. The content of Harlequins suggest that the readers, like the heroines, do not compartmentalize their lives in this way, becoming different people when they go to work. While the immediate concerns caused by workplace or home may be different, women's deeper abiding concerns remain the same, whether at home or on the job. To draw a strong division between working women and housewives comes perhaps from applying to women a male model. For the average man work and home really are very different. At work he must accept the power of his employer, while at home he is master of his family and finds relaxation. The average woman, on the other hand, finds herself contending with a masculine power both at home and at work. By combining the sexual domination of a lover and the economic domination of an employer in the same masculine figure, Harlequins draw attention to the specificity of the contemporary feminine situation.

In a sensitive study that explains the popularity of mass-market romances by interviewing a group of readers from one bookstore, Janice Radway says that women report they read the romances for relaxation and escape. "When asked to specify what they are fleeing from," she says, "they invariably mention the 'pressures' and 'tensions' they experience as wives and mothers" (p. 60). A group of working women I spoke to also said they read the romances to escape. But the escape portrayed in what are referred to in the trade as "career romances" also soothe job-related pressures and tensions.

The heroines' fantasy dilemmas compensate for those elements of women's work in the clerical factories, and for that matter in any factories, that critics of job automation find most oppressive. A reading of Harlequin Romances in the context of these critiques yields insights into the heroines' (and perhaps the authors' and readers') conflicts, their grievances against their living, working, and sexual situations, and the intensity with which they feel these grievances, but also into the extent to which the romances and their authors have adopted the basic corporate structure of present work relations as the invisible and unchallenged framework of a worldview.

Two themes of revolt and fantasy escape that run most strongly through the romances concern the depersonalization of the cybernetic world and the powerlessness of the feminine individual within it.

Surprisingly enough, the heroine's lack of power and freedom corresponds in some very precise ways to what sociologists have found out about the worker's lack of power and freedom in the computerized and bureaucratized workplace. According to Braverman, contemporary clerical workers, like low-paid factory workers, suffer from a lack of control over the work process, over the social use to which products will be put, over their own mental processes, and even over their own bodies. The assembly-line structuring of clerical work, says Braverman, results from applying to office work the techniques of Taylorism, which factory owners began using in the 1920s and 1930s to gain maximum efficiency by breaking down the unity of the labor process into its smallest discrete elements. While Taylorization yields greater productivity, its effects on the worker, whose tasks and bodily movements are also broken down to their smallest elements, are devastating.

With every movement of the office worker or lower-paid assembler controlled for maximum efficiency, and every moment of her day accounted for, she has lost all decision-making power not only over the products she is making, but even over her own bodily movements and the minutest scheduling of her own time. Braverman talks about clerical workers feeling "shackled" (p. 61) and quotes a vice president of an insurance company as saying of a room full of keypunchers: " 'All they lack is a chain!' " (p. 61). Ida Russakoff Hoos, in *Automation in the Office,* reports interviewing a supervisor who described keypunchers keeping supplies of tranquilizers in their desks and feeling "frozen."[13] And Ellen Cantarow cites findings of "appalling rates of coronary heart disease in women clerical workers,"[14] as a result of lack of control.

The force of the Harlequin Romance comes from its ability to combine, often in the same image, the heroine's fantasy escape from these restraints and her idealized, romanticized, and eroticized compliance with them. It does this through diverse types of story elements, which are remarkably consistent from romance to romance. A first and most simple compensation of the readers' situation is that by contrast to the jobs most working readers have, the jobs of Harlequin heroines, while greatly varied, almost always have in common that the work is meaningful in itself, challenging, has a direct effect on the well-being of other people, is a craft that requires skill or talent, and gains recognition for a job well done. A second, slightly more complex compensatory fantasy is that Harlequin heroines do fight for, and win, control over their jobs and a great deal of freedom.

A central, and one of the most attractive, compensations offered by Harlequin is that the romances respond to the depersonalization of the Harlequin reader's life, not only in her workplace, but in her shopping, her banking, in her relations to government, to school, and to all the services she now obtains from giant, faceless bureaucracies, which make her feel, as Tessa in *The Enchanted Island* thinks, "like a small, impersonal cog in a machine."[15] The relations between the heroines and their bosses may be love/hate relations, but they are intensely intimate. Although decisions about how the reader spends her time in the corporate workplace are made by real men, she never sees them. In the conglomerate the real decision makers may be in another state or another country, and in terms of the corporate hierarchy, they are in another universe. They are so removed from the secretary or assembler as to seem disembodied gods. In the world of Harlequin, the god descends from the executive suite and comes to her.

But in addition to this direct compensation for the depersonalized relations of the corporate world, the romances also idealize the working reader's sense that she herself has been reduced to one more interchangeable part of the office's "integrated systems." In *Battle with Desire* Gareth the hero, who is also violinist Anna's conductor, tells her: "'You and I together, Anna, will give them a performance they'll never forget. . . . the music will be a prelude to our love'" (p. 157). Yet Anna is hurt and asks herself: "But was it love for herself, or because she had been the instrument of such superb music?" While Anna's position is a highly idealized fantasy, it raises the same conflict experienced by those women in Hoos's study who feel their bosses regard them (if at all!) as an instrument or as part of the machinery.

A fourth and still more complex compensation directly concerns the theme of power. In the romances the heroine fights ardently against the power the hero has over her. Since the power figure represents both her lover and her boss, this power relation between one man and one woman reverberates on a larger network of social relations, all structured according to inequality of power. Thus the boss/lover can become an analogy for other men in the reader's life, such as her husband. The heroines reject the dependence or submissiveness that is most often forced upon their resisting spirit: Nicole in *Across the Great Divide* finds in her new boss Lang "something too suggestive of a rugged relentlessness . . . that she just couldn't bring herself to suffer meekly and which set her on the offensive" (p. 30). In her own mind, she rejects arrogant hierarchies, and when the board of the swim club threatens to fire her, "she was determined not to submit tamely. If she was going down, she would be going down fighting!" (p. 165).

In the most complex and contradictory of story elements, the romances combine in one image an escape from the "frozen" feeling of the working reader and an eroticized acquiescence to it. The heroine's struggle-filled, stormy relationship with the hero involves a strange combination of tempestuous physical movement and physical restraint by the hero. In one of dozens of examples, Nicole struggles with Lang.

> "I hate the lot of you!" she sobbed brokenly. "And don't touch me!" trying to jerk out of his hold. "You're all a load of two faced liars, only interested in your own egotistical aims." Then, when he didn't release her, "I said don't *touch* me!" as she began pummelling violently at his broad chest.
>
> "For God's sake, Nicky!" Lang gripped her wrists grimly in one hand and wrenched open the car door with the other. "Get in," he muttered, and bundled her flailing figure on to the back seat. Slamming the door behind them, he pinned her helplessly to his muscular form until she had exhausted her struggles and consented to stay there, crying quietly. (*Across the Great Divide*, p. 140)

The "shackles" of the office or factory job are on the one hand compensated for by vigorous movement, on the other hand romanticized and eroticized. The hero restrains the heroine not out of an impersonal desire for efficiency but out of a very personal desire to have her respond to him. He restrains her in an attempt to control her anger, to arouse her sexually, to fulfill his burning desire to have her confess her feelings for him, or all three. The heroine's anxiety no longer has its source in the cold, nagging, unpleasant fear that her boss will fire her if she rebels (or that her husband will reject her or worse) but in the warm, seductive, obsessive fear that she will not be able to resist his potent sexual magnetism, especially since he goes to considerable effort to create intimate situations where he can exert it. Transformed by the romances, the worker's restraint becomes on the one hand intermittent, and on the other hand emotionally and sexually gratifying. Instead of having to take tranquilizers to repress her internalized rage, like the office workers in Hoos's study and Cantarow's article, the Harlequin heroine is privileged to vent it violently and directly against her restrainer, even while this restraint takes an idealized form.

This strange mingling of protest and acquiescence to the situation of many contemporary women makes the Harlequin Romances so seductive and so contradictory. On the one hand, the heroine is empowered to revolt without risking masculine rejection, since the hero desires her more the angrier she becomes, but on the other hand, the romances also sexualize her impotence. This particular combination of elements intensifies our emotional involvement with a story that both arouses and nullifies the very subversive impulses that attracted us to it in the first place.

Changing Times, Changing Conflict

Harlequin's double message is all the more potent in that the heroine's conflict is also double. At stake for her in the romances that put the work situation at the center of the plot is both her social identity and the deepest core of her feminine self. A surprising number of Harlequins employ the same vocabulary to describe the inner conflict of the heroine as she struggles against the hero on his own grounds where he has all the weapons. His main weapon in this idealized world is his powerful sexual attraction, her main weakness her susceptibility to that attraction, which quickly becomes total love. Her struggle aims to prevent the hero from exploiting her love for his own sexual desires, and the conflict this struggle awakens in her is described by the key words "humiliation" and "pride." Nicole in *Across the Great Divide* finds that

> the most galling part of the whole episode had been her un-
> qualified surrender to Lang's lovemaking. That she should have
> so readily submitted—no, welcomed it was far more honest, she
> confessed painfully—was something she found impossible to ac-
> cept. The only thought left to salvage at least some of her *pride*

being the knowledge that Lang wasn't aware how deeply her feelings were involved. Her *humiliation* was bad enough now, but it would have known no bounds if she had inadvertently revealed how she really felt about him. (P. 144, emphasis added)

In *Stormy Affair* Amber faces the same problem.

She could not say: "I would love to live here and marry you but only if you say you love me. . . . " At least she still had sufficient *pride* to avoid the *humiliation* such a statement would cause.[16]

Through the heroine's impossible choice between two painful and destructive alternatives, summed up by the terms *humiliation* and *pride*, Harlequin Romances call attention to a feminine character structure that differs from the masculine one. Both Radway and Snitow have discussed this feminine character structure in the Harlequin heroine, and both have relied on Nancy Chodorow's theory to analyze it.[17] According to Chodorow, capitalist-patriarchal family structure and child-rearing practices produce in boys more strongly defined and closed-off ego boundaries, and in girls more fluid ego boundaries, so that men tend to define themselves as a separate, self-sufficient entity, while women tend to define themselves in terms of their relation to other people. Unable to adopt a rocklike, closed, thinglike self like the one the hero seems to possess, the Harlequin heroine's self alternates, until the end of the romance, between two forms of destruction: "humiliation," which signals a dissolution of her self into the masculine self, and "pride," a self-control that shrivels up her self by denying its needs and desires. Solution: the hero must recognize and adopt the relational, feminine form of the self.

This difference in character structure between men and women, which Harlequins emphasize as the cause of the heroine's problems, is inherited from the Industrial Revolution. With the separation of work from home, women were socialized to immerse themselves in the intense emotional world of the domestic sphere. Self-perpetuating family practices made that socialization seem like a "natural" feminine character. Now with the cybernetic revolution, women must also, like men, make their way in the rationalistic world of business, but they take with them the emotional makeup they have inherited from the past. They do not have, and in many cases do not want to have, a harder, more competitive, success-oriented emotional equipment with which men have been socialized in order to succeed, or even simply to survive.

If Harlequin heroines' character structure is inherited from the Industrial Revolution, their narrative structure is also inherited from one of the most prominent literary genres of the Industrial Revolution, the romantic novel. While Sally Mitchell and Tania Modleski have traced the genealogy of Harlequin Romances back to forms of nineteenth-century popular fiction such as seduction novels, historical romances, penny magazine aristocratic romances, and gothic novels,[18] the quest for self-fulfillment through love of the heroes and heroines of nineteenth-century high romanticism has also found a twentieth-century refuge in contemporary mass-market romances. As romance writer Louella Nelson told me of her romance *Freedom's Fortune:* "This book is about a woman's quest for courage and self-worth."

The inner conflict of the Harlequin heroines is a more explicitly sexualized version of feminine conflicts analyzed by authors writing during the Industrial Revolution, like Stendhal or Charlotte Brontë, but places it in a new sociohistoric context. In Stendhal's *The Red and the Black,* Julien Sorel lives a divided, compartmentalized life, because he must divide his activities between the domestic world and the economic/political world, and so must divide and compartmentalize his emotions between cold calculation and spontaneous passion. Since his beloved, Mme. de Rênal, is confined to the domestic sphere of society, it becomes a pseudo-whole for her so that her emotional life is partial, relating only to the domestic sphere, but intensely unified.

This sexual difference is also a subject of conversation between the heroines of Brontë's *Shirley,* where Caroline Helstone says: "Shirley, men and women are so different: they are in such a different position. Women have so few things to think about—men so many: you may have a friendship with a man while he is almost indifferent to you. Much of what cheers your life may be dependent on him, while not a feeling or interest of moment in his eyes may have reference to you." Shirley answers: "Caroline, . . . don't you wish you had a profession—a trade?"[19]

The Harlequin heroines do have a trade—and a lot of things to think about—but they still resemble the Stendhalian and Brontëan heroines in that for them sexual sensation, feelings of love, and rational thought are all intimately connected. They cannot be compartmentalized and sealed off from each other. When these heroines fall in love, they think about love and their lover all the time. The heroes of Harlequin Romances, like the heroes of *The Red and the Black* and of *Shirley,* are emotionally divided between the world of love and the world of business and public affairs, and therefore fragmented in their psychic structure. For them, or so it seems to the heroine, sex is divorced from other feelings, and love from other areas of their life. It seems that whenever he wills it, the hero can simply shut her image off and think about other things.

From this fragmentation, the Harlequin heroes, like their nineteenth-century brothers Julien Sorel and Robert Moore, draw their strength for success in the world. But since the Harlequin heroines must now also survive alone in that world, they can only, as Nicole says, attempt to conceal their feelings, try to pretend to be like the hero. But the heroine's wholeness, which is also her weakness, means that her outer appearance and actions cannot but reflect her inner emotions. The heroines are transparent where the heroes are opaque.

In fact the heroine frequently suspects until the end of the novel that the hero has no tender feelings under his harsh surface, and that therefore he does not have to exhaust all his energy in the fight for self-control the way she does. In *Stormy Affair,* for instance, Amber thinks that "she must pull herself together and not let Hamed Ben Slouma see that he in any way affected her" (p. 25). But "Hamed with his keen perception knew exactly what was going on in her mind. . . . 'Perhaps your desires were greater than mine, or do you think it could be that I have more self-control? You're very *transparent,* my charming one'" (p. 100, emphasis added). The effect of all these differences between the hero and the heroine is to increase the hero's power over this outsider in his world. But even this conflict contains within it wish-fulfilling compensations. If Ben Slouma finds Amber transparent, at least he cares enough to observe her transparency and is interested enough in her to notice what goes on inside her. If the heroine's anger is impotent, at least she has the chance to vent it with great rage at its rightful target, and at least he stays around to listen to it, even, as in the case of Tessa's boss Andrew, "with interest" (*The Enchanted Island,* p. 157).

Utopian and formulaic as they are, in Harlequin Romances the heroine's struggle and conflict serve to overcome something more than a merely psychological passivity or a role that a woman could simply choose to play or not to play. Although its roots in a total social situation are not so clearly shown as in the novels of Stendhal and Brontë, the Harlequin heroine's conflict is shown to be a very real lack of power to be herself in relations controlled by others. Her very activity and anger are signs of her impotence in the face of the more powerful male. Thus Nicole "seethed impotently" (*Across the Great Divide*, p. 99), and Debra "tried to control the rage and humiliation she was feeling," while Jordan's "composure wasn't disturbed by [Kathleen's] burst of anger."[20]

Like their nineteenth-century predecessors Jane Eyre, Caroline Helstone, and Lucy Snow, the Harlequin heroines seek recognition as a subject in her own right with her own point of view. And also like these earlier heroines, Harlequin heroines find that this recognition must take a different form than that sought by romantic heroes. Stendhal's hero Julien Sorel, in achieving this recognition, becomes closed in on himself, static, and self-sufficient as an absolute totality. Brontë rejects this form of the self and the narcissistic form of love it demands, and seeks fulfillment for a form of the self which is essentially fluid, essentially changing, and essentially involved in a dynamic, living network of intimate relations with others.

Like the Brontë heroines, although in a less reflective and more narcissistic way,[21] the Harlequin heroines find that women in our society are already endowed with this relational form of the self, but that it never achieves recognition or fulfillment. The cause of pain and obscurity rather than success, it in fact tends to get lost altogether in a relation with the hero's harder, closed self, and to merge into his. This is what Anna finds in *Battle with Desire:* "Anna knew she mustn't give in. . . . And it wasn't getting any easier to resist, the urge to fight was melting away, so she made one final attempt at self-respect" (p. 19). What really melts here are the boundaries of the heroine's personhood and her sense of individuality as she loses herself in the other. Solution: the hero must in the end adopt the feminine form of the self, recognize it as valid, and give the heroine the same tender devotion she gives to him.

The genius of the Harlequin Romances is to combine the struggle for the recognition of feminine selfhood and the struggle to make the work world a home for that self. As the cover blurb of *The Dividing Line* tells us of Kerry and Ross who have inherited interests in a department store: "She liked old fashioned friendliness and service. He was all for modern impersonal efficiency. Between them, Sinclair's was becoming a battle ground." Even the idealized form of Kerry's angry struggle against Ross, and violinist Anna's questioning resentment against Garth, suggest a need to go beyond an analysis like that in *Hearth and Home: Images of Women in the Mass Media,* edited by Gaye Tuchman, Arlene Kaplan Daniels, and James Benet. The book criticizes the mass media image of women for implying that "her fate and her happiness rest with a man, not with participation in the labor force,"[22] but it would be impoverishing even the impoverished romances to say that their heroines really want both. They want so much more besides. Not content with Helen Gurley Brown's rationalistic advice to "have it all," they don't want it the way it is now; they want the world of labor to change so that women can find happiness there, and they want men to change so that men will just as much find *their* happiness with women.

Hearth and Home sees hope for equality in "economically productive women who insist on the abandonment of old prejudices and discriminatory behaviors" (p. 4). But Harlequin Romances suggest women who insist on the abandonment of the present structures of economic production themselves, because those structures force women to give up their values, their ethos, and even their particular sense of self for success, or, more likely, for mere survival. The vastly popular Harlequin Romances implicitly and potentially pose a demand for profound structural transformations of the total social world we inhabit. And like their romantic forebears, the heroines desire that this new world be not just the same old world improved, but a different, better world. The problem is that Harlequin Enterprises, having learned these secrets to a woman's heart, exploited them by turning them into marketable formulae, which divorced the conflicts from their causes and cut off the path toward reflecting upon any realistic solutions.

Romantic Aspirations—Rationalized Form

In doing the needed work of finding out from readers themselves their reasons for reading romances, Radway says: "We would do well not to condescend to romance readers as hopeless traditionalists who are recalcitrant in their refusal to acknowledge the emotional costs of patriarchy. We must begin to recognize that romance reading is fueled by dissatisfaction and disaffection" ("Women Read the Romance," p. 68). Yet there is a crucial distinction to be made between dismissing the very justifiable fantasies and desires of Harlequin readers or the equally admirable achievements of romance writers, and criticizing a multinational publishing corporation that exploits those fantasies and achievements. As Radway says: "romance reading might actually elicit and then deflect protest about the character of patriarchal social relations" (*Reading the Romance,* p. 157). In this she echoes Modleski's observation that "their enormous and continuing popularity . . . suggests that they speak to very real problems and tensions in women's lives," but that the texts arouse subversive anxieties and desires, and then "work to neutralize them" (pp. 14 and 30).

The methods of editing, producing, marketing, and distributing Harlequin Romances are part and parcel of the depersonalized, standardized, mechanistic conglomerate system that the Harlequin heroines oppose. Harlequin heroines seek interconnectedness in the social, sexual, and economic world as a whole. Yet their very search is contained in a static, thinglike, literary structure, which denies their quest and turns it into its opposite.

A Harlequin reader enters into a relation not only with a text and an individual author, but also with the publisher. This relation, although distant and impersonal, remains a patriarchal relation of power. We are used to thinking of a publisher as a mediator between the readers and a book written by an individual author, but Harlequin has changed this. While Harlequin Romances are studied in very few university literature classes, Harlequin Enterprises is studied in management classes as a sterling example of successful business practices that students should learn to emulate. According to business professor Peter Killing, Harlequin's success is due precisely to its doing away with the reader-text and reader-author relation.

> Harlequin's formula was fundamentally different from that of traditional publishers: content, length, artwork, size, basic formats, and print, were all standardized. Each book was not a new product, but rather an addition to a clearly defined product line. The consequences of this uniformity were significant. The reader was buying a *Harlequin novel,* rather than a book of a certain title by a particular author. . . . There was no need to make decisions about layouts, artwork, or cover design. The standard-

ized size made warehousing and distribution more efficient. Employees hired from mass-marketing companies such as Proctor and Gamble had skills and aptitudes which led them to do well at Harlequin.[23]

Harlequin thought of everything—except the readers, the authors, and the creative freedom which has traditionally been the cornerstone of literature in Western culture. This publishing giant molded romantic aspirations into superrationalist forms of communication—the very antithesis of the readers' desires.

It is not the idealization of marriage in the romances, nor any specific content, that neutralizes their challenges to patriarchal ideology, but rather the form of the romances, and the form of communication Harlequin sets up between the corporate giant and the readers. Like the Stendhalian and Brontëan heroes and heroines, whose desires for sublime sexual communion were a protest against the rationalizing forces of the Industrial Revolution, the Harlequin Romances both protest against and compensate for their readers' dissatisfaction with the Taylorization of their lives as workers and consumers of goods and services. But when Harlequin instituted its new methods, the romantic quest and the sublime sexual communion were themselves Taylorized, so that the apparent escape from a depersonalized, coldly compartmentalized world led the reader right back into it.

Yet the effects of mass-market romance on its consumers are just as undecidable as were the effects of mass production for consumers in the nineteenth century. While industrialization increased alienation and exploitation, it also afforded many people some new kinds of freedom, broader horizons, and new opportunities. Likewise with mass-market romances: Does the romance industry cynically exploit its readers' deepest aspirations and seduce them into classic forms of addiction for the sake of profit? Or does it give readers greater access to justifiable fantasies? Similarly, does it exploit authors, making them write according to a formula? Or does it give hundreds of women opportunities previously unheard of to earn an independent living by writing fiction? The answer to all these contradictory questions is yes; and with the changes now promising to transform the romance industry, the contradictions are intensifying.

Harlequin's new marketing methods in the 1970s meant that romantic aspirations were reduced to the rational distillation of a formula. The *General Editorial Guidelines for Worldwide Library Super Romances* of 1982, in its directions to writers, broke down the fluid process of the romantic quest into its component set of static categories—"structure," "characters," "plot," "subplots," "romance," "sex," "viewpoint," and "writing style"—and even set forth each step in the plot.

- Introduction of hero and heroine, their meeting.
- Initial attraction or conflict between them.
- Romantic conflicts or heroine's qualms about hero.
- Counterbalance to developing romance (i.e., sensual scenes, getting to know each other, growth of love vs. conflicts).
- Hero's role in creating conflict.
- Resolution of conflicts and happy ending, leading to marriage.
- The development of the romance should be the primary concern of the author, with other story elements integrated into the romance.[24]

Sex (always of course coupled with "shared feeling rather than pure male domination" [General Editorial Guidelines]) is meted out in measured amounts and in measured doses of "sensuality" at measured intervals of the plot. As a further rationalization, the romantic quest can even be broken down numerically and quantified, so that, as "The [1982] Guidelines for Writing Harlequin's *New* American Romances" tell us, "parts of the plot can take place anywhere in the world provided that at least 80% of the novel takes place in the United States."

But in 1984, with changes in readers' tastes, and with the growth of the authors' professional association, Romance Writers of America, the Editorial Guidelines deny there is a formula: "Every aspiring Harlequin writer has a very clear picture of what makes these lines so successful, to the extent that some people have even tried to reduce it to a formula."[25]

A Changing Genre: The Author as Heroine

In fact, so much has changed and continues to change since 1980, when growth in the industry led authors to organize Romance Writers of America as a support group, that it is impossible to tell what will happen in the future. Present developments could lead not only to changes in the texts of the romances but to changes in the romance industry. Its very success could open up the potential contradictions inherent in the industry's methods. The same kinds of struggles against rationalizing power portrayed in the pages of the romances it markets could be turned against it. When Romance Writers of America held its first national convention in 1981, the organization saw as its main opponent a literary establishment and vaguely defined public that did not recognize the value of romance as "women's literature."[26] But as conditions governing author-corporation relations change, the industry itself might become another opponent.

Harlequin has responded to declining sales in face of competition by the classical strategy of buying out its major competitor (Silhouette Romances). But authors have had a quite different response to growth in the romance industry. While Harlequin's monopolizing strategy should work to make even more impersonal the author-publisher relation, authors have been seeking (as if in imitation of their own heroines) more affirming relations with the publisher and greater job satisfaction.

In her study of Harlequin Romances, Margaret Jensen reports that the experience of becoming writers has caused many romance authors to "identify themselves as feminists," to become self-assertive and to become more aware of themselves as working women who have succeeded in a profession quite difficult to break into. In addition to combating "the negative image of romance in the literary world," romance writers, she says, have two new concerns. They "are attempting to organize to improve the standards within their field"; they are also engaging in "an increasing outspokenness about the romantic fiction industry" and making "critical responses to it."[27] At a Romance Writers of America meeting in southern California, one candidate for office in the organization raised these same two issues. She spoke first of the need to "raise the standards of writing" and prevent "mediocre" writing. Then, after mentioning other writers' organizations which are more "militant," she spoke of the need to "increase our clout with publishers" and "improve the deal we're getting on contracts."[28] The question of authors' rights has received increasing attention from members of this group.

While authors still speak with indignation of the scorn that they face, saying that romances deserve the same respect as mysteries and science fiction, they also raise issues concerning the romance industry itself. Authors find themselves disadvantaged by the very marketing practice of Harlequin to which Peter Killing attributes Harlequin's economic success: Harlequin promotes its lines but rarely its authors. And Silhouette has followed suit. In a 1980 interview, Silhouette president P. J. Fennel said: "We're out to get brand name loyalty, so we're not selling individual titles."[29] The fierce competition among publishers to win brand loyalty has led them to make authors, except for the most famous, use a different pen name for each publisher she publishes with. The authors therefore have a difficult time establishing their own reputations. Because of this practice, and because a romance is on the market for only a month, romance authors have to hustle their own books and find their own markets. They can also, they report, have a difficult time getting royalties from publishers, with waits of up to two years. In fact, one of their main grievances is that they have no way of knowing whether or not their publishers are paying them their full royalties, nor of auditing the publishers to find out.[30]

While this kind of issue is just beginning to be addressed, the issues concerning quality of writing and personal creativity have already begun to be acted upon. Each product line in the romance industry has its own formula, and as the formulae have multiplied, they have also loosened. As a result, an author can pick the line that gives her the most freedom. More important, through Romance Writers of America, authors have formed their own critique groups, so that influences on their writing now also come from their peers and not only from the publishing institutions. Romances are beginning to be better and more carefully written, with more variety in the formulae, and more attention to detail. While some romances repeat a mechanical version of the formula, other romances like Leigh Roberts's *Love Circuits* are different. Roberts's work, where the hero, tender and loving from the beginning, wears a Charlotte Brontë t-shirt, and where the heroine has a witty sense of humor, brings some surprising transformations to the formula. Like any kind of formula writing—or any kind of writing—romance writing requires skill and talent.

As the corporations follow their destiny of expansion, conglomeration, and product diversification, differences between the mass-production needs of the corporations and authors' needs may prove to be potential cracks in the mass-marketing machine. The authors' own quest for creative individuality, for economic independence, and for recognition may make them the heroines of their own "real-life" romance, with conflicts and adventures outside the text just as gripping as those inside.

Chapter 8

Conclusion
Sexuality, History, Discourse

Romantic love narratives—twelfth-century romances, nineteenth-century novels, and contemporary mass-market romances—have enjoyed popularity in historical periods when forms of community based on direct personal relations, like the medieval clan, the nineteenth-century peasant village, or in our own day the nuclear family, were or are disintegrating and being replaced by institutions of the state which mediate, rationalize, and alienate these direct human relations.

While the narratives studied may not represent or reflect directly these historical changes, they incorporate the conflicting logics or codes of both the disintegrating and the emerging social forms. In *Tristan and Isolde* the multilogic of a feudal order, based on mixed matrilineal-patrilineal kinship networks and direct ties of personal dependence, comes into conflict with the emerging monologic of an order based on exclusive patrilineal systems of inheritance and the beginnings of a central state and of a codified system of law. In *Manon Lescaut* the code of a disappearing aristocratic order, enclosing people in stable social frameworks, and the code of an emerging bourgeois order, connecting people through unstable networks of money, combine to exclude the conflicting logic of middle-class femininity.

In *The Red and the Black* the linear logic of the post–French Revolution bourgeois state is disrupted by the various revolts of lower-class and women characters, while in *Shirley* the fragmentation of the Industrial Revolution is contrasted to the organic relations of the old English country estate. In *Big Meaulnes* the mediating forces of the centralized state and of consumer culture repress the culture of rural community; and Harlequin Enterprises tap into contemporary women's revolt against the depersonalizing force of huge faceless corporations and bureaucracies that have replaced family and community life.

Romantic love is a response to this disappearance of community, but that response is cut across by multiple contradictions. While human relations in the disintegrating forms of community are direct, they are imposed by the necessities of tradition, blood ties, and economic survival. They limit people rather than lead them to develop themselves and can often be oppressive. The new social structures alienate people from networks of immediate relations but they also create the *possibility* of building new human and sexual relations freed from economic determinism and based on conscious choice. Romantic love gives expression to this possibility but again in a contradictory way. The narratives harbor a passionate revolt against the newer, more alienating social structures, and also contain it in rationalizing discourses.

In the classic form of romance narrative, the central hero embodies this contradiction. He both seeks to live out the passions that would threaten the new order and also develops a form of subjectivity that supports and perpetuates that order. As a contradictory literary construct, he is what Lucien Goldmann calls the "problematic hero": a "madman or a criminal . . . whose degraded, and by that fact inauthentic, quest for authentic values in a world of conformism and convention, constitutes the content of this new literary genre which writers have created in our individualist society, and which has been called the 'novel.' "[1] While Goldmann cites Julien Sorel in *The Red and the Black* as a quintessential example of this problematic hero, Tristan, des Grieux, and Meaulnes are also, in the context of the laws of their world, crazy or criminal; and they are also problematic because of their ambiguity. As Goldmann points out, problematic heroes are both a part of and opposed to the inauthentic society in which they live, and while they protest against it, they ultimately perpetuate its values and structure.

The feminine narratives studied, *Shirley* and Harlequin Romances, center around heroines, but neither these heroines nor the heroines of the masculine romantic narratives are problematic in the sense that Goldmann gives to the word. Yet while their passions are not so "demoniacal," they nevertheless pose a more profound and thorough threat to rationalist order. Therefore feminine desires and an autonomous feminine voice are not simply contained by the narrative form, as in the case of the hero, but repressed to the textual unconscious. This difference between the hero and the heroine of a romantic narrative is a third contradiction of the genre.

While the hero develops the subjective structure for the new order, the heroine is excluded to its margins. Isolde is exiled from the matrifocal culture of Ireland, becomes the prisoner of a despotic marriage, and dies for the sake of her lover right after he dies; Manon is deprived of the opportunity to find work to maintain her autonomy and dies for the sake of her lover; Madame de Rênal is deprived of education, isolated in bourgeois domesticity, and dies for the sake of her lover right after he dies; Caroline Helstone is deprived of any meaningful activity or work, tries to face the isolated life of a spinster, and ends up in a marriage which is like death; Yvonne de Galais is the idealized version of the secluded petty bourgeois housewife, and dies shortly after her husband leaves her.

The Harlequin heroines provide fantasy compensations for this exclusion in a double way but are also doubly marginalized. They succeed in a man's world, and also force that world to recognize feminine values and feminine selfhood. Yet the romances work to recuperate women's subversive fantasies into structures of patriarchal power. In addition, while each romance places the heroine at its center, the genre as a whole remains at the margins of contemporary culture. While the masculine cultural pastime of equal popularity, the spectator sport of football, is shown on prime-time television, reading romances remains a quasi-secret activity for many readers. To read the cultural form which today shelters romantic ideals and desires is, as I discovered while working on this book, generally regarded with scorn.

In the narratives studied, the heroes' quest, however much it challenges or disrupts the social order in the content of the narrative, ends by his overcoming alienation in a return to a mythic and total identity. The heroines, living in a different, nonlinear, non-end-oriented historicity outside the dominant historical line of the narrative, have a different form of quest. Instead of seeking identity and totality, they seek connection between the fragments into which a rationalist social order has divided the organic network of lived experience. The texts of *Tristan and Isolde, Manon Lescaut,* and *The Red and the Black* harbor this other quest in the gaps of the linear quest. While the hidden quest differs from narrative to narrative, it seeks a sexuality that can heal the mind-body split as well as the split between immediate gratification and self-reflection. It expresses a feminine sexual desire that goes beyond both love as the fusion of two people into one (as in preoedipal sexuality or Victorian marriage) and phallic sexuality as an isolated genital act of penetration. As a sexual love, it fosters both difference and intimacy. It also refuses the separation between sociopolitical practice and erotic practice, and dissolves the illusory separation between the feminine sphere of domesticity and sentiment and the masculine sphere of politics and economics.

The contradictions of romanticism, and especially of feminine romanticism, have taken on a new configuration in contemporary romance. In Harlequin Romances the forms of rationalism that contain and control subversive feminine passion work more efficiently than in romance narratives of the past. They can therefore give more explicit expression to formerly forbidden passions for feminine sexuality and feminine historicity without their becoming a threat to order, unity, or identity, because they are more contained in a rationalized discourse.

The other romantic narratives from *Tristan and Isolde* to *Big Meaulnes* present a common contrast to Harlequin. In them disruptive sexual passions, historical processes, and feminine discursive practices all work together, and are all repressed together to a textual unconscious where they leave silent traces. In Harlequin, one of the elements, the workings of feminine discourse, is absent. Therefore, the other two of these elements, feminine sexuality and historicity, can have freer expression because they have been amputated from their own expressive form. This contrast suggests the necessary connections between sexuality, history, and the workings of language in any challenge to the universalist pretensions of an order that represses feminine difference, or any difference.

Harlequin translates the fantasies, conflicts, and anger of women who in their individual daily lives have had to battle against the separation between the "feminine" sphere of domesticity, intimacy, and sexuality and the "masculine" sphere of work, economics, and adventure. Expressing a desire to heal the split between the separate spheres, Harlequin introduces yet another contradiction into romantic love. It tends to neutralize the subversive force of that healing desire at a time in history when large numbers of people recognize a need to heal the split in practice. A romantic literature which could express feminine sexuality and historicity and also give room to feminine discourse, but which at the same time could be read, understood, and appreciated by large numbers of women, could give a powerful cultural voice to this desire.

Yet even in such a literature, romantic love would remain as it always has been, what George Lukács calls a "purely negative ideal."[2] Doubling patriarchal capitalism as its critical and unsettling other, romanticism gnaws at patriarchal-capitalist ideology from within. Its fictions act as a critical force that lays bare the spiritual deprivations of our society and provides an avenue for revolt from the stifling pressures of its totalizing rationalism. Yet it does not pose a positive alternative. Fulfilled romantic love cannot be narrated, and the great novels of romantic love, like *Manon Lescaut, The Red and the Black,* or *Shirley* also call into question romantic love itself as a model for human relations. As a negative force it moves people to aspire beyond our sociosymbolic order, albeit in vague and veiled ways.

Because it exists only in fantasy, and because that fantasy can be used to exploitative ends, romantic love is often denounced or scorned as an illusion and a myth. But all cultural forms of sexuality derive their power from the myths and fantasies that surround them, and romantic love is a form of sexuality whose power cannot today be denied. Instead of being scorned, it needs, like the heroines in the romances of old, to be liberated from captivity in the tower of patriarchal and corporate manipulation, but not by a Prince Charming.

Notes

Chapter 1

1. Pierre Lasserre, *Le Romantisme français* (Paris: Mercure de France, 1907), pp. 185 and 191. There have also been periods when romanticism found favor with intellectuals and was not so popular with the general public, such as the 1940s and 1950s. For a history of how romanticism fared with leading literary historians in different periods, see the articles collected in Robert F. Gleckner and Gerald E. Enscoe, eds., *Romanticism: Points of View* (Detroit: Wayne State University Press, 1970).
2. Irving Babbitt, *Rousseau and Romanticism* (Boston: Houghton Mifflin, 1919), p. 30.
3. Julia Kristeva, "La Femme, ce n'est jamais ça," in *New French Feminisms*, ed. Elaine Marks and Isabelle de Courtivron (New York: Schocken, 1981), p. 138.
4. Candace Lang, "Autobiography in the Aftermath of Romanticism," *Diacritics* 12, no. 4 (Winter, 1982): 2–16, quoted at p. 4.
5. Paul Zumthor, "Héloïse et Abélard," *Revue des sciences humaines* 91 (July–September, 1958): 316. Cited in Peggy Kamuf, *Fictions of Feminine Desire* (Lincoln: University of Nebraska Press, 1982), p. xv.
6. Harold Bloom, "The Internalization of Quest Romance," in *The Ringers in the Tower* (Chicago: University of Chicago Press, 1971); Northrop Frye, *The Secular Scripture: A Study of the Structure of Romance* (Cambridge: Harvard University Press, 1976); Georg Lukács, *La Théorie du roman* (Paris: Gonthier, 1963); Lucienne Frappier-Mazur, "Desire, Writing and Identity in the Romantic Mystical Novel: Notes for a Definition of the Feminine," Paper delivered to the Berkshire Conference for Women's History, June, 1984.
7. Some of the more prominent of these critics are: Terry Eagleton, *The Rape of Clarissa: Writing, Sexuality and Class Struggle in Samuel Richardson* (Minneapolis: University of Minnesota Press, 1982); Fredric Jameson, *The Political Unconscious: Narrative as a Socially Symbolic Act* (Ithaca, N.Y.: Cornell University Press, 1981); and Julia Kristeva, *La Révolution du langage poétique* (Paris: Seuil, 1974).

8. Lucien Goldmann, *Pour une sociologie du roman* (Paris: Gallimard, 1964), p. 345. Italics in original. Further references to this text will be cited in parentheses after the quotation. Translations are mine.

9. Jameson, *Political Unconscious*, p. 26. Further references to this book will be cited in parentheses after the quotation.

10. Louise A. Tilly and Joan W. Scott, *Women, Work and the Family* (New York: Holt, Rinehart and Winston, 1978); Joanne McNamara and Suzanne Wemple, "Sanctity and Power: The Dual Pursuit of Medieval Women," in *Becoming Visible: Women in European History*, ed. Renate Bridenthal and Claudia Koontz (Boston: Houghton Mifflin, 1977); Darline Gay Levy, Harriet Bronson Applewhite, and Mary Durham Johnson, eds., *Women in Revolutionary Paris, 1789–1795* (Urbana: University of Illinois Press, 1979); Bonnie G. Smith, *Ladies of the Leisure Class: The Bourgeoises of Northern France in the Nineteenth Century* (Princeton: Princeton University Press, 1981).

11. Roland Barthes, *S/Z* (Paris: Seuil, 1970); John Berger, *Ways of Seeing* (London: Pelican, 1972).

12. M. M. Bakhtin, *The Dialogic Imagination: Four Essays*, trans. Caryl Emerson and Michael Holquist (Austin: University of Texas Press, 1981), p. 262.

13. Julia Kristeva, "Le Texte clos," *Seméiotike: Recherches pour une sémanalyse* (Paris: Seuil, 1969). She defines the ideologeme as an "intertextual function," and calls it "the focal point in which knowing rationality seizes the transformation of *énoncés* (to which the text is not reducible) into a whole (the text), as well as the insertions of this totality into the historic and social text" (p. 114). Further references to this text will be cited in parentheses after the quotation. Translations are mine.

14. Simone de Beauvoir, *Le Deuxième sexe* (Paris: Gallimard, 1949), p. 234.

15. Frappier-Mazur, "Desire, Writing and Identity," p. 10.

16. Harold Bloom, "The Internalization of Quest Romance," in *The Ringers in the Tower* (Chicago: University of Chicago Press, 1971), p. 15. Further references to this work will be cited in parentheses after the quotation.

17. Northrop Frye, *The Secular Scripture: A Study of the Structure of Romance* (Cambridge: Harvard University Press, 1976), chap. 2. Further references to this book will be cited in parentheses after the quotation.

18. G. F. W. Hegel, *The Phenomenology of Mind* (New York: Harper and Row, 1967), p. 38. Further references to this work will be cited in parentheses after the quotation.

19. Critiques of phallocentric logic and also of Lacanian psychoanalysis are in: Hélène Cixous, *La Jeune Née* (Paris: Union générale d'editions, 1975) and "Le Rire de la Méduse," *L'Arc*, no. 61, pp. 39–54; Luce Irigaray, *Speculum de l'autre femme* (Paris: Editions de minuit, 1974) and *Ce Sexe qui n'en est pas un* (Paris: Editions de minuit, 1977); and Julia Kristeva, *Des Chinoises* (Paris: Des Femmes, 1975). For other critiques of Lacanian constructions of the feminine, see Jacques Derrida, "Le Facteur de la vérité," *Poétique* 21 (1975): 96–147; and Jane Gallop, *The Daughter's Seduction: Feminism and Psychoanalysis* (Ithaca: Cornell University Press, 1982).

20. See Juliet Mitchell, *Psycho-Analysis and Feminism* (New York: Vintage, 1975), p. 383; and Kristeva, *La Révolution*, pp. 44–45. See also Nancy Chodorow, *The Reproduction of Mothering: Psychoanalysis and the Sociology of Gender* (Berkeley: University of California Press, 1978). Her object relations analysis of the Oedipus complex shows that girls do not undergo this radical split (see for instance p. 169).

21. See Juliet Mitchell and Jacqueline Rose, eds., *Feminine Sexuality: Jacques Lacan and the école freudienne* (New York: Norton, 1982). In her introduction, Mitchell says: "A primordially split subject necessitates an originally lost object. Though Freud does not talk of the object as a lost object as Lacan does, he is absolutely clear that its psychological significance arises from its absence" (p. 25).

22. This expression is used by Sigmund Freud in "Femininity," in *New Introductory Lectures on Psychoanalysis*, trans. James Strachey (New York: Norton, 1965).

23. Mitchell, *Psycho-Analysis and Feminism*, p. 40. Further references to this book will be cited in parentheses after the quotation.

24. Jacques Lacan, "Guiding Remarks for a Congress on Feminine Sexuality," trans. Jacqueline Rose, in *Feminine Sexuality*, ed. Mitchell and Rose, p. 94. Further references to this essay will be cited in parentheses after the quotation.

25. Jacques Lacan, "The Field of the Other and Back to the Transference," in *The Four Fundamental Concepts of Psycho-Analysis*, trans. Alan Sheridan (New York: Norton, 1978), pp. 208 and 211. See also Julia Kristeva, *Histoires d'amour* (Paris: Denoel, 1983), pp. 35–36.

26. Jacques Lacan, "The Meaning of the Phallus," in *Feminine Sexuality*, ed. Mitchell and Rose, p. 79. For Lacan, combination and substitution are the operations of the two axes of language, metonymy and metaphor. They are also the two processes of the unconscious, displacement and condensation. In the romantic narrative the project of the hero's desire is the metonymic pole and his relation to the heroine the metaphoric pole of the narrative's language.

27. Jacqueline Rose, "Introduction—II," in *Feminine Sexuality*, ed. Mitchell and Rose, p. 32. Further references to this essay will appear in parentheses after the quotation.

28. Georg Lukács, *La Théorie du roman* (Paris: Gonthier, 1963), pp. 53–54. Translation is mine.

29. Paul de Man, "Georg Lukács's *Theory of the Novel*," in *Blindness and Insight: Essays in the Rhetoric of Contemporary Criticism* (New York: Oxford University Press, 1971), p. 58.

30. See the articles collected in Zillah R. Eisenstein, ed., *Capitalist Patriarchy and the Case for Socialist Feminism* (New York: Monthly Review Press, 1979).

31. The traditional literary history of the French canon locates in *Manon Lescaut* the origins of preromanticism.

32. Frappier-Mazur, "Desire, Writing and Identity," p. 1.

33. In this book, the author of the Harlequin Romances is considered ambig-

uous. While the writers of the particular romances are overwhelmingly women, each romance must conform to a formula, whose author is the masculine collectivity of the Harlequin Enterprises corporation.

34. Simone de Beauvoir, *Mémoires d'une jeune fille rangée* (Paris: Gallimard, 1958), pp. 260, 310–11, 371–73, and 484; *La Force de l'âge* (Paris: Gallimard, 1960), I:71.

35. This was suggested to me by Margaret Homans.

36. Susan Gubar, "The Genesis of Hunger according to *Shirley,*" in Sandra Gilbert and Susan Gubar, *The Madwoman in the Attic: The Woman Writer and the Nineteenth-Century Literary Imagination* (New Haven: Yale University Press, 1979).

37. Stanley Fish, *Is There a Text in This Class? The Authority of Interpretive Communities* (Cambridge: Harvard University Press, 1980). Further references to this book will be cited in parentheses after the quotation.

38. Wayne Booth, *The Rhetoric of Fiction* (Chicago: University of Chicago Press, 1961), p. 138.

39. On this notion, Judith Fetterley says: "Clearly, then, the first act of a feminist critic must be to become a resisting rather than an assenting reader and, by its refusal to assent, to begin the process of exorcizing the male mind that has been implanted in us" (Judith Fetterley, *The Resisting Reader: A Feminist Approach to American Fiction* [Bloomington: Indiana University Press, 1978], p. xxii).

Chapter 2

Portions of this chapter appeared in "The Establishment of Patriarchy in *Tristan and Isolde,*" *Women's Studies* 7 (1980): 19–38.

1. The versions of the romance consulted were: Béroul, *Le Roman de Tristan* (Paris: Firmin Didot, 1903); Eilhart von Oberg, *Tristant,* Edition diplomatique des manuscrits et traduction en français moderne par Danielle Buschinger (Göppingen: Alfred Kummerle, 1976); Friar Robert, *The Saga of Tristan and Isond,* trans. Paul Schach (Lincoln: University of Nebraska Press, 1973); Gottfried von Strassburg, *Tristan* (Darmstadt: Wissenschaftliche Buchgesellschaft); Gottfried von Strassburg, *Tristan,* trans. A. T. Hatto (Middlesex: Penguin Books, 1960); Joseph Bédier, *Le Roman de Tristan par Thomas,* 2 vols., vol. 1, Tome premier, texte (Paris: Firmin Didot, 1902).

2. For the difference between courtly love and "Tristan Love," see W. T. H. Jackson, "Faith Unfaithful—The German Reaction to Courtly Love," in *The Meaning of Courtly Love,* ed. F. X. Newman (Albany: State University of New York Press, 1968), pp. 55–71.

3. René Nelli, *L'Erotique des troubadours* (Paris: 10/18, 1974), 2 vols., 1:39. M. M. Bakhtin discusses the ancient Greek romances, which in many respects resemble the medieval romances, but he notes: "There is as yet nothing of that authentically solitary individual who makes his appearance only in

the Middle Ages and henceforth plays such an enormous role in the European novel" (M. M. Bakhtin, *The Dialogic Imagination: Four Essays*, ed. Michael Holquist, trans. Caryl Emerson and Michael Holquist [Austin: University of Texas Press, 1981], p. 145).

4. R. Howard Bloch, *Medieval French Literature and the Law* (Berkeley: University of California Press, 1977), pp. 238 and 249.

5. Georges Duby, *Le Chevalier, la femme, et le prêtre* (Paris: Hachette, Collection Pluriel, 1981). Discussing sermon literature of 1150, Duby says: "a primary theme, dominating the entire discourse, endlessly reappears: woman is bad, as lascivious as a viper, as sneaky as an eel, and in addition inquisitive, indiscrete and shrewish" (p. 224).

6. Joan Kelly-Gadol, "Did Women Have a Renaissance?" p. 144; and Joanne McNamara and Suzanne F. Wemple, "Sanctity and Power: The Dual Pursuit of Medieval Women," both in *Becoming Visible: Women in European History*, ed. Renate Bridenthal and Claudia Koontz (Boston: Houghton Mifflin, 1977); see also Duby, *Le Chevalier*, p. 228; and Susan Mosher Stuart, ed., *Women in Medieval Society* (Philadelphia: University of Pennsylvania Press, 1976).

7. For a summary of the source debate, see Rosemary Picozzi, *A History of Tristan Scholarship* (Berne: Herbert Lang, 1971), pp. 17 and 24–40; Roger Sherman Loomis, *Celtic Myth and Arthurian Romance* (New York: Columbia University Press, 1927), pp. 26–31; Loomis, *The Development of Arthurian Romance* (London: Hutchinson University Library, 1963), pp. 79–86; Bédier, *Tristan*, 2:106–16, 123–27.

8. Marc Bloch, *Feudal Society*, trans. L. A. Manyan (Chicago: University of Chicago Press, 1961), 2 vols., 1:115 and 172; Henri Pirenne, Gustave Cohen, and Henri Focillon, *Histoire du moyen âge* (Paris: Presses universitaires de France, 1933), pp. 40–59; Charles Homer Haskins, *The Renaissance of the Twelfth Century* (Cambridge: Harvard University Press, 1927), p. 130.

9. R. H. Bloch, *Medieval French Literature*, pp. 128–30; Michael Tigar and Madeleine R. Levy, *Law and the Rise of Capitalism* (New York: Monthly Review Press, 1977), pp. 97, 206, and 244; Karl Ferdinand Werner, "Liens de parenté et noms de personne," in *Famille et parenté dans l'occident mediéval*, ed. Georges Duby and Jacques le Goff (Rome: Ecole française de Rome, 1977), pp. 25–34.

10. David Herlihy, "Land, Family and Women in Continental Europe, 701–1200," in *Women in Medieval Society*, ed. Stuart, pp. 13–46.

11. "Sanctity and Power," pp. 107–8.

12. David Herlihy, "Life Expectancies for Women in Medieval Society," in *The Role of Women in the Middle Ages*, ed. Rosemarie Thee Morewedge (Albany: State University of New York Press, 1975), p. 11.

13. Eleanor Burke Leacock, *Myths of Male Dominance* (New York: Monthly Review Press, 1981), p. 67.

14. Denis de Rougemont, *L'Amour et l'occident* (Paris: 10/18, 1939). Translations are mine. Further references to this text are indicated in parentheses after the quotation.

15. Henri Hubert, *The Greatness and Decline of the Celts*, edited and brought up to date by Marcel Mauss, Raymond Lantier, and Jean Marx, trans. M. R. Dobié (New York: Benjamin Blom, 1972), pp. 232–37; Jean Markale, *La Femme celte* (Paris: Payot, 1976), p. 306; Alwyn and Brinley Rees, *Celtic Heritage: Ancient Tradition in Ireland and Wales* (London: Thames and Hudson, 1961), pp. 154ff.

16. Joseph Bédier, *Le Roman de Tristan par Thomas*, vol. 2: Introduction (Paris: Firmin Didot, 1905), p. 107; "Culhwch and Olwen," in *The Mabinogi and Other Medieval Welsh Tales*, ed. Patrick K. Ford (Berkeley: University of California Press, 1977), p. 131.

17. See Lady Augusta Gregory, *Gods and Fighting Men: The Story of the Tuatha de Danaam and of the Fianna of Ireland* (New York: Oxford University Press, 1970), pp. 139, 197, and 214. Further references to this text will be made in parentheses after the quotation.

18. "The King of Erin and the Queen of the Lonesome Island," in *Myths and Folktales of Ireland*, ed. Jeremiah Curtin (New York: Dover, 1975), p. 64.

19. "Finn MacCumhail and the Fenians of Erin in the Castle of Fear Dubh," in *Myths and Folktales*, ed. Curtin, p. 153. For legends of Finn and CuChúlainn see: *The Cattle Raid of Cualnge* (Tain Bo Cuailnge), trans. L. Winifred Faraday (London: David Nutt, 1904); Gregory, *Gods and Fighting Men;* and Jean Markale, *L'Epopée celtique d'Irlande* (Paris: Payot, 1971), pp. 75–138.

20. Gertrude Schoepperle Loomis, *Tristan and Isolt: A Study in the Sources of the Roman* (New York: Bert Franklin, 1963), p. 326.

21. Hubert, *The Greatness and Decline of the Celts*, p. 204.

22. Donncha O'Corráin, "Women in Early Irish Society," in *Women in Irish Society: The Historical Dimension*, ed. Margaret MacCurtain and Donncha O'Corráin (Westport, Conn.: Greenwood Press, 1979), p. 11.

23. See Carole L. Crumley, *Celtic Social Structure: The Generation of Archaeologically Testable Hypotheses from Literary Evidence*, Museum of Anthropology, University of Michigan, no. 54 (Ann Arbor: University of Michigan, 1974), p. 22; Hubert, *The Greatness and Decline of the Celts*, pp. 189–222; Markale, *La Femme celte*, p. 17; P. W. Joyce, *A Social History of Ancient Ireland* (New York: Benjamin Blom, 1968), 2 vols., 1:168; and Katharine Scherman, *The Flowering of Ireland: Saints, Scholars and Kings* (Boston: Little, Brown, and Co., 1981).

24. O'Corráin, "Women in Early Irish Society," p. 12.

25. Besides Leacock, *Myths*, the main writings on matriliny consulted were: Frederick Engels, *The Origin of the Family, Private Property and the State* (New York: International Publishers, 1973); Merlin Stone, *When God Was a Woman* (New York: Harcourt Brace Jovanovich, 1977); George Thompson, *Studies in Ancient Greek Society: The Prehistoric Aegean* (New York: Citadel Press, 1965); two articles were consulted in *Becoming Visible*, ed. Bridenthal and Koontz: Eleanor Leacock, "Women in Egalitarian Societies," pp. 11–35, and Ruby Rohrlich-Leavitt, "Women in Transition: Crete and Sumer," pp. 36–59; three articles were consulted in *Toward an Anthropology of Women*, ed. Rayna R. Reiter (New York: Monthly Review

Press, 1975): Kathleen Gough, "The Origin of the Family," pp. 51–76, Patricia Draper, "Kung Women: Contrasts in Sexual Egalitarianism in Foraging and Sedentary Contexts," pp. 77–109, and Karen Sacks, "Engels Revisited: Women, the Organization of Production, and Private Property," pp. 211–34.

26. "Pwyll, Prince of Dyfed," in *The Mabinogi,* ed. Ford, pp. 35–56.

27. "Math Son of Mathonwy," in *The Mabinogi,* ed. Ford, p. 98.

28. See, for instance, "Fair, Brown and Trembling" and "The Thirteenth Son of the King of Erin," in *Myths and Folktales,* ed. Curtin.

29. Gottfried, *Tristan,* p. 145. Words in brackets refer to alternative translations taken from the German edition. Help in translating the Middle-High German was received from Dr. Edith Potter. References to all versions of *Tristan* will be found in parentheses after the quotation.

30. Stone, *When God Was a Woman,* pp. 198–213, and Thompson, *Studies in Ancient Society,* pp. 114–19.

31. Markale, *La Femme celte,* pp. 19 and 26; and Robert Graves, *The White Goddess: A Historical Grammar of Poetic Myth* (New York: Farrar, Straus and Giroux, 1966), p. 64.

32. Curtin, ed., *Myths and Folktales,* pp. 142, 145, 176, and 204; Gregory, *Gods and Fighting Men,* pp. 206–7.

33. Clair Hayden Bell, *The Sister's Son in the Medieval German Epic: A Study in the Survival of Matriliny* (Berkeley: University of California Press, 1922), esp. pp. 69 and 68; William Oliver Farnsworth, *Uncle and Nephew in the Old French Chansons de Geste: A Study in the Survival of Matriarchy* (New York: AMS Press, 1966); Georges Duby, "Lignage, noblesse et chevalerie au XIIe siècle dans la région maconnaise," *Annales* 27, no. 4–5 (July–October, 1972): 803–24.

34. Graves, *The White Goddess,* pp. 315–16.

35. "Then by a final feminine ruse, exploiting this concession, the queen declares she will rejoin the knight" (de Rougemont, *Love,* p. 23); "How can they present us . . . as a virtuous lady this adulterous wife who does not even recoil before a clever blasphemy?" (p. 25).

36. Hatto, Introduction to *Tristan,* p. 23.

37. W. T. H. Jackson, *The Anatomy of Love: The Tristan of Gottfried von Strassburg* (New York: Columbia University Press, 1971), pp. 85–86.

38. Gustave Flaubert, *L'Education sentimentale* (Paris: Garnier, 1964), p. 9. Translation is mine.

39. La Chanson III du chatelain de Coucy, quoted in Paul Zumthor, *Essai de poétique mediévale* (Paris: Seuil, 1972), p. 194. Translation is mine.

Chapter 3

Portions of this chapter appeared as "History, Ideology and Femininity in *Manon Lescaut*" in the *Stanford French Review* 5, no. 1 (1981): 65–83.

1. To avoid repetition, I have decided not to analyze *La Princesse de Clèves* and to do a close study of *Manon Lescaut* instead since both are landmark

novels between twelfth-century romance and nineteenth-century romanticism.

2. Antoine-François Prévost d'Exiles, *Histoire du chevalier des Grieux et de Manon Lescaut,* ed. Henri Coulet (Paris: Garnier-Flammarion, 1967), p. 15. Further page references will be indicated in parentheses after the quotation. Translations are mine.

3. Paul Hazard, *La Crise de conscience européenne: 1680–1715* (Paris: Arthème Fayard, n.d.), p. 303.

4. Albert Soboul, *La Civilization et la révolution française,* Tome I, *La Crise de l'ancien régime* (Paris: Arthaud, 1970), pp. 17–18.

5. According to Franklin Ford, even though the aristocracy was more exclusive in the eighteenth century than under Louis XIV, it still intermarried with the most wealthy capitalist families; and even though it was still economically dependent on the land, it did invest heavily in the Law Scheme, in maritime commerce, and in manufacture for export. See Franklin L. Ford, *Robe and Sword: The Regrouping of the French Aristocracy after Louis XIV* (Cambridge: Harvard University Press, 1962), pp. 124–26, 144, and 160–61.

6. Joan Kelly-Gadol, "Did Women Have a Renaissance?" in *Becoming Visible: Women in European History,* ed. Renate Bridenthal and Claudia Koontz (Boston: Houghton Mifflin, 1977), p. 139.

7. See Alice Clark, *Working Life of Women in the Seventeenth Century* (London, 1919; reprint, New York: A. M. Kelly, 1968); Natalie Zemon Davis, *Society and Culture in Early Modern France* (Stanford: Stanford University Press, 1965), pp. 71–72; Madeleine Rebérioux, "L'Ouvrière," in *Misérable et glorieuse: La Femme au XIXe siècle,* ed. Jean-Paul Aron (Paris: Fayard, 1980), p. 60; Evelyne Sullerot, *Histoire et sociologie du travail feminin* (Paris: Gonthier, 1968), pp. 67–68; Louise A. Tilly and Joan W. Scott, *Women, Work and the Family* (New York: Holt, Rinehart and Winston, 1978), p. 31; Richard T. Vann, "Toward a New Lifestyle: Women in Preindustrial Capitalism," in *Becoming Visible,* ed. Bridenthal and Koontz, p. 203.

8. Olwen Hufton, *The Poor of Eighteenth-Century France: 1750–1789* (Oxford: Clarendon, 1974), pp. 12 and 26.

9. Abbé Prévost, *Histoire du chevalier des Grieux et de Manon Lescaut,* édition de Frédéric Deloffre et Raymond Picard (Paris: Garnier Frères, 1965), p. 17.

10. Nancy K. Miller, *The Heroine's Text: Readings in the French and English Novel, 1722–1782* (New York: Columbia University Press, 1980), p. 70; Lionel Gossman, "Prévost's Manon: Love in the New World," *Yale French Studies,* no. 40, pp. 91–102, esp. p. 101.

11. Roland Barthes, *Le Plaisir du texte* (Paris: Seuil, 1973), p. 14.

12. Wayne Booth, *The Rhetoric of Fiction* (Chicago: University of Chicago Press, 1961), pp. 158–59.

13. See Gérard Genette, "Vraisemblance et motivation," in *Figures II* (Paris: Seuil, 1969), pp. 74–75.

14. Raymond Picard, "L'Univers de Manon Lescaut," *Mercure de France* 1172 (April, 1961): 606–22, quoted at p. 610; and Jacques Proust, "Le Corps de Manon," *Littérature* 4 (1971): 5–21, p. 8.

15. Alain Robbe-Grillet, *Pour un nouveau roman* (Paris: Gallimard, 1963), p. 26.
16. Roland Barthes, *S/Z* (Paris: Seuil, 1970), p. 128.
17. Alfred de Musset, "Namouna," *Oeuvres complètes*, Tome I (Paris: Louis Conard, 1922), p. 387. Translation is mine.
18. There is an extensive and interesting discussion of this problem in Miller, *The Heroine's Text;* see also Proust, "Le Corps de Manon."
19. See chap. 1, p. 18.
20. See Julia Kristeva, *Des Chinoises* (Paris: Des Femmes, 1975), pp. 13–71; "Pratique signifiante et mode de production," *La Traversée des signes* (Paris: Seuil, 1975); and "La Fonction prédicative et le sujet parlant," in *Langue, discours, société pour Emile Benveniste,* ed. Julia Kristeva, Jean-Claude Milner, and Nicolas Ruwet (Paris: Seuil, 1975). Kristeva also adapts the Lacanian notion that this subjective structure is phallic, or as Luce Irigaray says: "Any theory of the subject will always be appropriated by the masculine" (Luce Irigaray, *Speculum de l'autre femme* [Paris: Editions de minuit, 1974], p. 165). See chapter 1 of this book for more discussion on the French feminist analysis of the phallocentric subject.
21. Kristeva, *Des Chinoises*, p. 27.
22. Kristeva, *La Révolution du langage poétique* (Paris: Seuil, 1974), p. 69.
23. Michal Foucault, *The Order of Things,* a translation of *Les Mots et les choses* (New York: Vintage, 1970), p. 231.
24. Robert Mauzi, *L'Idée du bonheur dans la littérature et la pensée au 18e siècle* (Paris: Armand Colin, 1969), p. 13. Translation is mine.
25. Julia Kristeva, "Le Sujet in procès," in *Artaud,* ed. Philippe Sollers (Paris: 10/18, 1973), p. 50.
26. Frédéric Deloffre and Raymond Picard, "Introduction," in *Manon Lescaut* (1965), p. xxxiv.
27. Applying to texts the symptomatic readings that Freud used in dream interpretation is now widespread. Among the first to develop this method of textual reading were Louis Althusser, "On the Young Marx," *For Marx,* trans. Ben Brewster (New York: Vintage, 1969), pp. 64–69; and Pierre Macherey, *Pour une théorie de la production littéraire* (Paris: Maspero, 1974).
28. This was not merely a tradition but a series of royal edicts concerning *dérogeance,* or as Ford says, the act of ceasing to "live nobly." According to an edict of 1669, renewed in 1701, "a nobleman still lost his noblesse and that of all progeny not yet conceived . . . if he adopted any manual craft save the famous exception of glassmaking or if he entered 'for sordid gain' into either retail commerce or the exploitation of another party's land." He could engage in maritime trade and export. Ford, *Robe and Sword,* pp. 25–26.
29. Tilly, *Women, Work and the Family,* p. 31.
30. This petition is in a collection of documents from the French Revolution: Darline Gay Levy, Harriet Bronson Applewhite, and Mary Durham Johnson, *Women in Revolutionary Paris, 1789–1795* (Urbana: University of Illinois Press, 1979), p. 19. The same petition is also in a collection of docu-

ments in the original French: Paule-Marie Duhet, *Les Femmes et la Revolution: 1789–1795* (Paris: Julliard, 1971), p. 34.

31. Speech of Chaumette to the Convention, in Levy, *Women in Revolutionary Paris*, p. 219.

32. Lionel Gossman, in "Prévost's *Manon*," has a different interpretation for the same phenomenon:

> Throughout the greatest part of the novel Manon is not only an incarnation of Regency worldliness but the very symbol of the shifting, indefinable nature of social reality. . . . Manon remains for him "une enigme." He recognizes a connection between her and the world, but he refuses to investigate it and persists instead in trying to define an essence or hard core of Manon, impervious to money and the world, behind her constantly changing appearances: ". . . elle est legère et imprudente, mais elle est droite et sincère." (P. 92)

33. Talleyrand in Duhet, *Les Femmes et la Révolution*, p. 187.

Chapter 4

1. Fredric Jameson, *The Political Unconscious: Narrative as a Socially Symbolic Act* (Ithaca, N.Y.: Cornell University Press, 1981), p. 35.

2. Erich Auerbach was the first critic to analyze the originality of Stendhal's incorporating history into the novel. According to Auerbach, the way *The Red and the Black* weaves "contemporary historical circumstances, contemporary political and social conditions" into a work of literature makes it "an entirely new and highly significant phenomenon" (Erich Auerbach, *Mimesis: The Representation of Reality in Western Literature*, trans. Willard R. Trask [Princeton: Princeton University Press, 1953], pp. 457–58).

3. The most recent of these critics are: Robert Alter and Carol Cosman, *A Lion for Love: A Critical Biography of Stendhal* (New York: Basic Books, 1979); Hans Böll-Johansen, *Essai sur la structure du roman stendhalien* (Aran, Suisse: Editions du grand chêne, 1979); and Elizabeth Tenenbaum, *The Problematic Self: Approaches to Identity in Stendhal, D. H. Lawrence, and Malraux* (Cambridge: Harvard University Press, 1977). They will be discussed later in this chapter.

4. Peter Brooks, "The Novel and the Guillotine; or Fathers and Sons in *Le Rouge et le noir*," PMLA 97, no. 3 (1983): 348–62, quoted at p. 349.

5. Stendhal, *Le Rouge et le noir*, Edition de Henri Martineau (Paris: Garnier frères, 1960), p. 231. Further references to this text will be in parentheses after the quotation. Translations are mine.

6. For more on this aspect of history in *Le Rouge et le noir*, see Juliet MacCannell, "Stendhal's Women," *Semiotica* 48, nos. 1 and 2 (1984): 4 and 9.

7. Julia Kristeva, "Le Texte clos," in *Seméiotike: Recherches pour une sémanalyse* (Paris: Seuil, 1969), p. 119. Translations are mine.

8. For Julien as a sexual androgyne, see Albert Sonnenfeld, "Ruminations on Stendhal's Epigraphs," in *Pre-Text, Text, Context: Essays on Nineteenth-*

Century French Literature, ed. Robert L. Mitchell (Columbus: Ohio State University Press, 1980), p. 102.

9. For a more extensive analysis of the Stendhalian heroines along this line, see Simone de Beauvoir's essay on Stendhal in the original French version of *Le Deuxième sexe,* vol. 2 (Paris: Gallimard, 1949), p. 365.

10. Alter, *A Lion for Love,* p. 191.

11. For similar interpretations of this letter, see Geneviève Mouillaud, *Le Rouge et le noir de Stendhal: Le Roman possible* (Paris: Larousse université, 1973), pp. 39–40; and Tenenbaum, *The Problematic Self,* p. 48.

12. Henri Martineau, *L'Oeuvre de Stendhal* (Paris: Divan, 1945), pp. 343–51. For a critique of this kind of psychological criticism, see Brooks, "The Novel and the Guillotine," p. 349.

13. Tenenbaum, *The Problematic Self,* p. 60.

14. Victor Brombert, *La Prison romantique* (Paris: Jose Corti, 1975), p. 75.

15. Luce Irigaray, *Speculum de l'autre femme* (Paris: Editions de minuit, 1974), pp. 9–161. Translation is mine.

16. Julia Kristeva, *La Révolution du langage poétique* (Paris: Seuil, 1974), p. 181.

17. A noteworthy exception to this critical practice is that of Julia Kristeva. Instead of taking sides, she critically analyzes the polarity itself from an exterior perspective, seeing it as an "eternal ruse of masculine sexuality" (*Histoires d'amour* [Paris: Denoel, 1983], p. 335).

18. Gérard Genette, *Figures II* (Paris: Seuil, 1969), pp. 178–79. Further references to this text will be in parentheses after the quotation. Translations are mine.

19. Hans Böll-Johansen, *Essai,* pp. 60–61. Translation is mine.

20. Martha N. Moss, "Don Juan and His Fallen Angel: Images of Women in the Literature of the 1830's," in *Pre-Text, Text, Context,* ed. Mitchell, p. 93.

21. Alter, *A Lion for Love,* p. 193.

22. René Girard, *Deceit, Desire and the Novel: Self and Other in Literary Structure,* trans. Yvonne Freccero (Baltimore: Johns Hopkins University Press, 1965), p. 22. Further references to this text will be in parentheses after the quotation.

23. Don Gruffot Papera, "Sur *Le Rouge et le noir,*" Appendix in Stendhal, *Le Rouge et le noir,* p. 525. Translation is mine.

24. Michel Guérin, *La Politique de Stendhal* (Paris: Presses universitaires de France, 1982), pp. 15–16. Translations are mine.

25. Moss, "Don Juan," p. 93.

26. Georg Lukács, *Studies in European Realism* (New York: Grosset and Dunlap, 1964), p. 79.

27. Christopher Prendergast, *Balzac: Fiction and Melodrama* (London: Edward Arnold, 1978), p. 139.

28. Roland Barthes, *S/Z* (Paris: Seuil, 1970), p. 112.

29. Kristeva, *Révolution,* p. 180. Further references to this text will be in parentheses after the quotation. Translations are mine.

30. Böll-Johansen, *Essai,* p. 60; and Mouillaud, *Le Roman possible,* p. 105.

31. Stendhal, *De l'amour* (Paris: Garnier-Flammarion, 1965), p. 46. For a more extensive discussion of this passage in *De l'amour,* see chapter 6 of this book.

32. Girard, *Deceit, Desire and the Novel.* The title of the first chapter is "'Triangular' Desire." It refers to desires which are not spontaneous but which are determined by an external model that the subject of desire wishes to imitate.

33. See *De l'amour,* pp. 149–50. Further references to this work will be in parentheses after the quotation.

34. Alter, *A Lion for Love:* "The proud Mathilde . . . resolves on a noble course of devotion unto death, consummating at the end her secret theatrical dream when she is privileged, like the mistress of her Renaissance ancestor, to carry off her lover's severed head" (p. 193).

Chapter 5

1. The major French women novelists of the 1830s and 1840s were George Sand, Marie d'Agoult (pseud. Daniel Stern), Hortense Allart, and Flora Tristan.

2. Sandra M. Gilbert and Susan Gubar, *The Madwoman in the Attic: The Woman Writer and the Nineteenth-Century Literary Imagination* (New Haven: Yale University Press, 1979), p. 48. Further references to this book will be in parentheses after the citation.

3. Elaine Showalter, *A Literature of Their Own: British Women Novelists from Brontë to Lessing* (Princeton: Princeton University Press, 1977), pp. 8, 27, 55, 73, 79, 81, and 92.

4. G. H. Lewes, "Currer Bell's *Shirley,*" *Edinburgh Review* 91 (January, 1850):106; A. S. A. Briggs, "Private and Social Themes in *Shirley,*" *Brontë Society Transactions* 13, no. 3 (1958): 203–19; Ivy Holgate, "The Structure of *Shirley,*" *Brontë Society Transactions* 14, no. 2 (1962): 27–35; J. M. S. Tompkins, "Caroline Helstone's Eyes," *Brontë Society Transactions* 14, no. 1 (1961): 18–28; Robert Keefe, *Charlotte Brontë's World of Death* (Austin: University of Texas Press, 1979), pp. 131–32, 206.

   For Terry Eagleton, the novel's amorphous form is connected to its conservative sociopolitical vision, in *Myths of Power: A Marxist Study of the Brontës* (London: Macmillan and Co., 1975); while Earl Knies sees the novel as being fragmented because "the social questions often temporarily displace the real story and distort the characters," in *The Art of Charlotte Brontë* (Athens: Ohio University Press, 1969), p. 162.

5. Those who argue to varying degrees in favor of the novel's feminine vision are: Helene Möglen, *Charlotte Brontë: The Self Conceived* (New York: Norton and Co., 1976), p. 134; Susan Gubar, "The Genesis of Hunger According to *Shirley,*" *Feminist Studies* 3, nos. 3 and 4 (Spring, Summer, 1976): 5–21, p. 5; Charles Burkhart, *Charlotte Brontë: A Psychosexual Study of Her Novels* (London: Victor Gollancz, 1973), p. 95; Carol Ohmann, "Charlotte Brontë: The Limits of Her Feminism," *Female Studies* 4 (Old Westbury: Feminist Press, 1972): 152–63, p. 156.

Those who argue against are: Mary Taylor, "Letter to Charlotte Brontë, April 25, 1850," in *The Brontës: Their Lives, Friendships and Correspondences,* ed. T. J. Wise and J. A. Symington, 4 vols. (Oxford: Shakespeare Head Press, 1932), 3:104–5; Patricia Beer, *Reader, I Married Him* (New York: Barnes and Noble, 1974), pp. 88, 98–100; Patricia Meyer Spacks, *The Female Imagination* (New York: Avon Books, 1975), p. 73.

6. Luce Irigaray, *Speculum de l'autre femme* (Paris: Editions de minuit, 1974). Further references to this book will be in parentheses after the quotation. Translations are mine.

7. Nancy Chodorow, *The Reproduction of Mothering: Psychoanalysis and the Sociology of Gender* (Berkeley: University of California Press, 1978), p. 196. Further references to this book will be in parentheses after the quotation.

8. M. M Bakhtin, *The Dialogic Imagination: Four Essays,* ed. Michael Holquist, trans. Caryl Emerson and Michael Holquist (Austin: University of Texas Press, 1981), p. 84. Further references to this book will be in parentheses after the quotation.

9. Charlotte Brontë, *Shirley* (Harmondsworth: Penguin Books, 1974), p. 120. Further references to this book will be in parentheses after the quotation.

10. Georg Lukács, "Reification and the Consciousness of the Proletariat," in *History and Class Consciousness: Studies in Marxist Dialectics,* trans. Rodney Livingston (Cambridge: MIT Press, 1971), pp. 83–222.

11. Sigmund Freud, "On Narcissism: An Introduction," *Standard Edition of the Complete Psychological Works,* 24 vols. (London: Hogarth Press, 1914), 14:69–102. See also Chodorow, *Mothering,* p. 63, and Paul Ricoeur, *Freud and Philosophy: An Essay on Interpretation,* trans. Denis Savage (New Haven: Yale University Press, 1970), pp. 127–29.

12. Charlotte Brontë, *Jane Eyre* (New York: Peebles Press, n.d.), p. 552. Further references to this book will be in parentheses after the quotation.

13. Elaine Showalter, "Feminist Criticism in the Wilderness," in *Writing and Sexual Difference,* ed. Elizabeth Abel (Chicago: University of Chicago Press, 1982), pp. 9–36, quoted at p. 34.

14. Burkhart, *Psychosexual Study,* p. 87.

15. Eagleton, *Myths,* pp. 58–59.

16. Jerre Collins, J. Ray Green, Mary Lydon, Mark Sachner, Eleanor Honig Skoller, "Questioning the Unconscious: The Dora Archive," *Diacritics,* Spring, 1983, pp. 37–42, quoted at p. 42.

17. Robert B. Heilman, "Charlotte Brontë's 'New Gothic,'" in *The Brontës: A Collection of Critical Essays,* ed. Ian Gregor (Englewood Cliffs, N.J.: Prentice-Hall, 1970), pp. 96–109, p. 103.

18. Carol Gilligan, *In a Different Voice: Psychological Theory and Women's Development* (Cambridge: Harvard University Press, 1983), p. 47.

19. Elaine Showalter, "Literary Criticism: Review Essay," *Signs* 1, no. 2 (Winter, 1975): 435–60, p. 435.

20. Fannie Elizabeth Ratchford, *The Brontës' Web of Childhood* (New York: Russell and Russell, 1964), p. 181. According to Burkhart, "the seven members of the Yorke family are granted more pages than their limited contribution to plot or theme justifies" (*Psychosexual Study,* p. 81).

21. René Girard, *Violence and the Sacred*, trans. Patrick Gregory (Baltimore: Johns Hopkins University Press, 1977), p. 8.
22. One line that could be explored is that in Freud's *Totem and Taboo* the scapegoat as surrogate victim is connected to the son's renunciation of his desire to kill the father and his acceptance of symbolic castration. Since *Shirley* rejects the problematic of symbolic castration and penis envy as the basis of a phallic representational system, this inversion of the scapegoat figure could be related to this rejection.
23. Among those who find Brontë's treatment of class struggle objective are Briggs, "Private and Social Themes," p. 214; Burkhart, *Psychosexual Study*, p. 88; Inga-Stina Ewbank, *Their Proper Sphere: A Study of the Brontë Sisters as Early-Victorian Novelists* (Cambridge: Harvard University Press, 1966), pp. 186–87; and Barbara Ward, "Charlotte Brontë and the World of 1846," *Brontë Society Transactions* 11, no. 10 (1946): 3–13. Möglen, *The Self Conceived*, pp. 117, 163, sees her as sympathetic to the workers. Among those who see the novel as, in the words of E. P. Thompson, "a true middle class myth" (*The Making of the English Working Class* [Harmondsworth: Penguin Books, 1963], p. 613), are Eagleton (*Myths*) and Ohmann ("Limits," p. 162).

Chapter 6

A shorter version of this chapter appeared as "Meaulnes' Search; François' Research" in *Michigan Romance Studies* 2 (1982): 101–38.

1. Simone de Beauvoir, *Mémoires d'une jeune fille rangée* (Paris: Gallimard, 1958), pp. 260, 310–11, 355, 371–73, and 484.
2. Simone de Beauvoir, *La Force de l'âge* (Paris: Gallimard, 1960), 1:71. Translation is mine.
3. Robert Gibson, *The Land without a Name: Alain-Fournier and His World* (London: Paul Elek, 1975), p. 283.
4. Alain-Fournier, *The Wanderer*, trans. Françoise Delisle, introduction by Havelock Ellis (New York: New Directions, 1928); reprinted with an introduction by Henri Peyre (New York: Heritage Press, 1958); *Meaulnes: The Lost Domaine*, trans. Sandra Morris (London: Blackie, 1966).
5. Marcel Schneider, *La Littérature fantastique en France* (Paris: Fayard, 1964), p. 243.
6. Henri Clouard, *Histoire de la littérature française du symbolisme à nos jours: 1915 à 1960* (Paris: Albin Michel, 1962), p. 77.
7. Jean Bastaire, *Alain-Fournier ou la tentation de l'enfance* (Paris: Plon, 1964), p. 38; Robert Gibson, *The Quest of Alain-Fournier* (New Haven: Yale University Press, 1954), p. 150.
8. Alain-Fournier, *Le Grand Meaulnes* (Paris: Fayard, 1971), p. 49. Further references to this text will be in parentheses after the quotation. Translations are mine.
9. See Charles Tilly, "Reflections on the History of European State-Making,"

in *The Formation of National States in Western Europe,* ed. Charles Tilly (Princeton: Princeton University Press, 1975); and Eugen Weber, *Peasants into Frenchmen: The Modernization of Rural France, 1870–1914* (Stanford: Stanford University Press, 1976). While Tilly emphasizes the importance of the sixteenth and seventeenth centuries for state consolidation, Weber emphasizes the importance of the period of the Third Republic. While Alain-Fournier's novel does not call into question Tilly's view, it does affirm Weber's view.

10. Nicos Poulantzas, *State, Power, Socialism,* trans. Patrick Camiller (London: Verso, 1980), p. 61.

11. For the role of the rural middle-class intelligentsia in promoting the ideological and cultural centralization of the French state, see: Madeleine Rebérioux, *La République radicale? 1898–1914* (Paris: Seuil, 1975), pt. 6, chap. 2: "Progrès et prospérité," especially p. 202; and Eugen Weber, *Peasants into Frenchmen,* chap. 18: "Civilizing in Earnest: Schools and Schooling," especially p. 333; and chap. 26: "Fled Is That Music," especially p. 441.

12. Paul Delarue, cited in Weber, *Peasants into Frenchmen,* p. 471.

13. Weber, *Peasants into Frenchmen,* p. 472. Further references to this work will be in parentheses after the citation.

14. Henry Cavaillès, "Problème de la circulation dans les Landes de Gascogne," *Annales de géographie,* pp. 561–82, cited in Weber, *Peasants into Frenchmen,* p. 205.

15. Karl Marx, *Capital,* trans. Samuel Moore and Edward Aveling (New York: International Publishers, 1967), 1:74.

16. Claude Lévi-Strauss, *Les Structures élémentaires de la parenté* (Paris: Mouton, 1968).

17. Athony Wilden, *System and Structure: Essays in Communication and Exchange* (London: Tavistock, 1980), p. 273.

18. Ferdinand de Saussure, *Course in General Linguistics,* trans. Wade Baskin (New York: Philosophical Library, 1959), p. 116.

19. Marx, *Capital,* p. 50.

20. Quoted in Bastaire, *Alain-Fournier,* p. 45.

21. For analyses of this form of subjectivity as a historically produced bourgeois form, see R. Howard Bloch, *Medieval French Literature and the Law,* pp. 283–94; Julia Kristeva, *La Révolution du langage poétique* (Paris: Seuil, 1974), pp. 151–87 and 481–85; Georg Lukács, *La Théorie du roman,* trans. Jean Clairevoye (Paris: Gonthier, 1963), pp. 49–90.

22. Poulantzas, *State,* pp. 51 and 56.

23. Rebérioux, *La République,* p. 43. Further references to this work will be in parentheses after the quotation.

24. Jean-Paul Aron, ed. *Misérable et glorieuse: La Femme du XIXe siècle* (Paris: Fayard, 1980), p. 16.

25. Martine Ségalen, "Femmes rurales," in *Misérable,* ed. Aron, p. 142.

26. Anne Martin-Fuguier, "La Maîtresse de maison," in *Misérable,* ed. Aron, p. 117.

27. Honoré de Balzac, *Le Lys dans la vallée* (Paris: Garnier-Flammarion, 1972), p. 217.
28. For the role of consumerism under the Third Republic, see Michael B. Miller, *The Bon Marché: Bourgeois Culture and the Department Store, 1869–1920* (Princeton: Princeton University Press, 1981).
29. de Beauvoir, *La Force de l'âge*, 1:71.

Chapter 7

1. Catering to an exclusively feminine audience, mass-market romances are an international phenomenon, with single romances or whole romance series being translated into as many as fourteen languages. Harlequin Enterprises, the best-selling and most successful publisher of this genre, has been imitated by many competitors both in America and in Europe. They publish a set number of romances per month, categorized into different series according to a carefully measured degree of explicit sex, known as "sensuality" in the trade. Harlequin, for instance, publishes *Harlequin Romances, Harlequin Presents,* and *Harlequin Temptations,* as well as a mystery-romance series, a gothic romance series, a longer series called *Superromances,* and an American romance series. Like any corporate consumer product, Harlequin Romances and its competitors are constantly "diversifying" their line, proliferating into a dizzying array of series.

   Other publishers now have romance series for more mature and/or divorced women, like Berkeley-Jove's "Second Chance at Love," or for adolescent girls, like Simon and Shuster's "First Love." This series shares the teen romance shelves with the "Sweet Dream" series from Bantam, "Young Love" from Dell, "Caprice" from Grosset and Dunlap, and two series from Scholastic Inc., whose "Wishing Star" and "Wild Fire" sold 2.25 million copies in 1982.

   Information from Brett Harvey, "Boy Crazy," *Village Voice* 27, no. 7 (February 10–16, 1982): 48–49; Stanley Meisler, "Harlequins: The Romance of Escapism," *Los Angeles Times,* November 15, 1980, pt. I, pp. 7–8; Rosemary Nightingale, "True Romances," *Miami Herald,* January 5, 1983; J. D. Reed, "From Bedroom to Boardroom: Romance Novels Court Changing Fancies and Adorable Profits," *Time,* April 13, 1981, pp. 101–4; interview with Jany Saint-Marcoux, Editor of *Collections sentimentales,* Editions Tallandier; "Romantic Novels Find Receptive Market," *Santa Ana Register,* July 26, 1979, Section E, p. 1; *Standard and Poor's Corporation Records* 43, no. 9 (New York, May, 1982): 8475.
2. Reed, "Bedroom." According to Margaret Ann Jensen, the very success of Harlequin has caused these figures to decline drastically. Since so many publishers are now imitating Harlequin and competing with it, Harlequin's "share of the market has dropped to 45 percent.... All signs indicate that Harlequin is a financially distressed corporation." Margaret Ann Jensen, *Love's $weet Return: The Harlequin Story* (Toronto: Women's

Educational Press, 1984). In order to offset this decline, Harlequin is purchasing Silhouette Romances.

3. Tania Modleski, *Loving with a Vengeance: Mass-Produced Fantasies for Women* (Hamden: Archon Books, 1982); Ann Barr Snitow, "Mass Market Romance: Pornography for Women Is Different," *Radical History Review* 20 (Spring–Summer, 1979): 141–61, reprinted in Ann Snitow, Christine Stansell, and Sharon Thomas, eds., *Powers of Desire: The Politics of Sexuality* (New York: Monthly Review Press, 1983); Janice Radway, *Reading the Romance: Women, Patriarchy, and Popular Fiction* (Chapel Hill: University of North Carolina Press, 1984), p. 20; Janice Radway, "Women Read the Romance: The Interaction of Text and Context," *Feminist Studies* 9, no. 1 (Spring, 1983): 53–78. Further references to these works will appear in parentheses after the citation.

4. Kerry Allyne, *Across the Great Divide* (1980); Ann Cooper, *Battle with Desire* (1980); Kay Thorpe, *The Dividing Line* (1980). All books published by Harlequin Books, Toronto, London, New York, Amsterdam, Sidney, Hamburg, Paris, Stockholm. Further references to these works will be contained in parentheses after the quotation.

5. Lynsey Stevens, *Race for Revenge* (Toronto: Harlequin, 1981).

6. Advertisement for Sara Jennings, *Game Plan* (Garden City: Candlelight Ecstasy Romances, 1984).

7. Marion Smith Collins, *By Any Other Name* (Harlequin Temptations, 1984); Sarah James, *Public Affair* (Harlequin American Romance, 1984); Leigh Roberts, *Love Circuits* (Harlequin Temptations, 1984). All books published by Harlequin Enterprises, Toronto. Further references to these works will appear in parentheses after the citation.

8. Advertisement for *Harlequin Temptations,* found in Harlequin books of July, 1984. (Toronto: Harlequin Enterprises, 1984).

9. Colette Dowling, *The Cinderella Complex: Women's Hidden Fear of Independence* (New York: Simon and Schuster Pocket Books, 1981), pp. 2, 54.

10. Harry Braverman, *Labor and Monopoly Capital: The Degradation of Work in the Twentieth Century,* Special Abridged Edition (Special issue of *Monthly Review* 26, no. 3 [July–August, 1974]), p. 50. Further references to this work will be in parentheses following the quotation.

   According to Braverman, by 1970 in the United States, clerical work was one of the fastest-growing occupations and had become one of the lowest paid, its pay "lower than that of every type of so-called blue collar work" (p. 51). Of its ten million members, by 1978, 79.6 percent were women. In 1970, clerical work included 18 percent of all gainfully employed persons in the United States, a percentage equal to that of production work of all sorts.

11. Roslyn L. Feldberg and Evelyn Nakano Glenn, "Technology and Work Degradation: Effects of Office Automation on Women Clerical Workers," in *Machina ex Dea,* ed. Joan Rothschild (New York: Pergamon Press, 1983), p. 62.

12. Radway reports that 42 percent of the women in her study work outside the home, and says that Harlequin claims that 49 percent of its audience works outside the home. Radway, "Women Read the Romance," p. 57.

13. Ida Rusakoff Hoos, *Automation in the Office* (Washington: 1961), p. 53, cited in Braverman, *Labor and Monopoly Capital.*

14. Ellen Cantarow, "Working Can Be Dangerous to Your Health," *Mademoiselle,* August, 1982, pp. 114–16.

15. Eleanor Farnes, *The Enchanted Island* (Toronto: Harlequin Enterprises, 1971).

16. Margaret Mayo, *Stormy Affair* (Toronto: Harlequin Enterprises, 1980).

17. Radway, *Reading the Romance,* pp. 94–96 and 135–38; Snitow, "Mass Market Romance"; and Nancy Chodorow, *The Reproduction of Mothering: Psychoanalysis and the Sociology of Gender* (Berkeley: University of California Press, 1978).

18. Sally Mitchell, *The Fallen Angel: Chastity, Class and Women's Reading, 1835– 1880* (Bowling Green, Ohio: Bowling Green State University Popular Culture Press, 1981); Modleski, *Loving with a Vengeance.*

19. Charlotte Brontë, *Shirley* (Baltimore: Penguin Books, 1974), p. 235.

20. Janet Dailey, *The Matchmakers* (Toronto: Harlequin Enterprises, 1978); Elizabeth Graham, *Come Next Spring* (Toronto: Harlequin Enterprises, 1980).

21. For the role of narcissism in the Harlequin Romances, see Modleski, *Loving with a Vengeance.*

22. Gaye Tuchman, Arlene Kaplan Daniels, and James Benet, eds., *Hearth and Home: Images of Women in the Mass Media* (New York: Oxford University Press, 1978), p. 18. Further references to this work will be found in parentheses after the quotation.

23. Peter Killing, *Harlequin Enterprises Limited: Case Material of the Western School of Business Administration* (London, Ontario: University of Western Ontario, 1978), p. 3.

24. *General Editorial Guidelines for Worldwide Library Super Romances* (Toronto: Harlequin Enterprises, 1982).

25. *Harlequin Romance and Harlequin Presents Editorial Guidelines* (Ontario: Harlequin Books, June, 1984), p. 1.

26. George Christian, "Romance Writers, Going to the Heart of the Matter (and the Market), Call for Recognition," *Publishers Weekly,* July 24, 1980. The first national conference of the Romance Writers of America was held in Houston, in June, 1981, with eight hundred participants, mostly women.

27. Jensen, *Love's $weet Return,* pp. 73–74.

28. Speech given at a meeting of Romance Writers of America, Orange County chapter.

29. Vivien Lee Jennings, "The Romance Wars," *Publishers Weekly,* August 24, 1984, pp. 50–55, quoted at p. 53.

30. Information gathered from conversations with authors at several meetings of Romance Writers of America, Orange County chapter.

Conclusion

1. Lucien Goldmann, *Pour une sociologie du roman* (Paris: Gallimard, 1964), pp. 24–25. Translation is mine.
2. Georg Lukács, *La Théorie du roman,* trans. Jean Clairevoye (Paris: Gallimard, 1963), p. 74. Translation is mine.

Selected Bibliography

Literature

Alain-Fournier. *Le Grand Meaulnes*. Paris: Fayard, 1971.
———. *Meaulnes: The Lost Domaine*. Translation of *Le Grand Meaulnes* by Sandra Morris. London: Blackie, 1966.
———. *The Wanderer*. Translation of *Le Grand Meaulnes* by Françoise Delisle. Introduction by Havelock Ellis. New York: New Directions, 1928.
———. *The Wanderer*. Translation of *Le Grand Meaulnes* by Françoise Delisle. Introduction by Henri Peyre. New York: Heritage Press, 1958.
Allyne, Kerry. *Across the Great Divide*. Toronto: Harlequin, 1980.
Balzac, Honoré de. *Le Lys dans la vallée*. Paris: Garnier-Flammarion, 1972.
Beauvoir, Simone de. *La Force de l'âge*. Paris: Gallimard, 1960.
———. *Mémoires d'une jeune fille rangée*. Paris: Gallimard, 1958.
Béroul. *Le Roman de Tristan*. Paris: Firmin Didot, 1903.
Brontë, Charlotte. *Jane Eyre*. New York: Peebles Press, n.d.
———. *Shirley*. Harmondsworth: Penguin Books, 1974.
Collins, Marion Smith. *By Any Other Name*. Toronto: Harlequin, 1984.
Cooper, Ann. *Battle with Desire*. Toronto: Harlequin, 1980.
Curtin, Jeremiah, ed. *Myths and Folktales of Ireland*. New York: Dover, 1975.
Daily, Janet. *The Matchmakers*. Toronto: Harlequin, 1978.
Eden, Laura. *Summer Magic*. New York: Simon and Schuster; Silhouette Special Editions, 1982.
Ellis, Janine. *Rough Justice*. Toronto: Harlequin, 1980.
Faraday, L. Winifred, trans. *The Cattle Raid of Cualnge*. London: David Nutt, 1904.
Farnes, Eleanor. *The Enchanted Island*. Toronto: Harlequin, 1981.
Firth, Susanna. *The Overlord*. London: Mills and Boon, Ltd., 1982.
Flaubert, Gustave. *L'Education sentimentale*. Paris: Garnier, 1964.
Ford, Patrick K., ed. *The Mabinogi and Other Medieval Welsh Tales*. Berkeley: University of California Press, 1977.
Graham, Elizabeth. *Come Next Spring*. Toronto: Harlequin, 1980.
Gregory, Lady Augusta. *Gods and Fighting Men: The Story of the Tuatha de Danaam and of the Fianna of Ireland*. New York: Oxford University Press, 1970.

James, Sarah. *Public Affair.* Toronto: Harlequin, 1984.

Jennings, Sarah. *Game Plan.* Garden City: Candlelight Ecstasy Romances, 1984.

Major, Ann. *Dream Come True.* New York: Simon and Schuster; Silhouette Desire, 1982.

Markale, Jean, ed. *L'Epopée celtique d'Irlande.* Paris: Payot, 1971.

Mayo, Margaret. *Stormy Affair.* Toronto: Harlequin, 1980.

Musset, Alfred de. "Namouna." In *Oeuvres complètes,* Tome I. Paris: Louis Conard, 1922.

Nelson, Louella. *Freedom's Fortune.* Toronto: Harlequin, 1984.

Oberg, Eilhart von. *Tristant.* Edited by Danielle Buschinger. Göppingen: Alfred Kummerle, 1976.

Prévost, Antoine-François. *Histoire du chevalier des Grieux et de Manon Lescaut.* Introduction by Frédéric Deloffre and Raymond Picard. Paris: Garnier, 1965.

Robert, Friar. *The Saga of Tristan and Isond.* Translated by Paul Schach. Lincoln: University of Nebraska Press, 1973.

Roberts, Leigh. *Love Circuits.* Toronto: Harlequin, 1984.

Scott, Isobel. *A Wild Sweetness.* New York: Bantam Circle of Love Romances, 1981.

Stendhal. *De l'amour.* Paris: Garnier-Flammarion, 1965.

——. *Le Rouge et le noir.* Edited by Henri Martineau. Paris: Garnier, 1960.

Stevens, Lynsey. *Race for Revenge.* Toronto: Harlequin, 1981.

Strassburg, Gottfried von. *Tristan.* Darmstadt: Wissenschaftliche Buchgesellschaft.

——. *Tristan.* Translated by A. T. Hatto. Baltimore: Penguin Books, 1960.

Thomas. *Le Roman de Tristan.* Edition by Joseph Bédier. Paris: Firmin Didot, 1902.

Thorpe, Kay. *The Dividing Line.* Toronto: Harlequin, 1980.

Criticism and Theory

Alter, Robert, and Carol Cossman. *A Lion for Love: A Critical Biography of Stendhal.* New York: Basic Books, 1979.

Althusser, Louis. *For Marx.* Translated by Ben Brewster. New York: Vintage, 1969.

Auerbach, Erich. *Mimesis: The Representation of Reality in Western Literature.* Translated by Willard R. Trask. Princeton: Princeton University Press, 1953.

Babbitt, Irving. *Rousseau and Romanticism.* Boston: Houghton Mifflin, 1919.

Bakhtin, M. M. *The Dialogic Imagination: Four Essays.* Translated by Caryl Emerson and Michael Holquist. Austin: University of Texas Press, 1981.

Barthes, Roland. *Mythologies.* Paris: Seuil, 1970.

——. *Le Plaisir du texte.* Paris: Seuil, 1973.

——. *S/Z.* Paris: Seuil, 1970.

Bastaire, Jean. *Alain-Fournier et la tentation de l'enfance.* Paris: Plon, 1964.

Beauvoir, Simone de. *Le Deuxième Sexe.* Paris: Gallimard, 1949.

Beer, Patricia. *Reader, I Married Him.* New York: Barnes and Noble, 1974.

Bloch, R. Howard. *Medieval French Literature and the Law.* Berkeley: University of California Press, 1977.

Bloom, Harold. "The Internalization of Quest Romance." In *The Ringers in the Tower.* Chicago: University of Chicago Press, 1971.

Böll-Johansen, Hans. *Essai sur la structure du roman stendhalien.* Aran: Editions du grand chêne, 1979.

Booth, Wayne. *The Rhetoric of Fiction.* Chicago: University of Chicago Press, 1961.

Briggs, A. S. A. "Private and Social Themes in *Shirley.*" *Brontë Society Transactions* 13, no.3 (1958): 203–19.

Brombert, Victor. *La Prison romantique.* Paris: José Corti, 1975.

Brooks, Peter. "The Novel and the Guillotine; or Fathers and Sons in *Le Rouge et le noir.*" *PMLA* 97, no. 3 (1983): 348–62.

Burkhart, Charles. *Charlotte Brontë: A Psychosexual Study of Her Novels.* London: Victor Gollancz, 1973.

Chodorow, Nancy. *The Reproduction of Mothering: Psychoanalysis and the Sociology of Gender.* Berkeley: University of California Press, 1978.

Christian, George. "Romance Writers, Going to the Heart of the Matter (and the Market), Call for Recognition." *Publishers Weekly,* July 24, 1980.

Cixous, Hélène. *La Jeune Née.* Paris: 10/18, 1975.

———. "The Laugh of the Medusa." *Signs,* Summer, 1976, pp. 875–94.

Clouard, Henri. *Histoire de la littérature française du symbolisme à nos jours.* Paris: Albin Michel, 1962.

Collins, Jerre, J. Ray Green, Mary Lydon, Mark Sachner, and Eleanor Honig Skoller. "Questioning the Unconsciousness: The Dora Archive." *Diacritics,* Spring, 1983, pp. 37–42.

Delesalle, Simone. "Lecture d'un chef-d'oeuvre: *Manon Lescaut.*" *Annales* 26, no. 3–4 (1971): 723–40.

de Man, Paul. "Georg Lukács's *Theory of the Novel.*" In *Blindness and Insight: Essays in the Rhetoric of Contemporary Criticism.* New York: Oxford University Press, 1971.

Derrida, Jacques. "Le Facteur de la vérité." *Poétique* 21 (1975): 96–147.

Dowling, Colette. *The Cinderella Complex: Women's Hidden Fear of Independence.* New York: Simon and Schuster, 1981.

Eagleton, Terry. *Myths of Power: A Marxist Study of the Brontës.* London: Macmillan and Co., 1975.

———. *The Rape of Clarissa: Writing, Sexuality and Class Struggle in Samuel Richardson.* Minneapolis: University of Minnesota Press, 1982.

Eisenstein, Zillah, ed. *Capitalist Patriarchy and the Case for Socialist Feminism.* New York: Monthly Review Press, 1979.

Engels, Frederick. *The Origin of the Family, Private Property and the State.* New York: International Publishers, 1973.

Ewbank, Inga-Stina. *Their Proper Sphere: A Study of the Brontë Sisters as Early-Victorian Novelists.* Cambridge: Harvard University Press, 1966.

Felman, Shoshana. *La Folie dans l'oeuvre romanesque de Stendhal.* Paris: José Corti, 1971.

Fetterley, Judith. *The Resisting Reader: A Feminist Approach to American Fiction.* Bloomington: Indiana University Press, 1978.

Fish, Stanley. *Is There a Text in This Class? The Authority of Interpretive Communities.* Cambridge: Harvard University Press, 1980.

Foucault, Michel. *The Order of Things.* A translation of *Les Mots et les choses.* New York: Vintage, 1970.

Frappier-Mazur, Lucienne. "Desire, Writing and Identity in the Romantic Mystical Novel: Notes for a Definition of the Feminine." Paper delivered to the Berkshire Conference for Women's History, June, 1984.

Freud, Sigmund. "On Narcissism: An Introduction." In *Standard Edition of the Complete Psychological Works.* London: Hogarth Press, 1914.

Frye, Northrop. *The Secular Scripture: A Study of the Structure of Romance.* Cambridge: Harvard University Press, 1976.

Gallop, Jane. *The Daughter's Seduction.* Ithaca, N.Y.: Cornell University Press, 1982.

―――. "Impertinent Questions: Irigaray, Sade, Lacan." *Sub-stance* 26 (1980): 57–67.

General Editorial Guidelines for Worldwide Library Super Romances. Hollywood: Harlequin Publishing Corp., 1982.

Genette, Gérard. *Figures II.* Paris: Seuil, 1969.

Gibson, Robert. *The Land without a Name: Alain-Fournier and His World.* London: Paul Elek, 1975.

―――. *The Quest of Alain-Fournier.* New Haven: Yale University Press, 1954.

Gilbert, Sandra, and Susan Gubar. *The Madwoman in the Attic: The Woman Writer and the Nineteenth-Century Literary Imagination.* New Haven: Yale University Press, 1979.

Gilligan, Carol. *In a Different Voice: Psychological Theory and Women's Development.* Cambridge: Harvard University Press, 1983.

Girard, René. *Deceit, Desire and the Novel: Self and Other in Literary Structure.* Translated by Yvonne Freccero. Baltimore: Johns Hopkins University Press, 1965.

―――. *Violence and the Sacred.* Translated by Patrick Gregory. Baltimore: Johns Hopkins University Press, 1977.

Giraud, Raymond. *The Unheroic Hero in the Novels of Stendhal, Balzac and Flaubert.* New Brunswick, N.J.: Rutgers University Press, 1957.

Gleckner, Robert F., and Gerald E. Enscoe, eds. *Romanticism: Points of View.* Detroit: Wayne State University Press, 1970.

Goldmann, Lucien. *Pour une sociologie du roman.* Paris: Gallimard, 1964.

Gossman, Lionel. "Prévosts's Manon: Love in the New World." *Yale French Studies* 40 (1968): 91–102.

Graves, Robert. *The White Goddess: A Historical Grammar of Poetic Myth.* New York: Farrar, Straus and Giroux, 1976.

Gregor, Ian, ed. *The Brontës: A Collection of Critical Essays.* Englewood Cliffs, N.J.: Prentice-Hall, 1970.

Guérin, Michel. *La Politique de Stendhal.* Paris: Presses universitaires de France, 1982.

Harlequin Romance Guidelines. Hollywood: Harlequin Publishing Corp., 1982.

Harvey, Brett. "Boy Crazy." *The Village Voice* 27, no. 7 (February 10–16, 1982): 48–49.

Hazard, Paul. *La Crise de conscience européenne: 1680–1715.* Paris: Arthème Fayard, n.d.

Hegel, G. F. W. *The Phenomenology of Mind.* New York: Harper and Row, 1967.

Holgate, Ivy. "The Structure of *Shirley.*" *Brontë Society Transactions* 14, no. 2 (1962): 27–35.

Irigaray, Luce. *Ce Sexe qui n'en est pas un.* Paris: Editions de minuit, 1977.

———. *Speculum de l'autre femme.* Paris: Editions de minuit, 1974.

Jackson, W. T. H. *The Anatomy of Love: The Tristan of Gottfried von Strassburg.* New York: Columbia University Press, 1971.

———. "Faith Unfaithful—The German Reaction to Courtly Love." In *The Meaning of Courtly Love,* edited by F. X. Newman. Albany: State University of New York Press, 1968.

Jameson, Fredric. *The Political Unconscious: Narrative as a Socially Symbolic Act.* Ithaca, N.Y.: Cornell University Press, 1981.

Jensen, Margaret Ann. *Love's \$weet Return: The Harlequin Story.* Toronto: Women's Educational Press, 1984.

Kamuf, Peggy. *Fictions of Feminine Desire.* Lincoln: University of Nebraska Press, 1982.

Keefe, Robert. *Charlotte Brontë's World of Death.* Austin: University of Texas Press, 1979.

Killing, Peter. *Harlequin Enterprises Limited: Case Material of the Western School of Business Administration.* London, Ontario: University of Western Ontario, 1978.

Knies, Earl A. *The Art of Charlotte Brontë.* Athens: Ohio University Press, 1969.

Kristeva, Julia. *Des Chinoises.* Paris: Des Femmes, 1975.

———. "La Fonction prédicative et le sujet parlant." In *Langue, discours société pour Emile Benveniste,* edited by Julia Kristeva, Jean-Claude Milner, and Nicolas Ruwet. Paris: Seuil, 1975.

———. *Histoires d'amour.* Paris: Denoel, 1983.

———. "Pratique signifiante et mode de production." In *La Traversée des signes.* Paris: Seuil, 1975.

———. *La Révolution du langage poétique.* Paris: Seuil, 1974.

———. "Le Sujet en procès." In *Arthaud,* edited by Philippe Sollers. Paris: 10/18, 1973.

———. "Le Texte clos." In *Seméiotike: Recherches pour une sémanalyse.* Paris: Seuil, 1969.

Lang, Candace. "Autobiography in the Aftermath of Romanticism." *Diacritics* 12, no. 4 (Winter, 1982): 2–16.

Lasserre, Pierre. *Le Romantisme français.* Paris: Mercure de France, 1907.

Levin, Harry. *Toward Stendhal.* New York: Haskell House, 1975.

Lévi-Strauss, Claude. *Les Structures élémentaires de la parenté.* Paris: Mouton, 1968.

Lewes, G. H. "Currer Bell's *Shirley. Edinburgh Review* 91 (January, 1850): 153–73.

Loomis, Gertrude Schoepperle. *Tristan and Isolt: A Study in the Sources of the Roman*. New York: Bert Franklin, 1963.

Loomis, Roger Sherman. *Celtic Myth and Arthurian Romance*. New York: Columbia University Press, 1927.

―――. *The Development of Arthurian Romance*. London: Hutchinson University Library, 1963.

Lotringer, Syvère. "Manon l'echo." *Romanic Review* 63, no. 2 (April, 1972): 92–110.

Lukács, Georg. "Reification and the Consciousness of the Proletariat." In *History and Class Consciousness: Studies in Marxist Dialectics*. Translated by Rodney Livingstone. Cambridge: MIT Press, 1971.

―――. *Studies in European Realism*. New York: Grosset and Dunlap, 1964.

―――. *La Théorie du roman*. Translated by Jean Clairevoye. Paris: Gonthier, 1963.

MacCannell, Julia. "Stendhal's Women." *Semiotica* 48, nos. 1/2 (1984): 143–68.

Macherey, Pierre. *Pour une théorie de la production littéraire*. Paris: Maspero, 1974.

Marks, Elaine, and Isabelle de Courtivron, eds. *New French Feminisms*. New York: Schocken, 1981.

Martineau, Henri. *L'Oeuvre de Stendhal*. Paris: Divan, 1975.

Marx, Karl. *Capital*, Vol. I. Translated by Samuel Moore and Edward Aveling. New York: International Publishers, 1967.

Mauzi, Robert. *L'Idée du bonheur dans la littérature du 18e siècle*. Paris: Armand Colin, 1969.

Meisler, Stanley. "Harlequins: The Romance of Escapism." *Los Angeles Times*, November 15, 1980, part I, pp. 7–8.

Miller, Nancy K. *The Heroine's Text: Readings in the French and English Novel, 1722–1782*. New York: Columbia University Press, 1980.

Mitchell, Juliet. *Psycho-Analysis and Feminism*. New York: Vintage, 1975.

Mitchell, Juliet, and Jacqueline Rose, eds. *Feminine Sexuality: Jacques Lacan and the école freudienne*. New York: Norton, 1982.

Mitchell, Robert L. *Pre-Text, Text, Context: Essays on Nineteenth-Century French Literature*. Columbus: Ohio State University Press, 1980.

Mitchell, Sally. *The Fallen Angel: Chastity, Class and Women's Reading, 1835–1880*. Bowling Green, Ohio: Bowling Green State University Popular Culture Press, 1981.

Modleski, Tania. *Loving with a Vengeance: Mass-Produced Fantasies for Women*. Hamden: Archon Books, 1982.

Möglen, Helene. *Charlotte Brontë: The Self Conceived*. New York: Norton and Co., 1976.

Mouillaud, Geneviève. *Le Rouge et le noir de Stendhal: Le Roman possible*. Paris: Larousse, 1973.

Nelli, René. *L'Erotique des troubadours*. Paris: 10/18, 1974.

Nightingale, Rosemary. "True Romances." *Miami Herald*, January 5, 1983, Section B, p. 1.

Ohmann, Carol. "Charlotte Brontë: The Limits of Her Feminism." *Female Studies IV*. Old Westbury: Feminist Press, 1972.

Papera, Don Gruffot. "Sur *Le Rouge et le noir*." Appendix in *Le Rouge et le noir* by Stendhal. Paris: Garnier, 1960.

Picard, Raymond. "L'Univers de Manon Lescaut." *Mercure de France* 1172 (April, 1961): 606–22.

Picozzi, Rosemary. *A History of Tristan Scholarship*. Berne: Herbert Lang, 1971.

Poulantzas, Nicos. *State, Power, Socialism*. Translated by Patrick Camiller. London: Verso, 1980.

Prendergast, Christopher. *Balzac: Fiction and Melodrama*. London: Edward Arnold, 1978.

Proust, Jacques. "Le Corps de Manon." *Littérature* 4 (1971): 5–21.

Rabine, Leslie W. "Searching for the Connections: Marxist Feminists in Women's Studies." *Humanities and Society* 6, nos. 2 and 3 (Spring and Summer, 1983): 95–222.

Radway, Janice. *Reading the Romance: Women, Patriarchy, and Popular Culture*. Chapel Hill: North Carolina University Press, 1984.

———. "Women Read the Romance: The Interaction of Text and Context." *Feminist Studies* 9 (Spring, 1983): 53–78.

Ratchford, Fannie Elizabeth. *The Brontës' Web of Childhood*. New York: Russell and Russell, 1964.

Reed, J. D. "From Bedroom to Boardroom: Romance Novels Court Changing Fancies and Adorable Profits." *Time*, April 13, 1981, pp. 101–4.

Ricoeur, Paul. *Freud and Philosophy: An Essay on Interpretation*. Translated by Denis Savage. New Haven: Yale University Press, 1970.

Rothschild, Joan, ed. *Machina ex Dea*. New York: Pergamon Press, 1983.

Rougemont, Denis de. *L'Amour et l'occident*. Paris: 10/18, 1939.

Saussure, Ferdinand de. *Course in General Linguistics*. Translated by Wade Baskin. New York: Philosophical Library, 1959.

Schneider, Marcel. *La Littérature fantastique en France*. Paris: Fayard, 1964.

Showalter, Elaine. "Feminist Criticism in the Wilderness." In *Writing and Sexual Difference*, edited by Elizabeth Abel. Chicago: University of Chicago Press, 1982.

———. *A Literature of Their Own: British Women Novelists from Brontë to Lessing*. Princeton: Princeton University Press, 1977.

Snitow, Ann Barr. "Mass Market Romance: Pornography for Women Is Different." *Radical History Review* 20 (Spring–Summer, 1979): 141–61.

Snitow, Ann Barr, and Sharon Thomas, eds. *Powers of Desire: The Politics of Sexuality*. New York: Monthly Review Press, 1983.

Spacks, Patricia Meyer. *The Female Imagination*. New York: Avon Books, 1975.

Tenenbaum, Elizabeth. *The Problematic Self: Approaches to Identity in Stendhal, D. H. Lawrence, and Malraux*. Cambridge: Harvard University Press, 1977.

Tompkins, J. M. S. "Caroline Helstone's Eyes." *Brontë Society Transactions* 14, no. 1 (1961): 18–28.

Tuchman, Gaye, Arlene Kaplan Daniels, and James Benet, eds. *Hearth and*

Home: Images of Women in the Mass Media. New York: Oxford University Press, 1978.

Ward, Barbara. "Charlotte Brontë and the World of 1846." *Brontë Society Transactions* 11, no. 10 (1946): 3–13.

Wilden, Anthony. *System and Structure: Essays in Communication and Exchange.* London: Tavistock, 1980.

Wise, T. J., and J. A. Symington, eds. *The Brontës: Their Lives, Friendships and Correspondences.* 2 vols. Oxford: Shakespeare Head Press, 1932.

Zumthor, Paul. *Essai de poétique mediévale.* Paris: Seuil, 1972.

––––––. "Héloise et Abélard." *Revue des sciences humaines,* July–September, 1958, p. 91.

History, Sociology, Anthropology

Aron, Jean-Paul, ed. *Misérable et glorieuse: La Femme du XIXe siècle.* Paris: Fayard, 1980.

Bloch, Marc. *Feudal Society.* Translated by L. A. Manyan. Chicago: University of Chicago Press, 1961.

Braverman, Harry. *Labor and Monopoly Capital: The Degradation of Work in the Twentieth Century.* New York: Monthly Review Press, 1974.

Bridenthal, Renate, and Claudia Koontz, eds. *Becoming Visible: Women in European History.* Boston: Houghton Mifflin, 1977.

Cantarow, Ellen. "Working Can Be Dangerous to Your Health." *Mademoiselle,* August, 1982, pp. 114–16.

Clark, Alice. *Working Life of Women in the Seventeenth Century.* London, 1919. Reprint. New York: A. M. Kelley, 1968.

Crumley, Carole L. *Celtic Social Structure: The Generation of Archaeologically Testable Hypotheses from Literary Evidence.* Museum of Anthropology, University of Michigan, no. 54. Ann Arbor: University of Michigan, 1974.

Davis, Natalie Zemon. *Society and Culture in Early Modern France.* Stanford: Stanford University Press, 1965.

Duby, Georges. *Le Chevalier, la femme, et le prêtre.* Paris: Hachette, 1981.

Duby, Georges, and Jacques le Goff, eds. *Famille et parenté dans l'occident mediéval.* Rome: Ecole française de Rome, 1977.

Duhet, Paule Marie. *Les Femmes et la Révolution, 1789–1795.* Paris: Julliard, 1971.

Ford, Franklin L. *Robe and Sword: The Regrouping of the French Aristocracy after Louis XIV.* Cambridge: Harvard University Press, 1962.

Haskins, Charles Homer. *The Renaissance of the Twelfth Century.* Cambridge: Harvard University Press, 1927.

Herlihy, David. "Life Expectancies for Women in Medieval Society." In *The Role of Women in the Middle Ages,* edited by Rosemarie Thee Morewedge. Albany: State University of New York, 1975.

Hubert, Henri. *The Greatness and Decline of the Celts.* Edited and brought up to date by Marcel Mauss, Raymond Lantier, and Jean Marx. Translated by M. R. Dobie. New York: Benjamin Blom, 1972.

Hufton, Olwen. *The Poor of Eighteenth-Century France: 1750–1789.* Oxford: Clarendon, 1974.

Joyce, P. W. *A Social History of Ancient Ireland.* New York: Benjamin Blom, 1968.

Leacock, Eleanor Burke. *Myths of Male Dominance.* New York: Monthly Review Press, 1981.

Levy, Darline Gay, Harriet Bronson Applewhite, and Mary Durham Johnson, eds. *Women in Revolutionary Paris, 1789–1795.* Urbana: University of Illinois Press, 1979.

MacCurtain, Margaret, and Donncha O'Corráin, eds. *Women in Irish Society: The Historical Dimension.* Westport, Conn.: Greenwood Press, 1979.

Markale, Jean. *La Femme celte.* Paris: Payot, 1976.

Miller, Michael B. *The Bon Marché: Bourgeois Culture and the Department Store, 1869–1920.* Princeton: Princeton University Press, 1981.

Pirenne, Henri, Gustave Cohen, and Henri Focillon. *Histoire du moyen âge.* Paris: Presses universitaires de France, 1933.

Rebérioux, Madeleine. *La République radicale? 1898–1914.* Paris: Seuil, 1975.

Rees, Alwyn, and Brinley Rees. *Celtic Heritage: Ancient Tradition in Ireland and Wales.* London: Thames and Hudson, 1961.

Reiter, Rayna, ed. *Toward an Anthropology of Women.* New York: Monthly Review Press, 1975.

Scherman, Katharine. *The Flowering of Ireland: Saints, Scholars and Kings.* Boston: Little, Brown, and Co., 1981.

Smith, Bonnie G. *Ladies of the Leisure Class: The Bourgeoises of Northern France in the Nineteenth Century.* Princeton: Princeton University Press, 1981.

Soboul, Albert. *La Civilization et la Révolution française.* 2 vols. Paris: Arthaud, 1970.

Standard and Poor's Corporation Records 43, no. 9 (May, 1982).

Stone, Merlin. *When God Was a Woman.* New York: Harcourt Brace Jovanovich, 1977.

Stuart, Susan Mosher, ed. *Women in Medieval Society.* Philadelphia: University of Pennsylvania Press, 1976.

Sullerot, Evelyne. *Histoire et sociologie du travail féminin.* Paris: Gonthier, 1968.

Thompson, E. P. *The Making of the English Working Class.* Harmondsworth: Penguin Books, 1963.

Thompson, George. *Studies in Ancient Greek Society: The Prehistoric Aegean.* New York: Citadel Press, 1965.

Tigar, Michael, and Madeleine Levy. *Law and the Rise of Capitalism.* New York: Monthly Review Press, 1977.

Tilly, Louise A., and Joan W. Scott. *Women, Work and the Family.* New York: Holt, Rinehart and Winston, 1978.

Weber, Eugen. *Peasants into Frenchmen: The Modernization of Rural France, 1870–1914.* Stanford: Stanford University Press, 1976.

Index